ACRL PUBLICATIONS

Teaching Literary Research: Challenges in a Changing Environment

Edited by
Kathleen A. Johnson and Steven R. Harris

Association of College and Research Libraries
A division of the American Library Association
Chicago, 2009

The paper used in this publication meets the minimum requirements of American National Standard for Information Sciences-Permanence of Paper for Printed Library Materials, ANSI Z39.48-1992. ∞

A previous version of the chapter, "Librarians Influencing the Literature Core Curriculum" appeared as "Where It Counts: Departmental Curriculum Committees and Librarians" in *Learning to Make a Difference: Proceedings of the Eleventh National Conference of the Association of College and Research Libraries, April 10-13, 2003, Charlotte, North Carolina*, ed. Hugh A. Thompson (Chicago : Association of College and Research Libraries, 2003.)

Library of Congress Cataloging-in-Publication Data

Teaching literary research : challenges in a changing environment / edited by Kathleen A. Johnson and Steven R. Harris.
    p. cm. -- (ACRL publications in librarianship ; no. 60)
 Includes index.
 ISBN 978-0-8389-8509-0 (pbk. : alk. paper) 1. Literature--Research--Methodology--Study and teaching (Higher) 2. Information literacy--Study and teaching (Higher) 3. Library orientation for college students. 4. Literature--Research--Data processing. I. Johnson, Kathleen A., 1950- II. Harris, Steven R. (Steven Robert)

PN73.T43 2009
807--dc22
            2009005525

Copyright ©2009 by the American Library Association.
All rights reserved except those which may be granted by Sections 107 and 108 of the Copyright Revision Act of 1976.

Printed in the United States of America.

13 12 11 10 09   5 4 3 2 1

Table of Contents

Introduction: Teaching Literary Research

Kathleen A. Johnson and Steven R. Harris

INFORMATION LITERACY AND LITERARY RESEARCH

Information literacy and literary research are two topics that have a great deal in common. This collection of essays grew from a desire to explore that relationship. The purpose of the collection is twofold: to gain the perspectives of both English professors and librarians on the significance of information literacy to the teaching of research methods in literary studies; and to meet the need for an expanded exploration of best practices in teaching literary research to students at various levels, undergraduate through graduate, and in various areas of literary focus.

"Information literacy" is a commonly used phrase that has come to represent any sort of instruction, orientation, or training directed at library users, but it also embodies a whole suite of professional values and philosophical principles within librarianship. From this place of prominence, the phrase and the concepts behind it become both a repository of professional hopes and the target of disdain. For example, the Instruction Section of the Association of College and Research Libraries (ACRL) says, "[i]nformation literacy is the solution to Data Smog." On the other hand, Stanley Wilder, in a *Chronicle of Higher Education* editorial, calls information literacy the "wrong solution to the wrong problem."[1]

Whether or not they are elements of the correct solution to an actual problem, library instruction and literary research have had a long and close, if at times uncomfortable, relationship. Information literacy, as a professional activity, can trace its lineage from the early years of library education through the changes in terminology to "bibliographic instruction" and then "library instruction" in the 1970s and 1980s. Students in English literature and related fields likewise have a pedigree of training which was once designated simply "bibliography" and then more generically "research methods." With changes in information technology, these kinds of courses have also experienced a change in content, moving away from training in practices like descriptive bibliography and toward instruction in database searching and other technologically centered applications. In fact, many English departments, which once saw a course in research methodology as essential to graduate education, have abandoned these courses altogether or replaced them with introductory surveys of criticism or literary theory.[2]

Thus, change is also one of the topics we strive to touch upon in this volume. Literary studies and their supporting library collections can, of course, be simultaneously conservative and cutting-edge. Literary studies continue to place great importance in "the book." Yet, electronic networks, databases, and digital texts all impact the research process of the literary scholar. Much of the impetus behind the creation of electronic texts (or etexts) and sophisticated mechanisms for interacting with etexts comes from the literary scholars themselves. The field has also undergone a proliferation of methodological approaches in recent years. In the early twentieth century, philology and literary history began to battle for prominence in English departments with the New Criticism, which later had to vie for ascendancy with postmodern approaches such as deconstruction and reader-response theory in the 1970s, and these in turn have given ground in recent years to feminist critique, the new historicism, and postcolonial studies. And yet, amazingly, all of these approaches might exist simultaneously in any given English department today.[3]

The students engaged in the literary research process have, likewise, changed with each generation, becoming greater consumers of technology, if, perhaps, remaining somewhat ignorant of effective research methods. Our contributors discuss the challenges instruction librarians and literature faculty face in this ever-changing environment. Perhaps, in the end, these essays demonstrate, as Altick and Fenstermaker state in *The Art of Literary Research*, that an "irreducible element of brain work that lies at the heart of productive research remains undiminished."[4]

This collection of essays grew out of a panel discussion program sponsored by the Literatures in English Section of the Association of College and Research Libraries at the 2002 American Library Association conference. The panel topic was "teaching literary research," and, like this volume, the topic was addressed by both librarians and literature faculty. Panelists included James K. Bracken, Assistant Director of Library Research and Reference Services and bibliographer for English and American literature at Ohio State University, and author of *Reference Works in British and American Literature* (Libraries Unlimited, 1998); James L. Harner, Professor of English, Texas A & M University, and author of *Literary Research Guide: An Annotated Listing of Reference Sources in English Literary Studies* (MLA, 2002); Helene C. Williams, English Bibliographer for the Humanities at

Harvard University, and co-author of *Teaching the New Library to Today's Users* (Neal-Schuman, 2000); and William A. Wortman, Humanities Librarian at Miami University of Ohio, and co-editor of a previous Publications in Librarianship volume, *Literature in English: A Guide for Librarians in the Digital Age* (ACRL, 2000). Steven R. Harris, co-editor of this volume and incoming chair of the Literatures in English Section at the time of the conference, served as the panel moderator.

The panelists held a lively conversation about teaching literary research, from which the audience gained numerous insights.[5] Following this panel presentation, the Publications Committee of the Literatures in English Section suggested that the Section sponsor a book on the topic of teaching literary research. With three of the original panelists taking part, this collection may be seen as a continuation of the conversation begun at that summer meeting.

STUDENTS, LITERATURE, AND INFORMATION LITERACY

The first four chapters in *Teaching Literary Research* address questions of how information literacy might advance the goals of the undergraduate literature curriculum. The opening essay, "Information Literacy as Situated Literacy" by Van E. Hillard, examines of the nature of "information" and "literacy" and their relationship "as context-specific within the universe of social activities of knowledge production and reproduction." Hillard's critique of the ACRL "Information Literacy Competency Standards for Higher Education" (2000) should inform subsequent revisions and adaptations of such standards and should advance the dialogue between professors of English and librarians about how they can best work together to teach and guide students. Hillard's description of a "library not as some vast storehouse of data, but rather as an elaborate house of argument, a site where users activate and reactivate conversations and disagreements across time and space..." reframes our understanding of the value and role of libraries.

"'I Couldn't Find an Article That Answered My Question': Teaching the Construction of Meaning in Undergraduate Literary Research," by John Bean and Nalini Iyer, focuses on teaching third year undergraduate English majors. A primary concern for the authors is for students to view research as inquiry; they argue that the "thesis question," rather than the "thesis statement" is the best approach to employ. In doing so, they critique the "information retrieval" model of research and emphasize the importance of making, not finding, an answer to the thesis question.

A complementary approach is described in Kate Koppelman's chapter, which uses the metaphor of students listening in on the critical conversations about literary topics via careful reading and guided research before joining in the conversation through their own literary essays. She describes a course for second year undergraduate English majors in which she introduces students "to some of the major theoretical movements in the field" and "to the expectations of the scholarly community" regarding research methods, use of library resources, and documentation styles.

In "The Printing Press and the Web: Modernists Teaching Postmodernists," Elizabeth Williams addresses the challenges to "modernist" professors and librarians of teaching undergraduates who are "post-modernists," untangling the many generational differences in world views, research approaches, and values between current students and their older mentors.

LITERARY SITUATIONS

The next group of chapters approaches the question of research within specific literary methodologies or genres. These include approaches to teaching non-majors and non-native English speaking populations.

Working with undergraduate students who are not English majors presents some interesting challenges and prompts creative solutions as described by Kate Manuel. Although her focus is on Southwestern Literature, the concepts and approaches may be applied more broadly to many different types of literature.

Miriam Laskin and José Díaz describe their approach to the challenges of working with first-generation college students, in a setting that allows students to begin studies in their native Spanish and then transitions the students into English as a second language. They concentrate on building a foundation in information literacy skills, which will then be reinforced and practiced during the literary research process. Their special focus is on "information literacy as a language-learning tool," a topic on which they say "virtually nothing" has been published.

Vickery Lebbin and Kristen McAndrews examine the use of folklore to expand students' research capabilities in their chapter "Ways of Knowing: Integrating Folklore Studies, Composition, and Information Literacy through a Learning Community." They incorporate the approach of using a learning community to link the worlds of folklore studies and of research.

Austin Booth and Laura Taddeo address approaches to teaching literary research within the context of cultural studies for graduate classes in the eighteenth century novel and the nineteenth century novel, and undergraduate classes in the twentieth century novel and in literary criticism. The authors also discuss technology and how electronic editions can be used in the research processes of cultural studies.

LITERARY LIBRARIANS

The remaining chapters illustrate various experiences of librarians in teaching literary research. Drawing on her dual experiences as an English Ph.D. and as a librarian, Meg Meiman offers insights into what a librarian can bring to teaching graduate students about research. Library education, she observes, enabled her to "see literary research from more than one angle at the same time," a "cubist" skill she hopes to impart to other students of literature.

As a librarian with many years of experience, William Wortman focuses on the "resources" of literary study and proposes a four-part program of instruction that addresses: texts and textuality, authors and authorship, criticism and theory, contexts and cognates. Throughout the program he emphasizes both book history and electronic resources, creating a context that encompasses the past and technological innovation.

The value of working with the English Department to integrate information literacy into the undergraduate curriculum is the focus of "Librarians Influencing the (Literature) Core Curriculum," by Sheril Hook and Verónica Reyes-Escudero. Approaches to assessing the students' progress toward meeting the goals are discussed, as are some of the challenges that face librarians and faculty members trying to integrate information literacy formally into coursework.

Helene Williams takes the matter of literary instruction in a different direction by asking who will train librarians. How will new and experienced librarians gain the skills they need to effectively assist in teaching literary research? She provides practical advice and specific recommendations to meet this need.

Dan Coffey's literature review identifies the few but significant works that deal directly with teaching literary research. His review was intentionally limited to materials with a literary focus, and does not address the general practice of bibliographic or library skills instruction. Kathleen Johnson extends this literature review through the year 2008. Many of the other authors in this anthology cite additional resources relevant to the matter of teaching literary research.

RESEARCH COMPETENCIES

We hope that this book launches further discussions of teaching literary research and continued examination of information literacy within the literary disciplines. In these discussions, the "Research Competency Guidelines for Literatures in English" (2007), which "address the need for a more specific and source-oriented approach within the discipline of English literatures, including a concrete list of research skills"[6] than offered by the ACRL "Information Literacy Competency Standards for Higher Education" (2000)[7] may prove to be a useful resource.

It has been a pleasure to work with each of the authors and we would like to express our gratitude to all of them for their contributions to this collection.

Kathleen A. Johnson
University Libraries
University of Nebraska-Lincoln

Steven R. Harris
University Libraries
The University of New Mexico

NOTES

1. See Association of College and Research Libraries, Introduction to Information Literacy. ACRL, 2003 [accessed September 19, 2005]. Available from: http://www.ala.org/ala/mgrps/divs/acrl/issues/infolit/overview/intro/index.cfm; and Stanley Wilder, "Information Literacy Makes All the Wrong Assumptions," *Chronicle of Higher Education* 51, no. 18 (2005): B13.

2. Susan Handelman, "Ending the Cold War: Literary Theory and the Bibliography and Methods Course," *Literary Research* 12, no. 2/3 (1987): 116-118.

3. Stephen Greenblatt and Giles Gunn, eds., *Redrawing the Boundaries: The Transformation of English and American Literary Studies* (New York: Modern Language Association, 1992). 1-11. Also see Terry Eagleton, *Literary Theory: An Introduction*, 2nd ed. (Minneapolis: University of Minnesota Press, 1996), 15-46.

4. Richard D. Altick and John J. Fenstermaker, *The Art of Literary Research*, 4th ed. (New York: Norton, 1993), vii.

5. A recording of this session was made. Association of College and Research Libraries, and American Library Association. 2002. *Teaching Literary Research: Challenges in a Changing Environment*. [Palm Desert, Calif.]: Produced and distributed by Teach'em Continuing Education.

6.   Association of College and Research Libraries. Literatures in English Section, "Research Competency Guidelines for Literatures in English," http://www.ala.org/ala/mgrps/divs/acrl/standards/researchcompetenciesles.cfm
The "Research Competency Guidelines for Literatures in English" are included in the Appendix in this book.

7.   Association of College and Research Libraries, "Information Literacy Competency Standards for Higher Education," http://www.ala.org/ala/mgrps/divs/acrl/standards/informationliteracycompetency.cfm

Part One: Students, Literature, and Information Literacy

Information Literacy as Situated Literacy

Van E. Hillard

Since the 1930s, American college and university libraries have increasingly located their library research instruction for first-year students within the first-year writing course, a course that typically has provided an introduction to those practices associated with academic writing: namely, the use of primary and secondary sources in the construction of intellectual argument and analysis.[1] Though library and writing faculty often hold a common interest in demystifying research and research writing for students new to the academy, library/writing instruction collaborations, usually congenial and well-intended, have not always been as efficacious as the participants might wish them to be. These events are often marked by anxieties related to proper timing of the instruction, appropriate tailoring of the instruction to satisfy students' particular needs, the availability of resources, as well as what might be termed an artificiality that accrues from marginalizing research methods instruction as an event superadded to the writing course itself, what a colleague of mine calls *guerilla teaching*, as it involves a stealthily targeted hit and run pedagogy.

Working collaborations between library and writing instructors, especially those involving the teaching of transdisciplinary research practices to undergraduates, are best achieved with a measure of symmetry to both sides of the relationship. If the research methods instruction is simply appended to the *real* course, it will most likely be unfairly trivialized by students and instructors. If writing instructors figure their research methods instruction merely as that which lubricates the machinery of the writing course, both parties suffer. As one scholar has recently put this:

> On virtually every college campus librarians and writing teachers can point to each other as classroom colleagues and curricular compatriots. Yet the conversation is often limited to this level—and thus dismissed as a matter of local lore and personal friendship. Our collegial rela-

tions tend not to be sustained by a broader, theoretically informed conversation between writing and information literacy as disciplines and fields of endeavor.[2]

The opportunity for librarians and writing faculty to reclaim an abiding intellectual alliance may be found as both partners reconsider and work to revive the latent implications of an elaborated notion of *information literacy*, understood as a social and cultural literacy that undergirds the workings of academic reading, writing, and research practices.[3] I speak of *latent* implications as a way to make overt the possibilities that lie dormant within the notion of information literacy, and to recognize that (1) writing instruction has tended to undertheorize the rhetorical nature of the library as a site of intellectual work and (2) library instruction has often been held to an abbreviated notion of literacy as merely the acquisition of functional skills, delimiting the very idea of undergraduate research itself.[4]

The Associate of College and Research Library's *Information Literacy Competency Standards for Higher Education* tend to figure research activities as skills disassociated from any particular context of application. They are generalizable skills, designed to be imported into any context of use with equal utility. Such an articulation of skills has been referred to as the "autonomous model" of literacy, which conceptualizes literacy "in technical terms, treating it as independent of social context, an autonomous variable whose consequences for society and cognition can be derived from its intrinsic character."[5] In contradistinction to the autonomous model, Street posits what he terms an "ideological" model of literacy, which "signals quite explicitly that literacy practices are aspects not only of 'culture' but also of power structures."[6] When applied to information literacy, Street's model holds the distinct advantage of explicitly defining research skills as learned behaviors particular to a distinct library culture, understood as a complex of social knowledges, distinctions, preferences, and values maintained and embraced by professionals (cultural insiders) who collectively set standards, develop and refine a specific research language, and invent the vast orders of classification schemes that enable access to its (even vaster) analog and digital archives. Students, at some moment in their undergraduate lives, stand as outsiders to this particular culture. If they are to become truly information literate, they must navigate its borders by developing a basic understanding of the elements making up the culture of the library.

I argue that this passage into understanding library culture can best be facilitated when we define information literacy as *situated literacy*, where literate practices shape and are shaped by social, cultural, political, and economic forces such that literacy events—a particular search for information, a specific occasion for composing an argument, a certain classification of a tradition of inquiry, the cataloguing of a monograph, the use and definition of a key term in writing—are understood as context-specific within the universe of social activities of knowledge production and reproduction. Situated literacy has been most prominently theorized and practiced by the New Literacy Studies group of social linguists, who examine literacy events as social, political, and material enactments, and seek to identify the ways in which literacy practices attain social value and distinction. Their work may help us to energize the efforts of research and writing instruction as it invigorates the important mandate of information literacy itself, guiding us to navigate a sharp social turn, writing instructors and library professionals together.[7]

Before turning to how information literacy may be conceptualized as a form of situated literacy, it may be useful to remind ourselves that the very name *information literacy* has fostered terminological troubles for librarians and writing instructors alike.[8] A first sticking point comes with the choice of the term *information* to represent the stuff of catalogs and databases. It is unlikely that most first-year Composition courses define writing as information management or information production, and even less likely that such courses conceive of reading and research as information recovery or retrieval. Certainly, academic argument calls at times for the inclusion of various data and facts as evidence in support of its claims, but such information must be written into the argument itself, shaped and contextualized to suit the occasion of its use. To be effective *as* evidence, information must be solicited in the service of larger judgments, guiding ideas, and intellectual or disciplinary values. This is all to say that though the concept of information literacy seems to work adequately to describe the activities of academic research from the librarians' perspective, it will likely not describe the rhetorical practices associated with academic writing. Written argument and analysis are typically not understood as predominately informational in nature. It is far more likely that research writing will be addressed in very different terms: documents, texts, traditions of inquiry and scholarship, debates and disagreements, studies—even knowledge production—but rarely as simply locating information.

At stake here is no small quibble over words. The historical shift from bibliographic instruction to information skills instruction is not trendy; it is a decades-old cultural shift from librarianship to information management driven by particular philosophical and institutional preferences. It may well be that university faculty other than reference and research education specialists have neither attended to nor reckoned with the profession's shift, finding themselves unable to connect their own expectations about undergraduate research to the workings of information literacy as a liberal-educational mandate. To work cooperatively on the shared intellectual project of teaching research practices, non-librarians might do well to acknowledge (perhaps even honor) the fact that nowadays information is the chief operating metaphor to describe what libraries contain, bringing to mind the institutional, political, and epistemologic preferences that have led to the ascendancy of the information paradigm. Likewise, librarians might acknowledge the strengths and limits of the term so as not to take its currency for granted, and not to be unwittingly captivated by its dominance in the library profession.

Another set of nominal (and therefore conceptual) issues cluster around the choice of the term *literacy* to represent the activity of using the library's resources. As a term of art, literacy is perhaps readily valued by librarians and writing instructors since it carries with it an invigorated notion of the purposeful use of language and operates as a value-laden and status-marking term. Some of its power can be felt if we envision what it will mean to classify someone as information *illiterate*, a quite radical characterization, but one that undoubtedly will be applied to some students who have not mastered or are unsuccessful with the practices of information retrieval.[9] Literacy is also a term that adumbrates a wide array of valuations of literate behaviors, ranging from the most functionalist and instrumental to the most critical and transformative. Interestingly, when linked to the term *information*, literacy operates on a number of points on a continuum of practices, from the utilitarian (as in the tool literacy of operating computers) to the political (as in analyzing sources and uses of information in order to critique some aspect of the status quo information environment). The Association of College and Research Libraries (ACRL) "Information Literacy Competency Standards for Higher Education" embraces a rather wide set of literate behaviors along this spectrum, maintaining that

An information literate individual is able to:
+ Determine the extent of information needed
+ Access the needed information effectively and efficiently

- Evaluate information and its sources critically
- Incorporate selected information into one's knowledge base
- Use information effectively to accomplish a specific purpose
- Understand the economic, legal, and social uses surrounding the use of information, and access and use information ethically and legally.[10]

The abilities to project need, to act efficiently, to evaluate critically, to use selectively in light of purpose, with a measure of ethical and legal awareness, constitutes an ambitious instructional project. Certain literate goals (planning, selectivity driven by purpose, ethical awareness) speak to a literacy driven by both criticality and a sense of the social and cultural uses of information. Efficiency, though, seems to come from a different set of interests—pragmatic, but also quantifiable, even mechanistic. To be fair, few, if any, librarians would value efficiency in locating sources at the expense of a prolonged critical evaluation of them. Still, we can expect uneven instructional attention to the objectives. Some information literacy instruction will attend dutifully to each behavioral variant, or (more likely perhaps) some will emphasize certain of the behaviors over others, or even jettison the higher order objectives (the less teachable, or more difficult to teach) altogether.[11]

The comprehensiveness of the ACRL standards also suggests a more troubling set of expectations insofar as they imagine information literacy as something that adheres to individuals, with full information literacy characterized as an achievement of independence in a user. This is not a social literacy, but a private one, a collection of learned behaviors that will provide the consumer an efficient and smooth experience composed of correct decisions. For, though *information* itself is understood as socially produced, as contextually significant, as contingent and partial, *literacy* is not. The ACRL document speaks characteristically in terms of *literate individuals*: Information literacy "enables learners to master content and extend their investigations, become more self-directed, and assume greater control over their own learning."[12] Nowhere is literacy defined as a *social* event so that curiously, the library—a communal space that requires a measure of social interaction, a place characterized by a complex of reference conversations and interactions between professional consultants and their constituent clients—disappears in favor of an interface between an independent user and the vast orders of information.

If, in constructing the ideal information literate individual, we di-
minish (or abandon) the recognition of the library as a site of complicated
social exchange, we run the risk of remaking the academic library into a
vast informational self-serve supermarket, and abbreviate the social role
of reference practitioners who, in directing and correcting the competencies of individuals, become consumer advocates rather than librarians. It
is difficult to envision the idealized information literate individual as a
viable participant in an intellectual culture since the ACRL's information
literacy performance indicators name each behavior as something that happens within a single mind, save for the moment when the user "validates
understanding and interpretation of the information through discourse
with other individuals, subject-area experts, and/or practitioners."[13] And
this is a moment of authorization rather than real conversation.

Despite such limits, we should recall that the information literacy
competency standards, like other such educational documents, are both
a product of their historical moment, and a response to a genuine set of
institutional needs. Numerous other academic literacies—reading and
writing among them—have traditionally been coded as sets of automous
skills to be mastered. Performance objectives are eminently assessable and
teachable. They can be applied to vast and diverse populations of learners.
From another perspective, we may appreciate the careful delineation of
library research activities that the competency standards offer—starting with their ground-setting classification of a vast array of intellectual
skills—and situate them against the social, historical, and political contexts
in which they will be used. When placed in its rich contexts of practice,
information literacy stands to become a powerful working concept for
teaching research reading and writing.[14]

One starting place for such recovery comes with thinking of the library
not as some vast storehouse of data, but rather as an elaborate house of
argument, a site where users activate and reactivate conversations and
disagreements across time and space, what one theorist has called "an
enormous sculpture in paper of the structure of knowledge, a sculpture
that is constantly changing because the parts grow at different rates."[15]
Classification makes the conversations possible, and provides the armature
upon which the sculpture rests.[16] Every time a student enters the library
(physically or virtually) she, in effect, involves herself in a vast community
of participants whose exchanges represent traditions of inquiry, public
controversies, disciplinary disputes, and schools of thought. As rhetoricians

Patricia Bizzell and Bruce Herzberg define this activity:

> [research is] a social, collaborative act that draws on and
> contributes to the work of a community that cares about
> a given body of knowledge... by the social definition of
> research, the solitary researcher is not at all solitary: the
> sense of what can and should be done is derived from
> the knowledge community.... his/her work of discovery
> is impossible without continuous recovery of the work of
> others in the community.[17]

In addition to recognizing the research act as collaborative in nature, bibliographies themselves can be read as social documents insofar as they provide a record of participants within specific conversations and provide a partial census of those who have shaped inquiry at a particular moment.[18] Students awaken and orchestrate these conversations in their own writing, as they bring others' texts into connection with one another and their own work. Such valuations of the social life of information are vital to students positioning themselves as active rhetorical agents whose responsibility as researchers is to access, define, and enter ongoing intellectual discussions and controversies. By defining information as contextually significant, the ACRL standards go far in establishing such practices as normative to undergraduates' use of the academic library.[19]

Robust treatments of the conversational and intertextual nature of writing from sources are central to refiguring writing and research as social activities. Important discussions in its theory and practice continue to unfold.[20] However, we might go a step further and envision what it might mean to treat information literacy as a situated literacy so that each of the many activities associated with the academic library's functionality—its production of instruction and instructional materials, its means of sustaining reference work, its classification and cataloguing, its modes of acquisition and document processing, its publications, and all of the opportunities for students to interface with persons and with information—are seen as composed of identifiable social practices, implicated in institutional and power relationships that change over time and locale.

A situated literacy perspective treats literate behavior not as the enactment of a set of skills to be mastered by an individual, but rather as a series of events that draw upon cognitive skills, but more importantly, are social and therefore richly contextual in nature. The study of situated literacy begins with the unit of a literacy *event*, the moment when persons enter and then negotiate (virtually or interpersonally, through reading or actual conversation) a communal occasion mediated by discourse. Literacy, then, is what one *does in practice* rather than what one *knows*, and unfolds as a set of behaviors adapted to the contingencies of any particular context of use.

As literacy scholars David Barton and Mary Hamilton put this, "*literacy events* are activities where literacy has a role. Usually there is a written text, or texts, central to the episodes which arise from practices and are shaped by them.... The notion of events stresses the situated nature of literacy, that it always exists in a social context."[21] Within a situated literacy, library users—from novice to professional—rarely, if ever, enact a full mastery of research skills as the information literate individual is idealized to hold in the ACRL competency standards. Rather, each information literacy event shapes and is shaped by the contingencies of each particular occasion of practice. One's literate practices are performed against an elaborate backdrop of provisional factors: the user's status within library culture; the user's (partial) memory of past experiences of use; the nature of the user's social encounters with particular members of the library profession; the user's fluency with the languages of classification and the library's specialized vocabulary; the user's feelings and attitudes toward the library as place; the user's comfort with—or resistance to—the frustrations of searching; and the user's improvisations as the information literacy event unfolds.

The working assumption is that information literacy necessarily requires a measure of adaptation to the variables of lived context which are, by nature, differently valued by its participants, historically-specific, marked by differential power relationships, and mediated by (differently interpreted) discourses and texts. Though information literacy certainly involves higher order cognitive skills (critical detection, reasoned analysis, judicious evaluation, inference-making, and critique), its practice requires something more: what might be called *dispositions* toward emergent occasions, where the library user calls upon and continues to assemble a repertoire of intellectual and social practices that sustain the library's culture.

From my distance, I envision these as rhetorical dispositions because they involve more or less strategic uses of language and other symbolic means to meet desired ends. Such dispositions might include, but are not limited to: a tolerance for ambiguity and indeterminacy (as research is inevitably messy, recursive, even inefficient at times); a preparedness to enter into and sustain conversations with others who, though relative strangers to one another, work to achieve mutually satisfying outcomes to their reference interactions; a readiness to revise procedures and modify principles to meet the exigencies of real-life situations (scant resources, dead end searches, unavailable materials, etc.); an historical sensibility, complemented by a political awareness that the library has evolved over time, and has both shaped and been shaped by the politics of knowledge-making (including the politics of classification; the partiality of cataloguers; the interests of those in acquisitions; as well as disciplinary and institutional pressures and agendas). But before we can codify such dispositions, we need to do our homework, to create a more fine-grained description of the specifics of research literacy as it is put to practice by students. We need, in other words, to attend first to the local.

Both library and writing instructors might collaborate to determine how to proceed with composing ethnographies of information literacy: How can we best observe and identify the complex of behaviors, attitudes, and social practices that constitute information literacy in use? What sorts of narratives of individual adaptation or improvisation might be uncovered? What characterizes reference conversations as discursive events? How is the physical place of the library perceived and valued? How is information literacy status conferred and encoded? How does the formal lexicon of professional terms of art coincide or differ from the ways in which conversations about research are managed in everyday situations? How does it feel to work within the library's system, and how do those feelings effect actions? Responses to such questions will almost certainly require of us a more careful humanistic study than we typically have engaged, one sponsored by close observation, the willingness to reconsider expectations and to revise our teaching of research and research writing practices in light of what our descriptions tell us. This is a project that undoubtedly will require time, energy, and resources.

We can assist our students in assuming their social roles if we treat research not simply as contact with information, but as participation within the professional culture we call the library. Since its coinage as a commonplace more than thirty years ago, the term *information literacy* has most often been viewed as a survival tactic: faced with the ever-growing, ever more confusing, omnipresent flood of information, how shall we train students responsibly and responsively to meet its power and force? A situated information literacy does not so much aim to tame that beast, but to honor the fact that all of us are in this together, that we have an important opportunity to invite our students to become participants in research culture when we enrich the very accomplishments of literacy as it is practiced.

NOTES

1.   A portion of this history is traced in Donald A. Barclay and Darcie Reimann Barclay, "The Role of Freshman Writing in Academic Bibliographic Instruction," *The Journal of Academic Librarianship* 20 (September 1994): 213-217.

2.   Rolf Norgaard, "Writing Information Literacy: Contributions to a Concept," *Reference & User Services Quarterly* 43, no. 2 (Winter 2003): 124-125.

3.   In his "Critical Information Literacy: Implications for Instructional Practice," *Journal of Academic Librarianship* 32, no .2 (March 2006): 192-199, James Elmborg has turned to an enriched concept of critical literacy to nourish information literacy as a more politically and socially conscious construct.

4.   Norgaard, 125, 126.

5.   Brian Street, "The New Literacy Studies," in *Cross-Cultural Approaches to Literacy*, ed. Brian Street, 5 (London: Cambridge UP, 1993).

6.   Street, 7.

7.   A comprehensive review of this literature (also grouped under the name of the "New London School") can be found in James Paul Gee's "The New Literacy Studies: From 'Socially Situated' to the Work of the Social," in *Situated Literacies: Reading and Writing in Context*, ed. David Barton, Mary Hamilton, and Roz Ivanič, 180-196 (New York: Routledge, 2000).

8.   A brief history of the professional reception of the term *information literacy* is provided in Shirley J. Behrens' "A Conceptual Analysis and Historical Overview of Information Literacy," *College and Research Libraries* 55 (July 1994): 309-322.

9.   C.H. Knoblauch reminds us that "The labels *literate* and *illiterate* almost always imply more than a degree or deficiency of skill. They are, grossly or subtly, sociocultural judgments laden with approbation, disapproval, or pity about the character and place, the worthiness and prospects, of persons and groups." "Literacy and the Politics of Education," in *The Right to Literacy*, ed. by Andrea A. Lunsford, Helene Moglen, and James Slevin, 74-80 (New York: Modern Language Association, 1990), 74.

10.   Association of College and Research Libraries, *Information Literacy Competency Standards for Higher Education* (Chicago: American Library Association, 2000), 2-3.

11.   We should remind ourselves that research methods instruction, as it is typically structured, is severely constrained by time, resources, and other delimiting variables, making full actualization of the various information literacy goals virtually impossible.

12.   *Information Literacy Competency Standards*, 2.

13.   Ibid., 12.

14.   Norgaard echoes this: "A robust sense of information literacy has at its heart evaluative and integrative concerns; no mere look up skill, it concerns how we judge and evaluate information and integrate it into effective communication," 126.

15.   O.B. Hardison, Jr., *Entering the Maze: Identity and Change in Modern Culture* (New York: Oxford University Press, 1981), 138.

16.   Hardison discusses the role and importance of classification in *Entering the Maze*, chapter 8, "From Knowledge to Information," 136-153.

17.   Patricia Bizzell and Bruce Herzberg, "Research as a Social Act," *The Clearing House* 60 (March 1987): 304; Barbara Fister elaborates upon the notion of research as collaboration in "Teaching Research as a Social Act: Collaborative Learning and the Library," *RQ* 29

(Summer 1990): 505-509.

18.   Building on work by Ilse Bry, Charles A. D'Aniello suggests "that bibliography is value laden." He further states that "the study of bibliographic reference sources cannot be divorced from political and sociologic considerations." "A Sociobibliographical and Sociohistorical Approach to the Study of Bibliographic and Reference Sources: A Complement to Traditional Bibliographic Instruction," in *Conceptual Frameworks for Bibliographic Education: Theory into Practice*, edited by Mary Reichel and Mary Ann Ramey, 109-133 (Littleton, CO: Libraries Unlimited, 1987), 109, 111.

19.   Two performance indicators in *Information Literacy Competency Standards* speak directly to this: "The information literate student compares new knowledge with prior knowledge to determine the value added, contradictions, or other unique characteristics of the information," and "The information literate student understands many of the ethical, legal and social issues surrounding the use of information and accesses and uses the information ethically and legally," 12, 14.

20.   From the library perspective, see Deborah Fink, *Process and Politics in Library Research: A Model for Course Design* (Chicago: American Library Association, 1989); Jeremy J. Shapiro and Shelley K. Hughes, "Information Technology as a Liberal Art," *Educom Review* (March/April 1996): 31-35; and Jean Sheridan, *Writing-across-the-Curriculum and the Academic Library: A Guide for Librarians, Instructors, and Writing Program Directors* (Westport, CT: Greenwood Publishers, 1995).

21.   David Barton and Mary Hamilton, "Literacy Practices," in *Situated Literacies: Reading and Writing in Context*, edited by David Barton, Mary Hamilton, and Roz Ivanič, 8 (London: Routledge, 2000).

"I Couldn't Find an Article that Answered My Question": Teaching the Construction of Meaning in Undergraduate Literary Research

John C. Bean and Nalini Iyer

Although the "research paper" has long been a ubiquitous undergraduate writing assignment, its definition varies widely from teacher to teacher and from discipline to discipline. Frequently undergraduate researchers, following a process quite removed from the knowledge-making practices of disciplinary scholars, produce informational reports rather than disciplinary arguments in response to a question, problem, or issue. For English majors, the problem of literary research is compounded by the unstable nature of literary studies itself, where the turn toward theory has yielded little disciplinary consensus about appropriate research problems for undergraduates.[1]

Our aim in this chapter is to address the question of how English departments, in partnership with academic librarians, might teach undergraduates to conduct literary research in a relatively sophisticated way as disciplinary insiders—at a level appropriate for undergraduates—within the discourse of literary studies. In the first part of this chapter we locate the problem of literary research within a four stage developmental theory proposed by Susan Peck MacDonald, whereby a successful undergraduate progresses from non-academic or pseudo-academic prose through generalized academic writing into novice approximations of disciplinary discourse and finally into expert insider prose.[2] Next we explore the special difficulties faced by English departments in trying to decide what constitutes "insider prose" for undergraduate English majors in light of the highly theorized and polyglot scholarship that characterizes contemporary literary studies. Finally we describe how the two of us, in collaboration with librarians, teach literary research as part of a team-designed junior level English major course entitled "Texts in Context," a course with the specific goal of teaching research writing while also introducing new English majors to critical theory.[3] We explain both the design of the course itself and the specific ways we collaborate with academic librarians. Our partnership with librarians is aimed at helping new English majors bridge the gap from generalized academic writing into the discourse of literary studies.

STAGES OF DEVELOPMENT: FROM NOVICE TO EXPERT

The problem of teaching literary research can be usefully placed within a developmental theory proposed by rhetorician Susan Peck MacDonald, who suggests that students pass through four stages in their progress from novice to expert within an academic discipline. Stage One entails pseudo-academic writing (for example, five-paragraph essays, high school book reports) or non-academic writing (personal essays, creative pieces), which often characterizes students' early writing instruction. In Stage Two, students learn, in MacDonald's words, "generalized academic writing concerned with stating claims, offering evidence, respecting others' opinions, and learning how to write with authority."[4] According to MacDonald, teaching generalized academic writing is often the goal of first-year composition courses and of general education curricula. Stage Three begins when students start advanced work in their majors. It encompasses what MacDonald calls "novice approximations of particular disciplinary ways of making knowledge"[5]—students' early attempts at thinking and writing like historians, chemists, psychologists, or literary scholars. MacDonald's Stage Four is "expert, insider prose," wherein students demonstrate— through a capstone senior project or a professional apprentice paper—an undergraduate-level mastery of the discipline's discourse.

An important insight from MacDonald's research is that the ability to write generalized academic prose does not prepare students for the demands of disciplinary research, which requires substantial insider knowledge. To demonstrate the extensive, subtle, and complex differences among disciplines, MacDonald analyzes published research in three academic sub-specialties: infant attachment research in psychology, family structure research in colonial American social history, and Renaissance new historicist research in literary studies. MacDonald shows how these specialties vary in the way they pose problems, in the extent to which they form communities to work on shared problems, in the ways they identify and use evidence, in their theoretical assumptions about methods and interpretive strategies, in the range and pattern of their citations, and in their understanding of the teleology of research (whether, for example, problems are to be "solved" by a research community or left endlessly open for hermeneutical play).

MacDonald's analysis helps us better understand a novice's cognitive and epistemological bafflement when assigned a research project in his or her newly chosen major. Her insights are usefully corroborated by research reported in library journals about the differences between novice and expert research strategies. Librarian Sonia Bodi's observations parallel MacDonald's:

> The primary difference between the research process of scholars and of undergraduate students is that scholars begin with an extensive body of knowledge of their discipline, whereas students often have little context for their topic. Scholars also know the theories and paradigms of their discipline and the methodologies that shape and answer research questions.... Furthermore, scholars know the names of their peers and the universities where major research is being done, they attend professional conferences where they hear the latest research, and they use bibliographies and footnotes extensively to lead them to sources of relevance and merit. Finally, scholars have the maturity to cope with ambiguity and self-doubt inherent in research. They are gratified to find nothing written on their topic; students are devastated.[6]

In contrast, Bodi continues, undergraduate students "have trouble comprehending the scholarly sources they might find because they are not yet conversant enough in the discourse of their discipline."[7] Undergraduate students, she explains, "do not have a sufficient body of knowledge to know the parts of a topic"[8] and they have little sense of what constitutes an arguable question or an unknown in the discipline. "Not until they are well into their major, or perhaps in graduate school, can they begin readily to identify schools of thought, important scholars, studies in their disciplines, and how they fit together."[9]

The observations of MacDonald and Bodi show why the problems of novice disciplinary researchers cannot be alleviated by more emphasis on the "research paper" in first-year composition. Before students can operate at Macdonald's Stage Four (expert insider prose) they must pass through the conceptual difficulties of Stage Three, where professors face the challenge of developing assignments and teaching strategies that help novices negotiate their new terrain. To build an instructional sequence leading from Stage Three to Stage Four, English faculty must first reach some resolution about Stage Four itself: What constitutes "expert insider prose" for undergraduate English majors? We address this question in the next section.

THE PROBLEM OF EXPERT INSIDER PROSE FOR UNDERGRADUATE LITERATURE MAJORS

From our experience it is no easy matter to reach faculty consensus about the kind of writing that might characterize expert, insider prose for undergraduate literature majors. For example, should a capstone paper in the senior year be an undergraduate version of a graduate seminar paper, or might it be something else? To what extent should undergraduates be expected to produce the theorized conversations that typify contemporary scholarship in literary studies?

Before we propose our own answers to these questions, let us examine several problems particularly relevant for literary studies. The first we might call the problem of genre. In contrast to a discipline like psychology, which valorizes the experimental report written in the style of the American Psychological Association (APA) as a prototype genre to be mastered by undergraduate psychology majors, literary studies lacks a prototype genre that might serve as a model or template for undergraduates. As MacDonald has pointed out, literary studies in the age of New Criticism revealed a greater consistency in genre. Typically, critics used what she calls an "epistemic" introduction in which the writer poses an interpretive problem (often already shared by the discourse community), reviews various attempts to solve the problem, and ends by stating his or her thesis, which purports to correct earlier misunderstandings or otherwise add something new to the conversation. In contrast, contemporary scholars regularly vary from this problem-thesis structure. Highly theoretical writers might emulate the discursive practices of the continental hermeneuticists, producing reflective, abstract, self-referential, often digressive pieces with no clearly summarizable thesis. Other scholars might follow the anecdotal, aggressively anti-epistemic practices of such New Historicists as Stephen Greenblatt, who, for example, might begin on article ostensibly on Shakespeare but not mention Shakespeare for the first dozen pages, which are devoted to a seemingly tangential historical anecdote.[10] Our point here is that there is no clear teachable genre for English majors analogous to the experimental report in the sciences, the marketing proposal in business, or the clinical observation in nursing.

A second problem, to which we have already frequently alluded, is the role of theory—problematic not only for its complexity for undergraduates but also for its permutations and variety. Undergraduates doing research on a primary text must negotiate their way through a plethora of theoretically varied conversations about the same text. Not all undergraduate English programs, and certainly not our own program at Seattle University, have made literary theory a mandatory part of their curriculum. Therefore, most undergraduates working on their first Stage Three writing project are mystified by theory. Consider, for example, the plight of an undergraduate doing research on Virginia Woolf's *To the Lighthouse*. In a search of the *Modern Language Association International Bibliography*, (*MLAIB*) which we conducted in March, 2005, the subject heading *To the Lighthouse* yielded 397 citations—a hopeless number for undergraduates to pursue. When we narrowed that search to "Virginia Woolf AND *To the Lighthouse* AND feminism," the number of citations was reduced to 14. However, the articles embraced a variety of highly theorized feminist topics from the Showalter-Moi controversy to Lesbian feminism, the Great War, and so on. Similarly, a search on Mary Shelley and *Frankenstein* yielded 605 citations. When narrowed to include "romanticism" as a key term, the number was reduced to 31 but the topics were wide ranging and included romantic suicide, revisions of the 1831 text, parody of romantic poetics, and so forth. An undergraduate who is reasonably adept at searching databases and wants to do something on Woolf and feminism or Shelley and Romanticism is capable of generating a list of resources but is not necessarily closer to a productive inquiry process than he or she was before the search. When undergraduates are confronted with such a diversity of theoretical approaches, they are often overwhelmed by the daunting gap in knowledge between their novice status and that of the experts they consult. Confronted with an often difficult and puzzling primary text that is itself embedded in theorized critical conversations shaped by postmodernism, deconstruction, cultural studies, new historicism, feminism, queer theory, and so on, the new English major struggles to find a position and a voice.

A final problem for research writing in literary studies we might call the explosion of possible primary texts. In the old days of New Criticism, an undergraduate research project typically asked a student to do a formalist analysis of a single text. The research component generally focused on secondary sources—what other New Critics had said about the text. In the age of theory, however, research can focus on an almost infinite number of primary texts ranging from contemporary reviews of a literary text to contemporary political documents, newspaper reports, cultural artifacts, and so forth. What a literary scholar seeks during the research process is substantially different now than it was thirty years ago.

Given these problems, what constitutes an appropriate Stage Four research project for an undergraduate literature major? Our own belief is that English departments should try to achieve only the loosest form of consensus. They should not impose on their majors any one mode or approach to scholarship but welcome a diversity of approaches depending on the interests of individual professors and the background and expertise of any particular undergraduate student. A capstone project might be a competent and extensive close reading of a text. (For example, how does one interpret the ending of Keats' "Ode on a Grecian Urn"? What have other scholars said about this work and what is new and original about my reading? [11]) It might be an intertextual analysis (how did Coleridge's "Rime of the Ancient Mariner" influence Mary Shelley's *Frankenstein*?), or it might be a very theoretical reading of the text (how does queer theory reinterpret E.M. Forster's *A Passage to India*?). The choice of research problem for a capstone project depends a lot on the professor's own scholarly approach and the student's base knowledge (i.e., how much expertise the student already has in Keats, in Coleridge's influence on later romantics, or in queer theory). The diversity of scholarly and critical approaches in the field and its representation in any given professor presents a valuable learning opportunity for students as they take courses from a variety of professors in the department.

Having recognized the importance of diverse approaches, it also becomes necessary for English faculty to acknowledge different ability levels among students. In our experience, a capstone project for departmental honors might require substantially more scholarship than that for a non-honors major. For an honors student, the process of inquiry might require a broad understanding of the author, the socio-historical context of the work, and the history of literary scholarship of that work. However, even with extensive reading and preparation for the capstone project, undergraduates acquire a different degree of expertise than graduate students or faculty conducting research into the same author or field. Therefore, it becomes important for departments to nuance for undergraduates the meaning of MacDonald's "expert, insider prose." In reality, most literary scholars approach expert levels only late in their graduate programs and receive recognition from their peers only when they begin publishing their work in peer reviewed arenas.[12] Therefore, if we expect our undergraduates to mimic the work of professors, we set them up (and ourselves) for disappointment and failure.

From our own perspective, for an undergraduate to write expert insider prose does not mean to produce work that imitates graduate seminar papers or is publishable in a scholarly journal but to demonstrate an ability to play with complex questions, to identify and use sources to support their interpretations of a text, to establish their own positioned voice within a conversation, and to provide the reader with a substantive and new reading of the text. The "new reading" in this case is one that is "new" for the class or for other undergraduate learners, not necessarily one that is new in the field. We often create a hypothetical case of a local undergraduate research conference where the audience's level of expertise matches that of students in our own classrooms as revealed in class discussions. For the best of our students, we also promote actual regional and national undergraduate conferences such as the National Conference of Undergraduate Research (NCUR) as venues where they might seek to present their work. Another possible standard, especially for those who are considering graduate school, is to have them write papers that will be a good writing sample for a graduate school application.

OUR OWN COURSE: DESIGNING ASSIGNMENTS AND INSTRUCTIONAL STRATEGIES FOR TEACHING LITERARY RESEARCH

Once faculty clarify the kinds of Stage Four tasks that students might be asked to tackle in 400-level courses or in a capstone research project, professors can design a Stage Three course that teaches the requisite skills. In the English major curriculum of our own department, faculty have designated a junior level course, "Texts in Context," as the place where disciplinary research writing is to be explicitly taught. The final assignment for the course is a major research paper (what we might call an apprentice Stage Four paper), which serves as a prototype of the kind of papers students will frequently be asked to write in 400-level English courses. Because the course is aimed specifically at Stage Three writers, instructors develop a sequence of smaller assignments that serve as scaffolding for the major assignment due the last day of class.

"Texts in Context" usually focuses on two primary texts from different historical periods (for example, we have paired *Jane Eyre* with *A Passage to*

India and *Frankenstein* with *To the Lighthouse*) set in biographical, historical, and cultural context. To design learning goals for the course, we identified four key misconceptions about the research process that new majors often bring to the study of literature. These comprise the novice assumptions or habits that English faculty, in partnership with academic librarians, need to help Stage Three writers "undo."

- *Privileging the "thesis statement" rather than the "thesis question."* New majors often think that a research project begins with a thesis statement that research will help them "prove." A concomitant factor is novices' desire for early closure—settling quickly on a thesis statement rather than dwelling with a problematic and significant thesis question. This emphasis on formulating a thesis at the beginning of the writing process has often been encouraged by older positivist models of the writing process as well as by "information retrieval" models for library research[13]—a problem we examine briefly later in this section. One goal of our course, therefore, is to help students learn to pose—and dwell with—a genuine literary question or interpretive problem.

- *Imagining that the purpose of research is to "find" an answer to their research question rather than to "make" an answer.* As the unhappy student lament in our title suggests, novice researchers think that the purpose of library research is to find answers to their research questions—as if research results in right answers rather than in claims supported by arguments. In reality, research often leads to ambiguity and doubt, often precipitated by crucial disagreements among critics. Another of our goals, therefore, is to help students make their own arguments in their own voice, a skill that requires them to speak back to critics and to position themselves in a conversation. Many of our short assignments help students learn to resist the authority of published scholars— to read them both with and against the grain. We teach them heuristic paradigms like the following: "Although many critics have said X, I am going to argue Y," or "Although critics have long asked Y, curiously they haven't asked Z." Thus, if a database search reveals no critical articles that directly address his research question, a novice has a strategy for proceeding rather than returning to the instructor, discouraged and dismayed, in search of a new "topic." Literary scholars go to the library, we tell our students, not to *find* an answer to their research question but to *make* their own answer in conversation with other scholars.

◆ *Thinking of evidence as quotations.* New English majors typically think of literary evidence as a series of quotations—often long block quotations—mined from a text to "prove" a thesis. To the dismay of the professor, this approach often subverts the text's subtlety, complexity, ambiguity, depth, and layers of potential meaning. Another of our goals, therefore, is to teach Stage Three writers an expert's more nuanced and contextualized ways of supporting points through an interweaving of summary, paraphrase, short quotation, references to key scenes or images, and other techniques. Similarly, when Stage Three writers read secondary sources, they look for quotations from critics to support a preconceived thesis (see the first two bullets in this list). The desire to quote reveals the undergraduate researcher's longing to take refuge in the words of a more credentialed scholar. (After all, the published author is often a professor with a Ph.D. and, therefore, in the student's opinion, someone who has found the answer to the problem/question at hand.) Teaching students to speak back to critics is thus a way of helping them overcome their search for quotations.

◆ *Using web search engines naively without understanding what is being searched:* Despite instruction on the "research paper" in many first-year composition courses, our new English majors do not understand distinctions among databases nor can they articulate what web search engines actually search. If we ask them, for example, to explain differences in what they are apt to find if they search "Mary Shelley" on *Google* versus *LexisNexis®* versus the *MLAIB* versus the library catalog, they reveal little understanding of how scholarly research gets published or how databases get compiled. They also have little sense of the difference between popular magazines and peer-reviewed journals or between print sources and cyber-sources that have never appeared in print. Another of our goals, then, is not simply to teach students how to search specialized databases such as *MLAIB* but to understand how the database got compiled—what the purpose of the database is and how included items got selected and why. Since the internet is evolving rapidly, providing more and more resources to students, we, as teachers, need constantly to update this section of the course.

Based on these specific problems and on the placement of "Texts in Context" within our overall curriculum, we try to help students achieve the following learning outcomes:

Students will be able to:

1.   analyze and interpret [the literary works selected for the course] within their historical and cultural contexts

2.   explain how their own reading practices—and the practices of other readers—are affected by personal, historical, and cultural contexts

3.   explain to a lay audience how the emergence of postmodern critical theory affected the field of literary studies

4.   demonstrate an introductory understanding of several postmodern critical approaches such as new historicism, feminist theory, and reader-response criticism and to use this understanding to read texts from multiple perspectives

5.   conduct independent critical research on a literary question by (a) posing their own research questions; (b) demonstrating skill at using the Seattle University library catalog and appropriate reference sources; (c) searching the *Modern Language Association International Bibliography* and other appropriate licensed and Web databases; and (d) reading and using sources rhetorically.

6.   write an insightful researched critical argument in response to their own interpretive problems, using appropriate primary sources and positioning themselves effectively within a conversation of secondary sources; students will cite and document sources, and format their formal papers, according to the conventions of the Modern Language Association (MLA).

In teaching this course, we generally front load the reading of the two primary texts. We spend the first weeks reading each text carefully, discussing them, and noting central themes, questions, and controversies that emerge from class discussion. To help students explore texts, we use a combination of informal non-graded writing (in-class freewrites, journal entries, out-of-class "thinking pieces") and short, formal skill-building assignments. An early assignment, which eventually leads to a research proposal, asks students to identify an issue or problem that puzzles them in one of the literary texts and to show how the question is both problematic and significant. We ask them to pose an interpretive question rooted in the text itself, one that requires close textual analysis without the initial need for library research. For example, we want students to distinguish between a broad research question such as "How does Forster understand Hinduism?" and a text-based interpretive question such as "What is Professor Godbole's role in *A Passage to India?*"

Once our students have immersed themselves in the literary texts, we move to critical articles provided in our course pack or in critical editions of the texts. These articles, representing different theoretical perspectives on the works, constitute a crucially important stage of the course. We want students to learn how to "read rhetorically"—that is, to read with the grain and against the grain of the articles—so that they engage in conversation with the critics. We ask students to pay attention to how the scholar constructs the argument (for example, how the central question is presented, where the thesis is stated) and how the article constructs its audience (how the author intends to change the reader's view of the text, how the author makes assumptions about the readers' background knowledge and beliefs). For example, we have used three different essays on rape and sexuality in *A Passage to India*: Brenda Silver's feminist reading, Jenny Sharpe's new historical /postcolonial reading, and Sara Suleri Goodyear's reading of homoeroticism.[14] Each of these essays offers a dramatically different and persuasive reading of the novel. From this exercise, students deepen their knowledge of the novel itself, learn how scholars construct knowledge and pursue ambiguity, and begin adding their own voices to the conversation. We emphasize that there is no "right" answer in literary research and that the goal of literary scholars is to construct a reading of a text and to support it with arguments.

In addition to the research proposal, we assign other skill-building papers that serve as scaffolding for the final project. Examples of these assignments are shown in Exhibit 1 (which asks students to summarize and "speak back" to a secondary source) and Exhibit 2 (which asks students to narrate their inquiry/research process). Sequenced through the term, assignments like these help students develop the critical thinking and writing skills needed for their final papers.

Once students formulate a preliminary proposal (about four weeks into the term), we schedule their crucial first work with reference librarians. Our goal is to integrate the library work seamlessly into the course so that students begin the library phase at a "point of need" eager for help.

At this stage of the course, librarians become co-teachers with us in three important ways:

- They collaborate with us to create example research scenarios based on materials from our course.
- They conduct an in-library class session on information resources and searching skills for literary scholarship.
- They provide one-on-one consultations with students sharing with us the language of inquiry that we have used in class.

We look at each of these activities in turn.

Several weeks before the in-library sessions begin we meet with reference librarians to explain our course goals and collaborate on the design of example research questions and search sequences to serve as models for the class. Because students have already formulated tentative research questions, they do not come to the library as blank slates in search of a topic. Rather, based on their previous class work with sets of scholarly articles, they understand their goals for doing research and have begun to understand the nature of academic publication in literary studies. Given this background preparation, they appreciate the librarians' research examples based on works they are currently studying in the course. In a typical case, a reference librarian, prior to the library session, will have already conducted her own database search on, say, "Charlotte Bronte and fathers" for a student speculating that Rochester may be a kind of father figure for Jane. She will show the results of her searches using a variety of key words such as "Charlotte Bronte" AND "fathers," "men," "masculinity," "patriarchy," "Rochester," and so forth. It is valuable for students to see the librarian modeling this trial and error research process, trying different combinations of keyword or subject searches, rather than immediately explaining some "correct" approach based on generic examples.

During the class session itself, a reference librarian teaches students how to use the *MLAIB* and explains advanced techniques for searching the library catalog. The librarian also explains other databases and contrasts these searches with Web searches using Google or other search engines. He or she also explains sources available on JSTOR, on other full text databases, or on specialized CD ROM collections owned by the library. Finally, the librarian introduces students to a wide range of reference materials related to literary scholarship (dictionaries of mythology, biographical indexes, concordances, specialized encyclopedias, and so forth). Near the end of the period, students begin hands-on exploration of the *MLAIB*, applying their new knowledge and skills to their own research questions. Reference librarians then become roving consultants, providing a wealth of individual advice to students, often referring them to different databases or to specialized reference materials in the library.

Following the initial session, librarians continue to consult with students throughout the rest of the term. A significant benefit of our partnership with reference librarians is our fruitful discussion of the epistemological differences between an information retrieval view of research, with its emphasis on topics and information, and a constructivist, inquiry model with its emphasis on questions and meanings. In our classrooms we stress research as inquiry: posing interpretive questions, reading rhetorically, positioning oneself in a conversation, evaluating sources for theoretical assumptions and perspectives, and making one's own meanings. From our perspective, literature students come to the library not primarily to find "information" but rather to join a critical conversation or to search for relevant biographical, historical, or cultural texts upon which to apply their own skills of analysis and synthesis. The language of research-as-information-retrieval doesn't match the cognitive processes we try to teach in the course.[15] We have found that when reference librarians use constructivist language they can communicate more effectively with our students and can intuit more accurately their research dilemmas. Particularly using constructivist language helps librarians employ consulting strategies analogous to those used by writing center personnel for coaching struggling writers such as asking for clarification of the assignment, listening empathically to a student's frustration, discovering where the student is in the research process, and asking inquiry-based prompts that might help the student clarify a research question or articulate the kinds of sources most needed at a particular stage of the student's research—for example, whether the student needs to find out what other critics said about a question, fill in background knowledge, or locate a certain kind of primary source.[16]

Once the initial library sessions have been concluded, we ask students to spend a week doing intense research on their projects and then to submit a revised proposal. At this point we try to schedule one-on-one or small group consultations with our students to make sure that each has focused a productive interpretive question and has a purposeful research plan. At this stage we occasionally consult with reference librarians ourselves for advice on helping students with certain kinds of research needs. From here on students know that they have two sources of support as they complete their research and begin the early drafts of their final papers: their course instructor and a helpful staff of research librarians. When students submit their final researched literary arguments at the end of the term, they have the satisfaction of knowing what an inquiry process feels like—inquiry as a thinking process wedded to the disciplinary skills of information literacy. Our hope is that students will take pride in their ability to add their own voices to a scholarly conversation.

CONCLUSION

In creating the course "Texts in Context," the English Department at our university set for itself the goal of helping new English majors negotiate the terrain between generalized academic writing and an undergraduate approximation of expert insider prose within literary studies. As we discovered, such an agenda places new demands on both literature professors and academic librarians. Literature faculty have the responsibility of defining, in some loose but coherent way, the kind of research-based writing they are looking for in Stage Four capstone projects. (The extent to which undergraduates should be conversant in contemporary critical theory is a decision to be made by individual departments.) Literature professors must then develop Stage Three strategies for helping novice majors learn the skills needed for the capstone project—particularly the skills of posing an interpretive question, conducting appropriate library and database research, positioning themselves within a critical conversation, and creating their own arguments using disciplinary strategies and conventions. In our version of a Stage Three course, the scaffolding provided by the early skill-building assignments helps students learn the skills needed for the major research paper at the end of the course. English faculty must also form new kinds of partnerships with reference librarians to develop strategies for teaching literary research. In our case we have been fortunate to work with a generous library staff willing to create special research examples based on our course content, schedule library sessions at the exact point of need for our students, and adapt an inquiry-based view of the research process that lets them enter into the full spirit of our students' learning. The partnership we forged with librarians remains one of the satisfying highlights of our experience.

EXHIBIT ONE: A Skill-Building Assignment in Which Students Incorporate A Secondary Source into their Own Argument

WHAT IS CHARLOTTE BRONTE'S VIEW OF WOMEN IN JANE EYRE?

Situation: Puzzled by Charlotte Bronte's view of love and marriage in *Jane Eyre*, you are researching Victorian cultural debates about love, marriage, and the role of women in society. While doing a bibliographic search, you happen upon an article titled "The Creation of the American Eve: The Cultural Dialogue on the Nature and Role of Women in Late Eighteenth-Century America" by Patricia Jewell McAlexander. This article explains four competing views of women in late 18th Century Europe and America. This article really sets you to thinking: *Which of these views, if any, does Charlotte Bronte espouse in Jane Eyre?*

Your Task: Write a 3 page paper (double-spaced, 11 or 12 point font) that includes the following features: (1) An introduction that sets up the interpretive problem to be addressed and gives your thesis (assume that your audience has not read this assignment); (2) a summary of the four views of women set forth in the McAlexander article; and (3) your own concise argument addressing the question of which of these four positions (if any) represents Charlotte Bronte's view as revealed in *Jane Eyre*.

Format: Follow the manuscript conventions of the Modern Language Association (MLA). Make your first page look like a professional scholarly manuscript in the MLA style and include a separate "Works Cited" page that accurately cites the McAlexander article and your edition of *Jane Eyre*. All internal citations should follow the parenthetical system of MLA. Your paper can be no longer than 3 pages of text. I will not read anything that spills over to a fourth page.

Purpose and Goals of This Assignment: This assignment will help you develop the following skills needed for your major paper.
1. The ability to write a title and an academic introduction that poses an interpretive question
2. The ability to summarize relevant portions of a scholarly article

3. The ability to attribute that summary to its appropriate source (through attributive tags such as "according to McAlexander" and "McAlexander claims further that …") and thus to distinguish the source's ideas from your own
4. The ability to cite the source in your text itself (using MLA's parenthetical style) and to give complete bibliographic information (using MLA conventions) in a separate "Works Cited" page
5. The ability to follow the MLA manuscript format for margins, paragraphing, placement of author's name and page numbers, placement of title, formatting of quotations, and so forth
6. The ability to use the source within your own argument.

EXHIBIT TWO: A Research Narrative Aimed At Delaying Closure And Promoting Inquiry[17]

The Task: Write a 7-10 page, chronologically organized, autobiographic account of your thinking process as you explore a research problem related to either *Jane Eyre* or *A Passage to India*. Your exploratory narrative should include both external details (how you found research sources, where and when you did your work, whom you talked to) and internal thinking details (summaries of your research sources, your responses to the arguments of critics, your wrestling with ideas, the evolution of your thinking). Make your exploratory narrative an interesting intellectual detective story—something your readers will enjoy. The key to this paper is to describe for your reader the evolution of your thinking, including times of frustration as well as excitement.

The Process: Your exploratory paper should be organized chronologically with narrative time cues ("The next day I …" "A couple of days later I again went to …" "Then on February 10th, while drinking coffee at Starbucks, I began to think about …"). Your narrative describes what you actually did and thought during the research period. You begin by describing your initial research problem and end up wherever you actually end up—perhaps at an unhappy dead end or perhaps at a productive place from which you can begin your final paper. *This is a "thesis-seeking" paper rather than a "thesis-supporting" paper. Your narrative describes your search for a thesis in response to a puzzling and significant problem.*

Format: Use the MLA style throughout and include a Works Cited list at the end.

Purpose and goals of the assignment: This assignment will help you develop ideas for your major paper that follows. It gives you a place to record your thinking-in-progress and to think metacognitively about your research process. It rewards you for periods of frustration and confusion and gives you space to explore complex ideas before they are fully formed and re-organized for readers. It also encourages you to work steadily on your research project throughout the middle of the term. If you don't do the research in a timely way, you will have no subject matter for this paper.

NOTES

1.   See J. Paul Hunter, "The Return to History in English Studies," in *Literature in English: A Guide for Librarians in the Digital Age*, ed. Betty H. Day and William A. Wortman (Chicago, American Association of College and Research Libraries, 2000), 289-299. The impact of literary theory on teaching of research is also pertinent to the education of graduate students according to Harrison T. Meserole in "The Nature(s) of Literary Research," *Collection Management* 13, no. 1/2 (1990): 68.

2.   Susan Peck MacDonald, *Professional Academic Writing in the Humanities and Social Sciences* (Carbondale, IL: Southern Illinois University Press, 1994).

3.   English departments vary widely in the way they teach research writing to their majors. At Seattle University, the English faculty developed "Texts in Context" specifically to employ the pedagogies described in this chapter. Although the curriculum has undergone two major changes in the last fifteen years, this course remains a required one.

4.   MacDonald, 187.

5.   Ibid.

6.   Sonia Bodi, "How Do We Bridge the Gap between What We Teach and What They Do? Some Thoughts on the Place of Questions in the Process of Research," *Journal of Academic Librarianship* 28, no.3 (2002): 109-110.

7.   Ibid., 111.

8.   Ibid., 110.

9.   Ibid., 111.

10.   MacDonald cites the opening sentences of Stephen Greenblatt's *Shakespearean Negotiations: The Circulation of Social Energy in Renaissance England* (Berkeley: University of California Press, 1988): 1 as an example of a non-epistemic introduction:

> I began with the desire to speak with the dead.
>
> This desire is a familiar, if unvoiced, motive in literary studies, a motive organized, professionalized, buried beneath thick layers of bureaucratic decorum: literary professors are salaried, middle-class shamans.

MacDonald argues that Greenblatt's departure from a conventional problem-thesis structure aims to critique not only the discursive practices of Shakespeare but also the socially constructed discursive practices of literary scholars themselves. (MacDonald, 127-28).

11.   A common misconception amongst undergraduates is that textual analysis is easy because it is not theoretical. Students need to be taught that there are theoretical assumptions underlying textual analyses and that many overtly theoretical analyses of literary works employ close textual readings.

12.   In his essay "Confessions of a Research Scholar," in *Symposium Humanists at Work: Disciplinary Perspectives and Personal Reflections* (Chicago: University of Illinois Press, 1989), 103-113, Gerald Graff recounts his own growth as a scholar after having been appointed to his first tenure track position. In Graff's humorous and somewhat self-deprecating essay, one can see that gaining expert status is a very long process. Therefore, it is useful to think of degrees or stages of expertise when one speaks of "expert insider" prose.

13.   For example, in the ACRL's *Information Literacy Competency Standards for Higher Education* (Chicago: Association of College and Research Libraries, 2000) Standard One, 1.b. specifies that the student "develops a thesis statement and formulates questions based on the information need" as an early step. We would like to see this rephrased to emphasize the early formation of an interpretive question rather than the early formation of a thesis statement.

14.   Brenda R. Silver, "Periphrasis, Power and Rape in *A Passage to India*," in *E. M. Forster*, ed. Jeremy Tambling (London: Macmillan, 1995), 171-194; Jenny Sharpe, "The Unspeak-

able Limits of Civility: *A Passage to India*," in *Allegories of Empire: The Figure of Woman in the Colonial Text* (Minneapolis: University of Minnesota Press, 1993), 113-136; Sara Suleri Goodyear, "Forster's Imperial Erotic," in *E. M. Forster*, ed. Jeremy Tambling (London: Macmillan, 1995), 151-170.

15. Many librarians have offered similar critiques of the information-retrieval model of research. See especially Barbara Fister, "Teaching the Rhetorical Dimensions of Research," *Research Strategies* 11, no. 4 (Fall 1993): 211-219. Mark Emmons and Wanda Martin used Fister's insights in developing a library instructional model at the University of New Mexico where students are taught to "take a critical stance toward sources, regarding authors as rhetorically situated contributors to the conversation about an issue (i.e. people with an interest and a point of view) rather than as disinterested sources of facts to be reported" ("Engaging Conversation: Evaluating the Contribution of Library Instruction to the Quality of Student Research," *College and Research Libraries* 63, no. 6 (Nov. 2002): 545).

16. Reference librarians, like writing center consultants, are often positioned as intermediaries between students and instructors. They observe first hand the struggles of students confronted with unclear assignments, blocked by frustration, or uncertain how to use the materials they are trying to locate in libraries. A promising direction for collaboration is to incorporate librarians more directly into the conversations of writing centers and more broadly the writing-across-the-curriculum movement. See James K. Elmborg, "Information Literacy and Writing Across the Curriculum: Sharing the Vision," *Reference Services Review* 31, no. 1 (2003): 68-80.

17. For a detailed explanation of exploratory narratives as a productive intermediate stage in the writing of a research paper, see John D. Ramage, John C. Bean, and June Johnson, *The Allyn and Bacon Guide to Writing*, 4th ed. (New York: Longman, 2006), 191-217.

Literary Eavesdropping and the Socially Graceful Critic

Kate Koppelman

> For years I have heard students complain about the gap
> between published criticism and the critical writing they
> feel able to produce. The professional essays remain a
> kind of foreign language, something that others write,
> something that can be quoted but seldom emulated.
> ~W.F. Garrett-Petts, *Writing About Literature*

> Read slowly ... not to devour, to gobble, but to graze,
> to browse scrupulously, to rediscover—in order to read
> today's writers—the leisure of bygone readings: to be
> *aristocratic* readers.
> ~Roland Barthes, *The Pleasure of the Text*

This chapter outlines a successful strategy for preparing students to produce engaged, original, and well-researched writing about literary texts.[1] The course I describe here is directed at sophomore-level English majors and has two primary goals: 1) an introduction to the context of scholarly literary analysis—this includes a brief introduction to some of the major theoretical movements in the field (New Criticism, New Historical or Biographical Criticism, Deconstruction, and Feminism); 2) an introduction to the expectations of the scholarly community in regard to research methods and forms—this includes library resources and documentation styles. As the quote from W. F. Garrett-Petts' *Writing about Literature* suggests, the expectation of written literary analyses in classes on literary research is often considered troublesome both for students and for instructors. He goes so far as to say that the analytical essay—most commonly the final (if not only) measurement of a student's success in a course on literature—"pales in comparison with the lively classroom discussion that may have preceded it."[2] According to Garrett-Petts (and, I would venture, anyone who has had the pleasure of a class discussion that "clicked," that was alive with enthusiasm), "critical [classroom] exchange can entertain and seduce even the initially uninterested student."[3]

Unfortunately, critical writing and research is too often seen as a threat to such seduction—such pleasure or enjoyment in the literary text. Insofar as this collection is intended for those directly involved in teaching students how to practice literary research—faculty members and librarians most immediately—the bulk of the chapter will speak to praxis: outlines for assignments, sequencing, local and global goals. However, this collection is also interested in how the current standards for information literacy can and should be used to teach students how to effectively function in an information-laden world. Consequently, the course as it is currently designed responds to the information literacy standards in quite specific ways: adhering to those standards at a number of discernable points while challenging other aspects of the standards and competencies as they are now written and understood. Most specifically, the second quote with which I began indicates that there is a more theoretical motivation behind the course as I see it: to *slow down* the research process for students in order to return to literary analysis the pleasure, seduction, and delight which is due to it. That process of slowing down is the primary way in which I see this course as challenging the ways in which information literacy is currently being discussed.

According to the *Information Literacy Competency Standards for Higher Education*, reviewed and approved by the Association of College and Research Libraries, students who have achieved information literacy will be "self-directed" and will be able to "assume greater control over their learning."[4] Further, the standards indicate that "Many of the competencies are likely to be performed recursively, in that reflective and evaluative aspects included in each standard will require the student to return to an earlier point in the process, revise the information-seeking approach, and repeat the same steps."[5] In the field of literary studies, self-direction and control cannot come without a focus on process and an emphasis on developmental learning. I believe that such an emphasis is best demonstrated by showing students the value of finding pleasure in the work and modeling for them the particular importance of recursive approaches to the reading of a literary text (in this course, the same literary text is read in various ways and from various perspectives for a bulk of the class time). Giving students a poem and asking them to read it and critically discuss it involves far more than asking that they understand the words on the page in front of them. While teaching students to read poetry is not the focus of this course (or this essay), the place of patient, leisurely, and recursive reading—a place to which I will ask students to return again and again when I teach this course—speaks directly to the standards of information literacy mentioned above.

In addition to the emphasis on self-direction and recursive learning, the information literacy standards claim that "An information literate individual is able to: … . Evaluate information and its sources critically [and] Incorporate selected information into one's knowledge base."[6] The approach to teaching literary studies that I advocate begins with a slight challenge or addendum to this definition or expectation. That is, it understands that the "knowledge base" of the beginning literature student must be significantly added to, polished, and exercised before that student is prepared to identify, evaluate, and incorporate information available to them through outside sources. It emphasizes the need for a more leisurely approach to the single literary text in order to build a "knowledge base" to which the student can actively add. Further, the field of literary studies—along with many of the other humanities—presents unique challenges to the idea of finding, collecting, and evaluating information. In literary studies especially, students are dealing not only with an abundance of current materials, but with, in many cases, hundreds of years of previous literary criticism and response of which they must both be aware and learn how to manage. Without emphasizing both the pleasure and the patience of what I am calling literary eavesdropping, such a task becomes overwhelming to students, leading them, I believe, to less of a self-directed approach to literary analysis and more of a self-preserving one. This course re-thinks the place of both faculty and librarians in the process of achieving information literacy by asking that we both model the ongoing process of "learning" the literary text by emphasizing activities stressed in the information literacy standards such as recursiveness and repetition. As such, most of the activities I describe here focus on the third of the five standards for evaluating information literacy: "The information literate student evaluates information and its sources critically and incorporates selected information into his or her own knowledge base and value system."[7] I am asking that faculty and librarians not rush the student into identifying a research topic or problem before the student has had the time and space to find the pleasure of a literary text and to hear its unique critical discourse.

Just as the information literate student should possess "critical discernment," the literary critic should be able to determine the meaning and the value of the literary text though a process of attentive judgment. It should not be surprising to find that, in describing the task of the literary critic (student or professional), the scholarly community has used metaphor and analogy to best characterize the actions of the attentive, attuned reader. I will here consider one such comparison—suggested by the title of this chapter: "eavesdropping"—which implies the presence of both pleasure and patience in the analytical process. This process focuses primarily on "inquiry" and "thinking critically," rather than on "problem-solving," the competency highlighted in the first of the information literacy standards.[8] Garrett-Petts makes reference to an analogy suggested by Kenneth Burke in *The Philosophy of Literary Form*: "the learning of new disciplines [is like] entering a room where others are busily engaged in heated discussion."[9]

For the student, as for the late arriver at a party, entering into a discussion that is already in progress has the potential to produce anxiety: what has already been discussed? What did I miss? Have there been rules of engagement established that I am unaware of? What are the political leanings of the group? The list of concerns is seemingly endless—as the vast amount of literary research might seem to the uninitiated student of criticism. However, Garrett-Petts is insistent that "becoming an active and successful participant within a college or university means learning the *academic discourse* or language of the community ... [F]ailing to learn it can have serious consequences."[10] The student is the late-arriving guest to the party, the instructor is the gracious host, and the two together must first engage in what Garrett-Petts briefly calls "'eavesdropping' on the profession" in order to equip the student with the social graces needed to avoid scholarly and analytical blunders.[11]

I find Burke's analogy quite apt for a number of reasons—though in talking to students about Burke's metaphor, I tend to turn the parlor discussion into a cocktail party, perhaps an image that might seem more accessible in twenty-first century America. First, the comparison insists that the instructor and the student establish a relationship from the start of this party banter. "Like a good host, the instructor can outline some of the stances taken, introduce the guests to one another, and perhaps even summarize what has been said and what issues have been addressed."[12] Further, it implies that in order to be an effective writer about literature, the student must be willing to put forth the effort required to participate in the multitude of ongoing discussions reflected in the research she will eventually be expected to do. "Only the most precocious or foolhardy would want to venture opinions or analyses in a room full of strangers, no matter how welcoming or stimulating the discussion—at least not until catching the drift and tenor of the conversation."[13] Most notably, however, the comparison allows that this introductory period might actually be enjoyable—it suggests that the period preceding full "engagement" in a literary discussion is like "eavesdropping," and further, that listening to (and watching) other partygoers puts the student in the position "of specta- tor."[14] Garrett-Petts rightly suggests that eventually, the student will want to move from this position—what he calls "passive observer"—"to that of participant" or "active learner."[15] However, I would argue that there is a benefit to highlighting the "passive" moment in the party-going—in fact, I would argue that this stage in the process of literary research and writing is not at all passive, but involves a different sort of activity than that with which students might be familiar.

For me, and for the students to whom I play host in this course, eaves- dropping is not an activity devoid of a certain amount of pleasure (and activity) in itself. According to the *Oxford English Dictionary*, to "eavesdrop" is "to stand within the 'eavesdrop' of a house in order to listen to secrets; hence, to listen secretly to private conversation."[16] As opposed to Garrett- Petts' estimation of this stage of "learning the *academic discourse*"—an estimation that presumes a drive to move beyond the "passive" and directly into the "active" mode of learning—I understand this moment in teaching literary research and analysis to be productive of its own sort of scholarly pleasure. As eavesdroppers, we get to watch the drama of others unfold before us, without having to risk our own reputations or opinions. Further, when we are effective eavesdroppers, we learn things that others might not know—we are put in a position of privilege with regard to texts, individuals, or histories. Finally, the position of eavesdropping does not foreclose the more "active" element of literary analysis—in fact, it insists that, in order to effectively produce writing about literature, we must all have passed through the stage of attuned listening—a process with which we must be *actively* engaged in order to be successful.

We can then turn to the critical essay as a forum not only for sharing our own ideas about a text, but also as a place to compare those ideas with at least some that have come before—we have listened well not only to learn the history of a text, but also to learn the style with which the community discusses that text. Students who, as Garrett-Petts correctly notes, are "confused or frustrated by the way academics talk and write" can, through leisurely eavesdropping, learn the form of literary analysis.[17] It is enjoyable to learn to "talk like" members of a community—moving from a position of isolated individual to that of fully engaged member of a group.[18] However, this element of eavesdropping should not be seen as teaching mimicry skills. In fact, the ease with which students will often resort to mimicry is, in my estimation, a symptom of a rush to produce the critical analysis most students see as the end point in their literary education. Instead, I advocate a program that allows students and the instructor to talk not only about the content of literary discourse, but about its form as well.

M. Keith Booker observes that "the rise of theory in literary studies consists largely of a rise in the self-consciousness with which texts are read and interpreted."[19] This fullness of awareness is achieved, I believe, when the stage of eavesdropper is allowed to proceed leisurely. In order to fully appreciate the pleasure of the text—and the eventual pleasure of the criticism produced *about* the text—the reader, the student, must slow down the process of reading, of viewing, of listening. Therefore, although many of the information literacy standards emphasize "efficiency," I would caution teachers of literary research against valuing the efficient research strategy over the research strategy based upon patient criticism practiced recursively. Disciplined observation organizes the progression of how I teach literary research and analysis. The remainder of this chapter outlines this progression by describing the sequence of main (and minor) assignments I give to students in this sophomore-level course.

FIRST CONTACT: EXPLICATION AND THE NEW CRITICISM

The final product for this course is a ten to twelve page argumentative interpretation of a specific literary text. Students are expected to provide a thorough close reading of the text at hand, as well as a bibliography that indicates careful and far-reaching library research. However, the course begins with much more modest goals: to teach students to slow down in their reading of a literary text so that they might allow themselves the time to find an interpretation that feels like their own, as opposed to a meaning that is imposed by an instructor, a text book, or a professional critic. For this reason, I tend to de-emphasize standard one ("to identify a research topic").[20] In order to effect this response to literature, the course begins with a self-conscious attention to the process of explication or close reading. The main assignment for this portion of the class is the Explication Essay, a three to four page close reading of John Donne's poem, "The Canonization."

I begin the course with a discussion of New Critical methods of analysis, including an in-depth presentation of formal tools for such an analysis: metaphor, image, meter, rhyme, etc. While New Criticism might seem to be a relatively "old" method of literary analysis—and one that, in the fullness of its formality, feels restrictive and limiting to students—it still provides the most basic tools used in academic discourse about reading literature. According to M. Keith Booker, "many college students are essentially New Critics without even knowing it, and the same might be said of their teachers."[21] More specifically, Booker argues that "characteristics such as close reading and detailed interpretation of specific texts were eventually broadly perceived as central to the critical enterprise."[22] Steven Lynn argues a similar ubiquity for New Criticism when he notes that "even in the midst of a cornucopia of critical options, New Criticism is still essentially the only approach on the menu, its principles so pervasive that they seem natural and obvious—and therefore remain, often enough, unarticulated."[23] The first few weeks of this course serve not only to articulate these principles, but also to equip students to use them effectively. In addition, by first introducing and then leisurely modeling New Criticism, the course can produce student readers who feel empowered in their ability to offer careful analyses of literary texts—without having to master entire histories of those texts' critical reception.

In this first unit of the course, the discussion of New Criticism proceeds in a very general way. I assign a book such as Steven Lynn's *Texts and Contexts* in order to provide students with an easy to digest definition. Lynn's text is especially useful for this course because after providing a brief introduction to the theory, he also provides models for how to read and write as a New Critic. Here is what Lynn has to say at the beginning of his text about what New Criticism is:

> So how does one do New Criticism? Begin by reading closely. Since everything should contribute to the work's artistic unity—figures of speech, point of view, diction, imagery, recurrent ideas or events, and so forth—then careful analysis of any aspect of the work should be revealing. Look for oppositions, tensions, ambiguities. These add complexity to the work's unity. A mediocre work might be unified but have little complexity; or it might be complex but never really come together. The

New Critic, finally, shows how the various elements of a
great work unify it.[24]

This method of critical involvement assumes a certain basic literary
vocabulary—a vocabulary that is not always shared by all the sophomore
level English majors in the class. Therefore, much of the first few class
periods are devoted to discussions of metaphor, rhyme, meter, and other
formal aspects of poetic or literary discourse. M. Keith Booker also references this aspect of New Criticism when he notes that it is "a 'formalist'
approach to literature—that is, it pays close and careful attention to the
language, form, and structure of literary texts while regarding individual
texts (rather than historical context or broad generic trends) as the principal
object of critical investigation."[25]

The work of formalist criticism is best supported in the course by introducing students to the only external resource they will use for the first
unit of the course: the *Oxford English Dictionary (OED)*. This introduction
is the occasion for our first trip to the library. Again, I stress that during
the first visit to the library, students are not being asked to formulate a
research question or topic. Instead of seeing the library as a place at which
they might practice their "treasure hunting" skills, I emphasize that their
initial library work should involve active and patient listening. At this point,
my goal is simply to show the students the main reference materials available in the library, including the *OED*. With the guidance of the reference
librarian, students will, at this point (usually somewhere near the end of
the first week or beginning of the second week—in either a semester or a
quarter) complete a basic library assignment that asks them to locate the
reference section, the bound and current periodicals, and the literature
section of the collection. This exercise also asks them to go directly to the
OED and look up a word that has appeared in one of the poems we have
been reading. I ask that students photocopy the relevant pages from the
dictionary and bring them to class the following day. At this point in the
course, I am insistent that students only use the print resources available
to them. This is a difficult restriction for some of them. There is a general
inclination to hover around the computer terminals, looking for analogous
information there, as opposed to in the stacks of the library itself. For example, the *OED* is available, in many libraries, online. Some students are
aware of this and try to do their exercise electronically. Though there is an
initial accusation of "nerdy conservativism" on my part, I try to point back

to the place of leisure and "browsing" in the course, encouraging students to take their time with the material text of the dictionary: hold its weight in their hands, feel the pages.

At this point in the course, I assign both the first paper and a more detailed *OED* exercise. Both assignments ask that students apply to Donne's poem some of the more basic principles of New Criticism. Steven Lynn outlines these principles by presenting students with three main questions with which a New Critical reading should be concerned:

1.   What complexities (or tensions, ironies, paradoxes, oppositions, ambiguities) can you find in the work?

2.   What idea unifies the work, resolving these ambiguities?

3.   What details or images support this resolution (that is, connect the parts to the whole)?[26]

Donne's poem becomes our main concern for the remainder of the unit. Students who are shocked to find that we will, on average, spend one to two weeks doing close readings of Donne's poem as a class sometimes meet this attention with groans. However, as the *OED* assignment asks that students explore the full range of meanings for four or five words from Donne's poem, it quickly becomes clear that the "symbolic polyphony" of the poem easily generates extended class discussion.[27] Of course, Donne's poem has occupied a central place in the history of New Criticism—it lends a line to the title of Cleanth Brooks' *The Well-Wrought Urn: Studies in the Structure of Poetry*, as well as being the main object of inquiry in his first chapter, "The Language of Paradox." Brooks' text, as well as his position as a major figure in New Criticism, is introduced to students in the second unit of the course—notably, after they have already produced their own critical explications of Donne's poem using New Critical methods. By that point in the course, students have already explored many of the details of the poem that occupy Brooks' time in his first chapter.

A brief look at the often paradoxical semantic range of three words from Donne's third stanza demonstrates the fruitfulness of such a leisurely reading. The stanza is as follows:

Call us what you will, we are made such by love;
> Call her one, me another fly,
We're tapers too, and at our own cost die,
> And we in us find the Eagle and the Dove.
> The Phoenix riddle hath more wit
> By us; we two being one, are it.

So to one neutral thing both sexes fit,
    We die and rise the same, and prove
    Mysterious by this love.[28]

By this point in our investigation, students have established the main paradox of the poem: Donne's effort to canonize—sanctify—an earthly love in a manner presumably reserved for religious figures. Three words in the third stanza that occupy our attention at this point are: "tapers," "die," and "phoenix." According to the *OED*, a "taper" is "A wax candle, in early times used chiefly for devotional or penitential purposes."[29] Students quickly see that this simple comparison further places the lovers in a devotional scene. Additional discussion about this word reveals that candles are, perhaps like the mortal lives of these lovers, ultimately ephemeral—they will burn out eventually. This leads students to more carefully attend to Donne's use of the word "die" in the poem. Like Brooks before them, students are struck by the word's semantic history. While initially suggesting the literal termination of life—nicely fitting with the reading of "taper" offered above—definition 7d of the verb form of "die" suggests a further interpretive layer: to "die" can mean "To experience a sexual orgasm. (Most common as a poetical metaphor in the late 16th and 17th cent.)."[30] This meaning allows students to see the strength of the suggestion Donne is making in this poem: the sexual act by two lovers is just as sacred and divine as a religious devotion. Finally, keeping in mind the range of the words "taper" and "die," students find the word "phoenix" to be of central importance in the poem.

As with Brooks before them, students note the ambiguity of this image—the bird represents both death and life—adding to the larger paradox established by Donne's main theme. Many students find this image one of the poem's most telling and work on furthering their interpretation of it in their first papers—for example, expanding upon how the image of the mythical bird serves as a reference to the death and rebirth of Christ—again elevating earthly love to the sphere of the divine. Such a careful close reading can be performed on any number of other words throughout Donne's poem.

After this in class investigation of Donne's poem, work proceeds on the first paper assignment proper. The Explication Essay asks that students articulate the logic of Donne's poem using close reading techniques. The details of the assignment are outlined in terms that should, by this point in the course, sound familiar to students. In their papers, they need to perform the following tasks:

1. Find and examine at least two poetic elements in Donne's poem.

2. Use the *OED* to consider the semantic range of at least two key terms in the poem.

3. Offer a clearly stated claim about the problem of the poem—one of its main paradoxes or ambiguities—and the solution the poem itself offers to that problem.

These three tasks adhere to the principles of New Criticism with which the unit began. Most notably, the assignment asks that students be able to identify a main theme of the poem in terms of paradox and ambiguity. Lynn's text is again useful here: "[T]he critic will want to recover the idea, or principle, or theme, that holds the poem's parts together, and thereby reveal how the parts relate to each other and to the whole."[31] Our careful work with the *OED* enforces the idea that a New Critical reading cannot offer an argument about a poem's themes without taking its formal elements into account.

> The strategy of a New Critical reading, then, would involve showing how the details of the poem support and elaborate this complex or ironic unity. Your structure [in a critical essay] involves arranging this evidence in a coherent way, grouping kinds of details perhaps, or moving logically through the poem. That is, throughout the poem, a New Critical reading would find oppositions reinforcing and supporting in some way the poem's central ambiguity.[32]

The first formal assignment in the course addresses the outcomes of information literacy standard three: "The information literate student ... Reads the texts and selects main ideas; Restates textual concepts in his/her own words and selects data accurately; Identifies verbatim material that can be then appropriately quoted."[33] In addition to this work on explication, I introduce students to some basic editing techniques. Most notably, we spend at least one class period discussing the proper MLA method for quoting poetry within their papers and one other period learning editing notations to be used in future paper workshops. As with all three main assignments in the class, an entire period is devoted to peer review of student drafts.

THE EAVESDROPPING ESSAY: BROOKS AND DONNE ON TOUR

The second unit of the course is its heart. By this point in the term, students are likely fairly tired of Donne's poem—after all, they have spent weeks becoming experts, of a sort, on the intricacies of Donne's language and imagery. However, if Kenneth Burke's metaphor of the parlor discussion is to be taken seriously, students must now take their own careful observations of Donne's poem into a more public forum. Standard three for information literacy asks that the student "Recognizes interrelationships among concepts and combines them into potentially useful primary statements with supporting evidence."[34] This is achieved with the second essay—a writing assignment that builds directly upon the first. In order for this second assignment to work correctly, the instructor must respond to the Explication Essays in a careful and timely manner. Though it may be difficult, essays should be returned to students—with full marginal and end comments—no later than a week after they are turned in. In my comments to students I focus on their ability to pay sustained and careful attention to the form of Donne's poem—connotations, metaphor, rhyme—as well as their efforts to make an argument about the larger problem and internal resolution of the poem—their claim. The most common difficulty that students present at this point in the course is an inability to write a fully argumentative (and risky) claim about literature. For the most part, the first papers begin not with an argument, but with statements about general observations. For this reason, my comments on the first papers try to take the observations students have made and suggest ways in which those observations might lead, in the second paper, to an argumentative position—a claim—about Donne's poem.

Teaching students to recognize the difference between a claim and an observation about literature has been, without a doubt, one of the most difficult tasks in this and other courses that foreground the critical essay. Garrett-Petts notes this challenge and devotes a chapter in his text to "Writing the Critical Essay: Form and the Critical Process."[35] He describes the main task of the analytical essay in terms of a "critical issue": "In its simplest form, the *critical issue* is a problem (usually presented in your introduction) your essay resolves through careful interpretation of the literary text. The more focused your problem, the better your chance of writing a successful essay."[36]

I encourage students to push this idea further by thinking about what they think the *argument* of the text itself actually is. For example, in the case of John Donne's "The Canonization," class discussion about the *poem's* argument will reveal that the speaker in the poem truly does seem to be making a case—arguing a point—to a specific audience (to those who he addresses in the first line, "For God's sake hold your tongue"). The details of the case are varied (opening the possibility of multiple student claims about the poem's "meaning"), but it is vital to get students to see that there is, indeed, a case being made. This encourages them to formulate claims about the poem that are equally argumentative. However, before students return to their initial close readings of Donne's poem, the class turns directly to the "eavesdropping" activities described above. We begin, in fact, by eavesdropping on the form of the scholarly essay with an ear (and eye) to identifying how claims sound (and look) in professional essays about literature. The need for this sort of careful teaching of how to distinguish claims from statements is one of the primary reasons that I do not focus on standard one (again, the identifying of a research topic) at an early point in the course.

Our text for eavesdropping at this point in the course is Cleanth Brooks' first chapter of *The Well-Wrought Urn*, "The Language of Paradox." Brooks begins by articulating some of the main principles of New Criticism with which students are, by this point, quite familiar. I usually read to them from his preface: "But the 'miracle of communication' as a student of language terms it in a recent book, remains. We had better not ignore it, or try to 'reduce; it to a level that distorts it. We had better begin with it, by making the closest possible examination of what the poem says as a poem."[37]

His first chapter proceeds in a similar vein, insisting that in poetry "terms are continually modifying each other, and thus violating their dictionary meanings."[38] Brooks then uses Donne's poem as his "concrete case" of how the language of paradox works in poetry.[39] Students move through Brooks' explication quickly, since they have already discovered many of the paradoxes he highlights. Brooks' essay is useful as a forum for literary eavesdropping though, not because it confirms what students have themselves already discovered about Donne's poem, but because it allows them a chance to respond to the strictures of New Critical methods that they have, up until this point, been forced to adopt as their only available method of literary analysis. Students are quick to note that, while he argues for a method of analysis that limits itself to "what the poem says as a poem,"

Brooks actually uses a fair amount of historical and cultural information in his analysis. Despite opening his book with the sort of statement that lead New Historicists to discount the restrictive nature of New Critical readings, Brooks is unable to fully practice that kind of analysis. "The temper of our times is strongly relativistic. We have had impressed upon us the necessity for reading a poem in terms of its historical context, and that kind of reading has been carried on so successfully that some of us have been tempted to feel that it is the only kind of reading possible."[40]

However, when he gets to his analysis of Donne's poem, Brooks must make reference to historically specific meanings for certain key terms, most notably, the word "die," whose sexual connotation is, according to the *OED*, specific to sixteenth- and seventeenth-century poetic language.

At this point in the term, we turn again to Steven Lynn's text and read his chapters on "New Historicism" and "Biographical Criticism"—both of which are, at least in part, responses to the New Criticism that came before them. In addition, I usually ask students to read the introduction ("Introduction: What is Literature") and first chapter ("The Rise of English") from Terry Eagleton's *Literary Theory: An Introduction*. Eagleton encourages students to find fault with some of the larger theories supporting New Criticism, while insisting that the practice of close reading should still be integral in any analytical investigation of the literary text. According to Eagleton, New Criticism "encouraged the illusion that any piece of language, 'literary' or not, can be adequately studied or even understood in isolation. It was the beginnings of a 'reification' of the literary work."[41] Armed with these reactions to New Criticism, along with a basic awareness of the forms of the scholarly essay, the class returns to the library for the second and third times in the term. At this point, the students have two main tasks ahead of them: to find specific print references to Donne's historical, cultural, or biographical milieu, and to begin searching for scholarly responses to Donne's "The Canonization" with which they can, in their second paper, compare their own.

Our second and third trips to the library involve introducing students to resources such as *The Dictionary of Literary Biography* and asking them to perform another library exercise—this time making specific use of those print resources that would help in a New Historical or Biographical reading of Donne's poem. This is fairly easy for them to do, and I set up simple search and find exercises with librarians that ask students to find the answers to questions about Donne's love life, his relationship with the Church, and the history of the reception to his poem during and immediately after his lifetime. Additionally, before going to the library, I assign the second of the shorter assignments in the class, their first annotated bibliography. This assignment is meant to be a place for them to eavesdrop on a few (2-3) scholarly essays about Donne's poem. The annotations they are asked to provide should demonstrate an awareness of the scholarly form (a discussion of the source's claim, key assumptions, and evidence) as well as a record of their personal reactions to the essay's main argument. They should think about how the sources they find support or differ from the reading of the poem they worked out in their first paper. In order for them to effectively complete this exercise some discussion is usually needed—in either the second or third visits to the library—of how to evaluate the sorts of sources they are likely to find in completing the first annotated bibliography. Since I am still asking them to use only the print resources and the university's main catalog (as opposed to the discipline specific databases such as *MLAIB*), this discussion involves introducing students to the difference between peer-reviewed and non peer-reviewed journals, making them aware of the value of dates in establishing the reliability of a particular source, and getting them to pay attention to an essay's bibliography in order to evaluate the depth of the research being presented to them. Finally, with the help of the research librarian, there is usually time to do a brief brainstorming about themes related to Donne's poem and how students can use them to locate even more sources. For example, doing a catalog search on John Donne will produce far more entries than students are able to handle, whereas qualifying that search by reference to the title of the poem will often narrow the search too much. So, brainstorming about themes can help students find sources that may not be about "The Canonization" per se, but might have something to say about Donne's treatment of religion, love, or sexual union, for example.

These library exercises, and the annotated bibliography, set up students nicely for the Eavesdropping Essay—a comparison of their initial close reading of "The Canonization" with one scholarly reading of the poem. The second paper is longer than the first (5-7 pages) and involves, of course, reference to an outside source. However, students are encouraged to cut and paste directly from their first paper whenever possible. Chances are that students will need to revise their main claim about Donne's poem, but they may be able to keep entire sections of close reading. This revision, as I have suggested above, is meant to bring the student's isolated reading of the poem into the open—the public parlor room discussion. I describe the main intent of the assignment in the following way:

> If we are to describe the field of literary studies as an extended parlor-room discussion, this assignment asks you to move away from the corner of the room—where you have gathered your thoughts about "The Canonization" and begun to make an argument about how to properly interpret it—and engage one other person in a discussion about the poem, one of the themes you have identified within the poem, or Donne himself.

I try to have students turn in their annotated bibliography far enough before the second paper is due so that I can help decide which essay might best work for the Eavesdropping assignment. In addition to another peer-review workshop, I devote an entire class period to more extensive MLA citation and formatting details.

THE FINAL FRONTIER

After weeks of reading and evaluating John Donne's "The Canonization," students are relieved to find that the final assignment for the course has nothing to do with either Donne or seventeenth-century poetry. The last weeks of the course give students the opportunity to critically engage a text on their own—the final product of this engagement is a ten to twelve page argumentative research paper that uses three or four outside sources. At this point in the course, I am asking that students engage in those "'Higher Order' thinking skill[s]" described in the information literacy standards: "Extends initial synthesis, when possible, to a higher level of abstraction to construct new hypotheses that may require additional information."[42] It is finally, at this point in the term, that I will ask that both students and librarians consider how to identify and work with a well-articulated research topic or question (standard one). Though I have seen versions of this class in which students are allowed to choose their own text for this final analysis, I have found it successful to limit their choices by giving students a list of possible texts toward the middle of the first unit. In my case, the list includes the following texts: *Beowulf*, *Mankind*, Theodore Dreiser's *Sister Carrie*, Raymond Chandler's *The Big Sleep*, Zora Neale Hurston's *Their Eyes Were Watching God*, and any three poems by Langston Hughes.

Primarily this limitation assures that the texts upon which students will write have been thoroughly analyzed by scholars—for all of the texts I choose, there is an active parlor-room conversation already underway. In addition, I limit their choices to texts with which I am, at least in part, familiar. It is difficult to be a proper host when you have never met any of the guests before. Students need to choose the text for their final paper fairly early in the term, since they should have it completely read by the time the final unit begins.

For the final paper, students are, in the main, released to do much of their remaining work on their own. We visit the library at least one more time as a class in order to introduce students to the more discipline specific databases available to them. Before this trip, I usually provide the reference librarian with a list of the texts students will be choosing from. This way, the library instruction on the *MLAIB* database can direct students to essays and sources that are directly relevant to the work they are being asked to do in the final paper—this is yet another reason for limiting their final choices. It is perfectly feasible for the librarian to work through four or five main topics or texts, as opposed to thirty different ones. There is a second annotated bibliography assigned early on in the unit as well, and students can begin work on this during the final supervised library visit. Finally, I usually schedule group study rooms in the library for three or four class periods in order to have individual conferences with students on the direction they are taking in their final papers. Scheduling these conferences in the library assures that students can ask and address any final research questions in a place at which most of those questions can be adequately answered. The final week or two of class is devoted to individual presentations of the work students have done towards their final papers. These presentations are fairly informal, though I do ask that each student bring a copy of their claim—as it stands—with them so that class comments and questions can react specifically to the argument the student plans to make about his or her chosen text. Presentations usually last about ten minutes, so depending on the size of the class, this final element can be rather time consuming. However, I find it invaluable for being sure that students have progressed adequately not only in their research—this can be checked when they turn in their second annotated bibliography assignment, as well as when I meet with them in conference—but in the development of an argumentative claim. By this point in the term, their fellow students are very attentive to the requirements of such a claim, and are fully able to offer constructive and suitably critical responses to the arguments being presented. For me, this final element of the class is often the most rewarding and enjoyable. The analogy of a parlor-room discussion or a cocktail party comes to life when students begin and sustain lively and informed discussion about literary texts. Again, by limiting the choices for the final paper, I am assured that each student presenter will have at least one other student present who is familiar with the text being discussed. As I suppose is the case with a successful party host, my role in this final stage of the course is to simply watch as discussions unfold and the enjoyment of analytical exchange is made manifest.

"WE'LL BUILD IN SONNETS PRETTY ROOMS": THE WELL-WROUGHT CRITICAL ESSAY

The method of introducing students to literary research that I have explained here assumes that there is both a desire on the part of students to participate in the conversation—the field of literary studies—as well as a pleasurable effect to such participation: the transformation of the student from reclusive wall-flower to engaged member in the discourse of literary analysis. My experience in teaching versions of this course to sophomore-level English majors has been that the criticism produced at the end of the term is "pleasure spoken," it proceeds from an engagement with the literary text that is attentive on two levels: "private" explication and "public" exchange. As such, the student feels as though she has truly gained the skills to be "self-directed" in their further interactions with literary texts.

Although her investigation centers primarily on the place of medieval studies in the humanities, L.O. Aranye Fradenburg speaks to some of the same issues I have addressed here and that organize my thinking about and teaching of a class like the one I have described. She argues that as teachers and scholars "what we try to deliver to our audiences is the excitement of knowledgeable discourse (or 'pleasurable analysis')."[43] Hers is an argument in favor of locating and maintaining this excitement in all fields of the humanities, as opposed to ignoring such "pleasurable analysis" because it might seem to be in opposition to production—to a final scholarly product. "When the humanities seeks to define the social and historical efficacies of its work, we too often elide the issue of our enjoyment by repeating oppositions between productivity and pleasure that privilege the former term at the expense of the latter—oppositions many of us would be unlikely to tolerate in our work."[44]

The class I have described here is one that presents library resources as a way to enlarge and supplement a student's reading of a literary text. Instead of seeing the library as a place to locate a viable, scholarly reading of literature, students should see it as one place among many to share their own thoughts about particular pieces of literature. The "work" of critical analysis, for undergraduates no less than for "professional" scholars, should be infused with the pleasure and enjoyment of leisurely exchange. When students come to realize this, they produce critical writing about literature that is graceful, confident, unhurried, and ultimately, more insightful than writing from which they feel alienated as "outsiders" and "amateurs."

NOTES

1.   The strategy has developed from two main sources. First, from a class entitled "Literary Research and Writing" that I taught at DePaul University. Many of the general goals for the course were designed by the Department of English at DePaul, and it was there that I was introduced to the idea of teaching not only literary analysis, but also library research tailored especially for students of literature. Additionally, the faculty at DePaul encouraged the use of W.F. Garrett-Petts' textbook in teaching these skills to English majors. Second, from various experiences I have had in teaching "Introduction to Literature" classes at the University of California, Santa Barbara, DePaul University, and most recently, The University of Montevallo. In my position at Montevallo, I helped to design a course which was more directly modeled on the one taught at DePaul. This chapter then, is a description of how I approached the goals set by DePaul while adding assignments and methodologies I used previously in courses that were not solely dedicated to teaching literary research.

2.   W.F. Garrett-Petts, *Writing About Literature: A Guide for the Student Critic* (Peterborough, Ontario, Canada: Broadview Press, 2000), 3.

3.   Garrett-Petts, 3.

4.   *Information Literacy Standards for Higher Education* (Chicago: Association of College and Research Libraries: 2000), 2. http://www.ala.org/ala/mgrps/divs/acrl/standards/standards.pdf

5.   *Information Literacy*, 6.

6.   *Information Literacy*, 3.

7.   *Information Literacy*, 11.

8.   *Information Literacy*, 8.

9.   Garrett-Petts, 14.

10.   Garrett-Petts, 13.

11.   Garrett-Petts, 16.

12.   Garrett-Petts, 15.

13.   Ibid.

14.   Ibid.

15.   Ibid.

16.   *Oxford English Dictionary*, 2nd ed., s.v. "eavesdrop."

17.   Garrett-Petts, 3.

18.   Sigmund Freud discusses this movement in detail, most notably in *Group Psychology and the Analysis of the Ego*, trans. James Strachey, (New York: W.W. Norton and Company,

1959), 22, in which he argues that "The most remarkable and also the most important result of the formation of a group is the 'exaltation or intensification of emotion' produced in every member of it ... it is a pleasurable experience for those who are concerned."

19.   M. Keith Booker, *A Practical Introduction to Literary Theory and Criticism* (New York: Longman, 1996), 3.

20.   *Information Literacy*, 8.

21.   Booker, 13.

22.   Ibid.

23.   Steven Lynn, *Texts and Contexts: Writing about Literature with Critical Theory*, 3rd ed. (New York: Longman, 2001), 34.

24.   Lynn, 14.

25.   Booker, 14.

26.   Lynn, 41-42.

27.   "Symbolic polyphony" is a term used by Jacques Lacan, "Aggressivity in Psychoanalysis," in *Écrits: A Selection*, trans. Alan Sheridan (New York and London: W.W. Norton and Company, 1977), 17.

28.   John Donne, "The Canonization," in *The Love Poems of John Donne*, ed. Charles Fowkes (New York: St. Martin's Press, 1982), 8.

29.   *Oxford English Dictionary*, 2nd ed., s.v. def. 1a. "taper."

30.   *Oxford English Dictionary*, 2nd ed., s.v. def. 7d. "die."

31.   Lynn, 40.

32.   Lynn, 47.

33.   *Information Literacy*, 11.

34.   Ibid.

35.   Of course, almost every text directed to introductory literature courses deals with the question of how to write the critical essay. Steven Lynn ends every chapter in his book with a sample critical essay. Two other texts that I have found useful are John R. Trimble's *Writing with Style: Conversations on the Art of Writing*, 2nd ed. (Upper Saddle River, N.J.: Prentice Hall, 2000), and David R. Williams' *Sin Boldly: Dr. Dave's Guide to Writing the College Paper*, 2nd ed. (New York : Basic Books, 2004). Both are general guides to writing at the university level, but can act as useful supplements to a course devoted entirely to writing the critical essay about literature.

36.   Garrett-Petts, 62.

37.   Cleanth Brooks, *The Well-Wrought Urn: Studies in the Structure of Poetry* (New York: Harcourt Brace & World, Inc., 1947), xi.

38.   Brooks, 9.

39.   Brooks, 11.

40.   Brooks, x.

41.   Terry Eagleton, *Literary Theory: An Introduction* (Minneapolis: University of Minnesota Press, 1983), 44.

42.   "Information Literacy," 7.

43.   L.O. Aranye Fradenburg, *Sacrifice Your Love: Psychoanalysis, Historicism, Chaucer* (Minneapolis: University of Minnesota Press, 2002), 244.

44.   Fradenburg, 241.

The Printing Press and the Web: Modernists Teaching Postmodernists

Elizabeth M. Williams

> All's changed, changed utterly/A terrible beauty is born.
> ~W. B. Yeats in "Easter, 1916"

All that stuff out there! They won't know what to do with it! It will only add fuel to their discontent! Anybody will be able to publish anything! How will they know the truth? What will happen to all of the manuscripts? What will happen to me?

Sound familiar? The dismay in the academy today over students' use of the Internet for research is reminiscent of what the monks in the scriptoriums must have felt when they heard the clacking of the printing presses and saw the broadsides being nailed up in the streets. Consider how most professors of literature conduct research, how librarians do. Compare our methods and the very different approach that students use and bear in mind the differences in the intended goals. Most librarians and most English professors are dyed-in-the-wool modernists. English professors tend to work alone; they need to browse; they need special access points, such as historical period; they rely on monographs for retrospective coverage. Knowing the literature is the defining aspect of their professional identity.[1] Students, however, come into higher education with their own priorities, experiences, and values, which often markedly differ from those of academics. This chapter will analyze the thought processes of the present generation of college students and will suggest that teachers of literature apply postmodernist theories to demonstrate the universality of the human experience and to engage students and meet them where they are.

Problematic assumptions on the part of both faculty and students contribute to the confusion. Most faculty assume that students will bring some research expertise with them when they come to the university. They also expect all students to be proficient computer users. Both of these assumptions are often false. First year college students rarely know how to broaden or narrow a topic or how to search effectively for resources. The computer skills they possess have not been used for searching academic materials. They are good at making choices, but those skills have not usually been applied to academic resources. Students in general have no concept of what a professor means by the terms *scholarly literature, literary criticism,* or *plagiarism.* Their primary purpose in the research process is to get the paper or project finished in the quickest way possible. And that is usually accomplished by using the Internet.

We will have to revolutionize our thinking and our teaching if we expect postmodernist students to pay attention to us. We can begin by respecting their opinions and admitting that our students have much to teach us. Their free-fall approach to research may not be all bad. Many of them produce acceptable research papers with no help from us at all. However, accepting these facts may be difficult and, worse, threatening. English professors in their ivory towers and librarians in their organized, automated, and digitized information castles are, after all, the experts here. But today's students are coming from a different perspective; they are growing up in a different world and they have different goals.

Wilson and Ryder compare the rise of the Internet with other educational revolutions throughout history. The history of education is inseparable from the history of technology. Before the invention of the printing press, writing was for the elite. The manuscript was an instrument of power, and literacy was the means of social control. Afterward, story telling and rhetoric were enhanced by written text. After the Reformation came the Enlightenment, then democracy. In the new millennium the lecture and the research paper are giving way to "learning environments where students define the central tasks, including how the learning should be monitored, assessed and adjusted to achieve the desired outcomes."[2]

A wake-up call for academic librarians is sounded by Barbara Mac-Adam in "From the Other Side of the River: Re-Conceptualizing the Educational Mission of Libraries." Reference and instruction librarians will fail to provide meaningful service to their primary patrons unless they can reach today's postmodern students. They need to teach what students want to learn and they need to understand what students value. Today's students have a lot to offer: they confront the world they live in energetically and engage it head-on; they are curious, willing to investigate; they love to talk, are interested in ideas, and like to collaborate. MacAdams reminds us, "Students are naturally critical in everyday life."[3] We have the ability to help them use their critical thinking skills for academic research.

WHAT IS POSTMODERNISM?

For a course on literary theory, Mary Klages of the Department of English at the University of Colorado at Boulder created a web page that has a lucid definition and discussion of postmodernism. She reminds us that modernism came about as a rejection of the Victorian view of the creation and the use of art, music, and literature. Major literary figures, such as Joyce, Eliot, Woolf, Proust, and Kafka redefined literature and poetry. Postmodernism, like modernism, rejects boundaries between low and high art and favors ambiguity and self-consciousness. It differs from modernism in that it does not consider ambiguity and self-consciousness to be tragic, but, rather, celebrates them: "The world is meaningless? Let's not pretend that art can make meaning then, let's just play with nonsense." Modernism was equated with science, as contrasted to narrative. Knowledge was good for its own sake; hence, the argument for a liberal arts education. Postmodernism, on the other hand, sees knowledge as a function; you learn things to use them. How many English majors are asked, "What are you going to do with your degree?"[4]

The difference between modernists and postmodernists is that modernists present the TRUTH in capital letters. Wilson and Ryder explain:

> To the modern mind, there is too much information. The
> world is exploding with ideas and perspectives that cannot
> possibly be consumed. We must control what people read
> so that the truth might prevail over misinformation, so
> that quality might prevail over mediocrity, so that correct
> ideas might prevail over anarchy.[5]

To the postmodernist, however, efforts to control what people read is futile. There is no handbook or manual to guide one through this postmodern world.

Postmodernism continues to wield influence today because it is impossible to ignore the mass media and the consumerism of this present age. Terry Eagleton writes:

> Postmodernism is doubtless the most widely touted term
> in cultural theory today. It means the end of modernism,
> those grand narratives of truth, reason, [and] science. Our
> lives are relative, ungrounded, self-sustaining, made up

of...cultural convention...without any identifiable origin or...goal. Knowledge is relative to cultural contexts. Truth is the product of interpretation.[6]

Theories come and go, but the influence of postmodernism has remained strong in literature and philosophy.

POSTMODERNIST LITERATURE

Writings on postmodernist writers and literature abound. Brian McHales's 1987 *Postmodernist Fiction* is a classic in the field. He states that postmodernism does not exist, "precisely in the way that 'the Renaissance' or 'romanticism' does not exist...these are all literary-historical fictions, discursive artifacts constructed either by contemporary readers and writers or retrospectively by literary historians."[7] He maintains that the "dominant of postmodernist fiction is *ontological*," that is concerned with the nature of being and existence, rather than about what can be known, understood, and communicated.[8] Its strategy of "integrating history and the fantastic is a flagrant violation of the realistic norms of historical fiction."[9]

Peter Brooker's *Modernism/Postmodernism* is cited frequently in discussions. Brooker suggests that postmodernism presents an argument for "sensuous response and the languages of the body over intellectual analysis," making it compatible with the youth and drugs counter-culture.[10] The book includes essays on postmodernist fiction by Umberto Eco, Carlos Fuentes, and Linda Hutcheon. In his essay "Postmodernism, Irony, and the Enjoyable," Eco observes that postmodern literature ironically looks at the past. Since it can't be destroyed, it must be revisited and rethought, with irony. He relates this concept to his novel *The Name of the Rose* and ponders whether or not a novel could be enjoyable without being escapist.[11] Carlos Fuentes, in "Words Apart," writes about the novel:

> In dialogue, no one is absolutely right; neither speaker holds an absolute truth or, indeed, has an absolute hold over history. Myself and the other, as well as the history that both of us are making, still are not. Both are unfinished and so can only continue to be. By its very nature, the novel indicates that we are becoming. There is no final solution. There is no last word.[12]

Linda Hutcheon's "Telling Stories: Fiction and History" asserts that postmodernist fiction reveals the past with irony and paradox and prompts the question, not about what is true, but about whose truth it is.[13]

TEACHING LITERATURE TO POSTMODERNISTS: A LITERATURE REVIEW

There is a lot of discussion in scholarly literature about modernism versus postmodernism or about teaching literature in a changing world, but little of it is specific to the teaching of literary research to the postmodern generation. One book that does discuss the implications of the changes faced by teachers of literature adjusting to postmodern trends is *Margins in the Classroom: Teaching Literature*, edited by Linda and Kostas Myrsiades. In the introduction to the collection of essays they discuss the present dilemma: how to teach literature to the postmodern generation. They propound the view that the teacher-student relationship should be "subjectivized" in order to question and discuss the established order.[14] In his essay Henry Giroux maintains that the teacher of literature has political responsibilities that remove education from the comfortable role of passive onlooker in the greater cultural debate and place the academic squarely on the site of the struggle. The purpose of pedagogy should be about linking "teaching and learning to forms of self- and social empowerment…that move beyond the particularistic politics of class, ethnicity, race and gender."[15] Postmodernism questions reason and universality; reason and science make no sense without considering the broader implications imposed by history, politics, and culture.

Karen Coats makes an interesting point as she describes why teaching children's literature can demonstrate the intellectual stimulus possible for college students when they make connections between children's literature and social issues. Thought provoking themes are presented, such as the racist and colonialist implications in *Curious George* and *The Story of Babar*, or gender considerations in *Little Women* and *Little House on the Prairie*. Censorship is a topic close to the heart of librarians and it can be creatively discussed in regard to books that students may not think are fit for childish consumption. Coats has found that teaching children's literature at the university level engages students' interest and helps them gain intellectual and personal insights that can be related to other academic work and to their lives after college.[16]

Peter Carino has found that John Updike's "A & P" provides an opportunity for reading multiple meanings into texts, such as issues of class and gender. Postmodern strategies of learning teach students that meaning is best conveyed traditionally or pedagogically, but is related to the text and the context in which it is read and understood. He thinks that the postmodern perspective can present a richer understanding for beginning literature students. They may realize that neither life nor literature can be understood from a single perspective, that everything is open to interpretation and revision.[17]

Brubacher and Payne have more suggestions for English teachers in "Cooperative Learning and Postmodern Approaches to Teaching Literature" that librarians can use in the teaching of literary research. They suggest that the classroom should be conceptualized as a workshop. Group projects and discussion should be encouraged, and students should have some control over the selection of topics they will study. Enabling students to determine what beliefs and values are under discussion and why is a way of turning collaborative learning into postmodernist theory."[18]

Additional insight about teaching the postmodern student is presented in *Generation X Goes to College: An Eye-opening Account of Teaching in Postmodern America* by Peter Sacks. Sacks believes that the parts of modernity that are not effective can be eliminated while standing firm on academic standards. He presents an analogy: it is possible to package something good and nutritious in a bottle that looks like a Pepsi. Sacks describes ways to do that, saying that the professor is no longer the "classroom monarch," the know-all and be-all of the educational process. He has too much competition in the information business from electronic resources. Like the librarian, he is no longer the gatekeeper to knowledge, but more like the expert consultant. He is the "cultural producer" that provides the raw materials…leaving it open to the student to assemble them and discover meanings. The postmodernist asks, not "is it true," but "what good is it?"[19]

POSTMODERNISM IN LIBRARIES

Postmodernism in relation to libraries and library instruction is a topic of interest as well. Melody Burton has written an article on postmodernism in libraries which is applicable to literary research. "The Knee-Bone Is Connected to the Thigh Bone" discusses the barriers that libraries impose on student research. She proposes an instructional method that uses critical pedagogy, and an active learning and teaching method to "empower the researcher." She suggests that the traditional research path has changed; description and interpretation are more difficult for the postmodern student.

Reality to them is subjective, and knowledge is no longer the prerogative of the teacher, as there can be more than one answer to a research question. Accuracy and authenticity of texts can be questionable because textual sources can be customized. First editions online can have no resemblance to the print item. Burton felt compelled by the information explosion and the reality of postmodern students to revise her instruction to include more active classroom strategies.[20]

In the midst of the hullabaloo about the "The Death of the Librarian in the (Post) Modern Electronic Age," Robert H. Kieft offers some "rules or assumptions" for librarians. Parts of them are quoted:

- Students do not want to learn how to use a library—they want to get their work done....
- Librarians are not in the business of teaching students how to use a library. Rather, they are in the business of teaching them how to think critically about research problems and papers.
- Students have difficulty abstracting from experience with ...one research project to others.
- Students tend to cast all their relationships in the mode of social relationships. What adults think of as working relationships... responsibility, accountability... are mostly foreign to them.
- Students do not receive enough, let alone systematic, instruction in information literacy to go about doing the work assigned to them...very little in U.S culture does much...to encourage that they seek such training.
- Academic librarians are not nor have they ever been "major players" in the information game...most people find what they want or what they are willing to settle for without the direct intervention of most of the people who work in libraries.[21]

He suggests that librarians are in the education business, not the information business: "Librarians should look to functions other than those of gathering, storing, or delivering information as their true functions." As educators, they should be achieving other goals. They should be more interested in "enhancing human capacity" than in providing students with information or technological skills. "To emphasize technology...is to value means over end, information over knowledge."[22]

Taylor Hubbard would agree. He advocates focusing on educating about knowledge rather than how to find information. In "Bibliographic Instruction and Postmodern Pedagogy," he suggests that libraries should be "learning laboratories" to study information in the context of the literature of an academic discipline, making the process a discovery experience, not information gathering. To do this effectively, library instruction should be integrated into the curriculum.[23] We keep track of our gate-counts and the number of books circulated, but when asked how these numbers support the academic disciplines, we have no evidence. Postmodernism encourages the consideration of the purpose of our existence. Hubbard sees the Internet as the working model of postmodernism, demolishing physical and textural dimensions: "If all knowledge is local, should not our instructional focus be on those who create it rather than the subsequent acts of other who publish, collect, and organize it?"[24] Our traditional bibliographic instruction is modernistic: we legitimize our organized collections and discourage students from questioning the authority of established literary works. Students should be encouraged to be conscious of the role they play in information creation, for knowing about knowledge implies knowing how and why it is created and used.[25]

Academic librarians everywhere are re-evaluating their instruction and reference services. In "The Postmodern Condition: Students, the Web, and Academic Library Services," Harley, Dreger, and Knobloch discuss some of the causes and concerns in the evaluation process. They characterize the postmodern condition as one of "consumerism, superficiality, and knowledge fragmentation."[26] Students often find it difficult to ask for help, feeling self-conscious or ignorant. The primary goal of librarians should be to increase their interaction with students to make them feel comfortable in a library atmosphere. Above all, both inside and outside of the library, they should be trying to integrate critical thinking into the learning process. Instruction librarians should be teaching students how to think through their research problems, rather than merely showing them how to use a library.[27]

TEACHING LITERATURE IN A CHANGING ENVIRONMENT

A number of publications examine teaching literature in a changing environment, even though the words modernism and postmodernism are not used. Marcel Cornis-Pope hints at the terms when he talks about post-structuralist criticism. He notes that the new hypertext and networked communication have allowed readers to interact with the text and among themselves, resulting in "perceptual and conceptual breakthroughs." The creative logic of "patterning" is replacing the linear logic of reading and writing. The reader and writer make the patterns.[28] He continues, "hypertextuality is a nonlinear mode of reading/writing that mimics the way the brain works: associating, cross-referencing, and networking data."[29]

The editor of *English in the Digital Age: Information and Communications Technology and the Teaching of English*, Andrew Goodwyn, contributed a chapter in which he maintains that we are between generations, that today's students are unwilling to make the effort required of previous generations and are looking for easier entertainment than reading literature. They are very comfortable in a media environment and are uncomfortable in the classroom. If professors dare to question the validity of computer literacy and new technology, they are likely to be considered "antiquated luddites, as opposed to critical professionals."[30] Goodwyn goes on to observe that the computer can provide fresh and innovative ways of teaching literature. Communication between students themselves and with their teachers has been facilitated by e-mail, and students are writing more than ever. Teachers can create a communicative learning environment in the medium that is preferable and familiar to their students.[31]

Hickey and Reiss report that some teachers are encouraging students to be active, rather than passive, in understanding literature. In *Learning Literature in an Era of Change: Innovations in Teaching* they suggest that students be asked to use their imaginations and write their own hypertexts or poetry in different genres and then to discuss their contributions with their peers. They comment that ours is an increasingly visual culture and add that nothing is new, as illuminated manuscripts were the very things replaced by the printing press. They advocate cross-disciplinary partnerships, such as science in literature, to achieve a more satisfying and complete appreciation and understanding of literature.[32]

Marlowe Miller calls for a rededication to teaching in the academy. In "Figuring Literary Theory and Refiguring Teaching: Graphics in the Undergraduate Literary Theory Course," he maintains that students do not respond favorably to the traditional lecture; they prefer concrete, practical, relevant topics and active learning methods. He thinks that English teachers need to be "problem posers." They should encourage students to make mental and visual connections between the subjects they are studying and their contemporary lives: a survival skill in a changing world. He provides sample assignments to help them evaluate and make connections between ideas.[33]

RESEARCH METHODS: FACULTY & STUDENTS

In a presentation at LOEX in 1999, Donna Gunter outlined some assumptions that are barriers to effective library instruction, such as the idea that library instruction should be general; it doesn't need to have a context. Other assumptions that are sometimes held by teaching faculty, library directors, librarian colleagues, and students include the idea that bibliographic instruction is public relations, not teaching; that it is redundant and can be accomplished at the reference desk.[34]

Gloria Leckie has contributed an article to the professional literature that outlines the fundamental differences between modernist faculty and postmodernist students and the methods each uses for their research. Most faculty are expert researchers. They have gone through a long process of acculturation, they have an in-depth knowledge of their discipline, they rely heavily on contacts and bibliographies, and they don't expect research to be sequential or linear. Undergraduates rarely have any of those characteristics. "Students do not think in terms of an information-seeking strategy, but rather in terms of a coping strategy."[35]

When professors assign a research paper, they often make problematic assumptions. Some of them are paraphrased:

+ Faculty expect students to focus on a specific interest when reading a broad overview. Research has shown that students don't know how to narrow either their reading or the topic and don't have confidence in their ability to do so. This problem is compounded by library anxiety; they often see the library as intimidating.
+ Faculty make assumptions about students' knowledge of scholarly literature and how to use the sources, but students do not know what is scholarly and how or why it is. They do not know which databases to use for their topic or which ones have scholarly journals.
+ Students have had little experience in evaluating a body of work. They often are frustrated to the point that they will just pick one view when the professor is expecting them to present both sides.
+ Assumptions are made about information-seeking strategies, that students have one. They do not know how to follow the citation trail, nor do they have any knowledge of the literature on the topic and are embarrassed to ask.

‣ Faculty assume that students know how to use computers for research. Even if they do, they don't know how distinguish between the options they have for finding information, and they do not know how to use them effectively. They do not know the difference between keywords and controlled vocabulary. Faculty has had enough experience to get around those kinds of hindrances.

‣ Assumptions are also made about librarians: Librarians are nice people, use them if you need them. There is seldom real partnership between librarians and faculty, and students are reluctant to ask for help.[36]

Leckie makes several suggestions about what faculty and librarians can do about the problems that students encounter when conducting research. Information literacy and critical thinking skills can be integrated into course content. The assignment can be structured so that the separate components of the assignment are worked on individually, for example: narrowing the topic, demystifying scholarly research, finding and using the scholarly literature in the discipline, understanding legitimate shortcuts, and developing a strategy and time frame for completion of the paper.[37]

TEACHING THE POSTMODERN STUDENT

What, then, can we offer the postmodern student?

We can show them the easiest and quickest ways to get to the best resources. We know how to do that. We can help them develop their ideas and point out that the subjects they are researching have most certainly been written about before, that their dilemmas are the themes of great literature. Hardy's Tess was at the mercy of nature and fate. The brothers Karamazov were psychological case studies. Hamlet, after all, was the quintessential postmodernist, questioning everything.

In the introductory classes we can concentrate on the basics: researching one topic for one assignment. First year students need to be guided in the right direction. That is about all that can be absorbed. When students have chosen majors and have settled into a discipline, we can collaborate with departmental faculty to teach them the best resources for literature, linguistics, or literary theory—online and in print. Even more importantly, we can teach them how their discipline interacts with others, such as science in literature, psychology in literature, education in literature, and so on. We can encourage English departments to include advanced information literacy instruction in their curriculum and give them reasons why they should.

Catherine Lee points out that the present generation does not generally feel comfortable in libraries, so it is our job to make them feel at home. We cannot appear to be busy at the reference desk; we should be smiling at them, asking if they need anything.

Postmodern students like to see the connection, the reason for what they are doing. Partnering with faculty helps make that connection between library instruction and classroom teaching. We should be maximizing the library's role in their lives—in college and out. Lee makes suggestions for the design of instruction sessions, which include presenting short sessions using hands-on, active learning, and using their skills and interest in technology. Focus on an assignment they are working on, so they will know they can use what they are learning. We should try to stimulate and entertain them and encourage questions and comments. We need to keep handouts to a minimum, as students think paper guides are dull. Making a web page for their class is helpful, if appropriate, and we should show them library electronic subject guides.[38]

At a Library Orientation Exchange (LOEX) conference in 1999, Lori Ricigliano made a presentation, "After Generation X Comes Y: Teaching the Next Generation." Generation Y has been called the Net Generation or the Millennials. They are generally happy and optimistic, everything that Generation X was not. They like to be independent and in control. Both generations have had life experiences that set them apart from previous age groups: working parents, single parent families, day care, and part-time jobs.[39]

However, Ricigliano observes that understanding the present generation does not guarantee instructional success. They must be ready, willing, and engaged. She agrees that using a range of learning styles can make instruction more meaningful and suggests taking a cue from the media: keep up a fast pace, be clear, concise, and relevant. Make sure the instruction is customized and flexible. The library can be an exciting place; use their interest in technology to show them practical ways it can work for them and how it can make their work easier. And show them the point; they want to know *why* they need to learn what you are teaching and what they will be able to do with the information strategy you are demonstrating.[40]

Chris Dede at the Harvard Graduate School of Education has written a body of work about the learning styles of the Neomillennial student. He touts the need for "multiuser virtual environments," balancing "experiential learning, guided mentoring, and collective reflection," and maintains that educational institutions that recognize and support the shifts in student learning will gain the competitive advantage, attracting the finest and the brightest and will teach them more effectively.[41] In "Disconnects Between Library Culture and Millennial Generation Values," Robert McDonald and Chuck Thomas warn libraries to consider changing their policies if they mean to "remain relevant to the next generation of students." Library culture, they maintain, "despite a few encouraging exceptions, such as RLG's RedLightGreen Catalog interface and OCLC's Open WorldCat," most libraries have failed to provide services such as personalization and recombination of information sources.[42] A balance must be found between traditional library services and the expectations and values of a new generation.

TEACHING WITH TECHNOLOGY

Articles about teaching with technology are helpful to those trying to reach computer-dependent students. EDUCAUSE provides an excellent web site for "transforming education through information technologies," including numerous resources for working with Millennials and technology.[43] Brent Wilson has written a body of work addressing instructional development. In "The Postmodern Paradigm," he discusses both postmodernism versus modernism and instructional theory versus practice of design. He provides a set of useful guidelines for postmodern instructional design, among which are:

- Be willing to break the rules.
- Place principles above procedures, and people above principles.
- Allow instruction and learning goals to emerge during instruction.
- Don't sacrifice educational goals for technical training.
- Emphasize problem solving.
- Present content in multiple ways to accommodate different learning styles
- Appreciate the value-ladenness of all analysis
- Distinguish between instructional goals and learners' goals; support learners in pursuing their own goals.
- Think of instruction as providing tools that teachers and students can use for learning; make these tools user-friendly.
- Consider strategies that provide multiple perspectives that encourage the learner to exercise responsibility.

+ Allow for the 'teaching moment.'[44]

Wilson also suggests that assessment should be incorporated into the learning experience and that informal assessments such as observing student reaction can be useful.

In his preface to the *Literary Text in the Digital Age*, Richard Finneran discusses the revolution resulting from the access that computers can give to the study, creation, and preservation of literary texts. Although electronic texts can never replace the printed word, there is no denying the future, and there is much to gain from embracing the new technology: "If the achievement that we have come to value is to remain a viable part of our cultural inheritance, it needs to be made accessible to future generations in the form that they will understand as the standard way of interacting with 'monuments of magnificence.'"[45] In the same work, John Unsworth wrote an essay saying that electronic scholarly communication "permits the individual scholar, the teacher, the student to have a near-firsthand experience of manuscripts formerly available only to the few."[46] Moreover, users can contribute to electronic archives. At the University of Virginia, private family collections have added significantly to the Civil War collection. In another essay, Simon Gatrell envisions an "Electronic Hardy," whereby two or three editions of the same novel can be on a compact disc, complete with images, sounds, and Hardy's own notations.[47]

TEACHING THE INTERNET

In addition to teaching on the Internet, we should be teaching the Internet itself. It is both hopeless and unproductive to forbid students to use the most significant medium of information dissemination since the printing press. We should, instead, be teaching them to use it properly and effectively. In "To Cope, to Contribute, to Control," Jane O'Donoghue realizes that few modernists feel the same thrill about the Internet as they do over a big book, but we need to think about the fact that our students will be making and shaping the future by means of their participation in an electronic environment. This generation is very fond of the Internet, and we will have to admit that it does offer reading and writing. It offers technical, designing kinds of writing and a not-as-isolated kind of reading. She warns: "Most people cope, some contribute, and a few are in control."[48] She continues by observing that we can be using it to find information, to publish ourselves, to communicate with other individuals and groups, and to write collaboratively.[49]

An enlightening study done by Kibirige and DePalo helps modernists understand how current academic users perceive search engines and electronic databases. The study revealed that the primary qualities that they require are accessibility, timeliness, readability, relevance, and authority. The Internet is good at the first three. The last two require critical thinking expertise that most undergraduates do not possess.[50]

The study found that users need to be re-educated:

+ Search engines index only a fraction of possible sites.
+ Anyone can publish on the web; no one is checking authority.
+ Web sites are unstable; they are here today and gone tomorrow.
+ Subject-oriented library databases can provide good sources with all five of the qualities, and can do it quicker.[51]

Instead of roaming around ineffectually on the Internet, students can usually (and more easily) find appropriate resources from a library database. Early intervention for the re-education of first year English classes is paramount, but structured discipline-oriented research instruction must follow at more advanced levels.

Kate Manuel notes that while Millennials share some similar characteristics with Generation X, they are more secure and have more optimistic worldviews. It is also the most ethnically diverse generation yet; one in three is not Caucasian.[52] Having grown up in the midst of a technological explosion, they are confident in their computer expertise and often overestimate their ability to search for information and evaluate it. They ignore the teacher who cautions against information gained from the Internet, thinking that he or she is "trashing" the new technology because they are not familiar with it. Manuel suggests using some of the same techniques that Lee and Ricigliano have touted for reaching and teaching this generation and recommends replacing lectures with active learning exercises designed to demonstrate that the Internet could be both effective and ineffective, depending upon the purpose of the search.[53]

CONCLUSION

After postmodernism, what next?

By definition, we would assume that there is no literature after or beyond postmodernism, the "self-reflective, end-of-the-line works of fantasy and fabulation."[54] However, Robert Rebein, writing about current American fiction, maintains that there has been a broadening of the perception of what constitutes literary postmodernism, because the classic novels generally associated with the term are finding few new readers. The editors of *Postmodern American Fiction: A Norton Anthology*, published in 1998, translate the term broadly, including "those authors who...shared a new cultural sensibility as a response to an altered world."[55] Along with the obvious postmodern literature like that of Barth, Barthelme, and Pynchon, the anthology includes others not usually associated with postmodernism, such as Toni Morrison and E. L. Doctorow.

James Sosnoski goes so far as to question the existence of literary criticism as a discipline and suggests that there needs to be an alternative way of describing literary studies. In *Modern Skeletons in Postmodern Closets*, he suggests a turn toward person-orientation from text-orientation that would "address a profound contradiction in the...discipline of literature—an aspiration to impersonally study the intensely personal." He continues, "From a postmodern perspective, literary research is ad hoc; results are aimed at very specific social changes."[56] Envisioning the university of the future, Sosnoski sees primarily electronic environments. With an emphasis on conflict rather than consensus and a tolerance of difference and dissent, the future university will be decidedly postmodern. The author concludes by asserting: "Imagination and emotion are 'fields' we all too often neglect in cultural studies...they are indispensable in electronic educational environments."[57]

The increased concern with postmodern theory has precipitated an interest in the study of folklore, as well as cultural and ethnic studies. Minority literature and the oral tradition have benefited from the literature department's desire for an interdisciplinary focus. Margaret Brady writes in *The Journal of Folklore Research* that scholars are focusing on the social connotations implied when connections are made between oral and written texts. She describes her own enlightenment: "The effects of this class were as varied as the narrative experiments of the American Indian writers who consciously manipulated and complicated the received distinctions between oral and written forms...The significance of various features of cultural context became inseparable from the traditional 'close reading' of a text."[58] After her folklore class, her students began to see the relationship between folklore and the literature they were reading.

As a graduate student teaching literature, David Anthony was dismayed that graduate school provided little help in creating assignments for his students. In the process of designing an assignment for a graduate school workshop, he realized that many of the historical narratives we rely on to define ourselves are subjective and often unstable. He therefore designed an assignment which would require students to choose a literary work about American identity, construct a history of an individual, then write a rationale for why they chose to include certain facts, photos, interviews, or articles in their papers. They were to explain what they were trying to prove, to whom, and why, to get the connection between the form and content of their presentation. This kind of exercise can help students see how the present affects their interpretation of the past. For Anthony, "the notion of American identity...depends upon the act of storytelling."[59]

Is the great literature of the past obsolete? Are books old-fashioned? Of course not. We need to help our students discover that for themselves. And they will. Today's students have passed rigorous admission requirements and are highly intelligent. We should use their curiosity, their eagerness to investigate and question things, their love of hanging out, their dedication to ideas and causes. Let us take advantage of their energy and their willingness to meet today's world head-on. If we continue to try to teach them what we think they should know instead of what they want to know, we may end up teaching them nothing at all.

NOTES

1. Debora Shaw, "Bibliographic Database Searching by Graduate Students in Language and Literature: Search Strategies, System Interfaces, and Relevance Judgments," *Library & Information Science Research* 17, no.4 (Fall 1995): 330.

2. Martin Ryder and Brent Wilson, "Affordances and Constraints of the Internet for Learning and Instruction," Presentation at a joint session of the Association for Educational Communications Technology (Indianapolis, February 14-18, 1996), cited 26 November 2002, (http://carbon.cudenver.edu/~mryder/aect_96.html).

3. Barbara MacAdam, "From the Other Side of the River: Re-conceptualizing the Educational Mission of Libraries," in *Future Teaching Roles for Academic Librarians*, ed. Alice Harrison Bahr, 92 (New York: Haworth P, 2000).

4. Mary Klages, "Postmodernism," in *Introduction to Literary Theory* (University of Colorado, Fall Semester 2001), 1-2, cited 2 July 2003, (http://www.Colorado.edu/English/engl2010mk/2010syllabus.2001.htm). See also Klages' "Postmodernism" (http://www.colorado.edu/English/courses/ENGL2012Klages/pomo.html), viewed March 2007.

5. Martin Ryder and Brent Wilson, "Affordances and Constraints of the Internet for Learning and Instruction," presentation at a joint session of the Association for Educational Communications Technology (Indianapolis, February 14-18, 1996), cited 26 November 2002, (http://carbon.cudenver.edu/~mryder/aect_96.html).

6. Terry Eagleton, *Literary Theory: An Introduction* (Minneapolis: University of Minnesota Press, 1996), 200-203.

7. Brian McHale, *Postmodernist Fiction* (New York: Methuen, 1987), 4.

8. Ibid., 10.

9. Ibid., 94.

10.   Peter Brooker, *Modernism/Postmodernism* (London: Longman, 1992), 2.

11.   Ibid., 226-27.

12.   Ibid., 244.

13.   Ibid., 229.

14.   "Introduction," in *Margins in the Classroom*, ed. Kostas and Linda S. Myrsiades, xii (Minneapolis: University of Minnesota Press, 1994).

15.   Henry A. Giroux, "Rethinking the Boundaries of Educational Discourse: Modernism, Postmodernism, and Feminism," in *Margins in the Classroom*, 48.

16.   Karen Coats, "Fish Stories: Teaching Children's Literature in a Postmodern World," *Pedagogy* 1, no. 2 (2001): 406.

17.   Peter Carino, "Making Meaning in the Postmodern Market: Teaching John Updike's 'A & P,'" *Teaching English in the Two-Year College* 28, no. 2 (2000): 197.

18.   Mark Brubacher and Ryder Payne, "Cooperative Learning and Postmodern Approaches to Teaching Literature," in *Handbook of Cooperative Learning Methods*, Shlomo Sharan, ed., 221-224 (Westport, Connecticut: Greenwood Press, 1994).

19.   Peter Sacks, *Generation X Goes to College: An Eye-opening Account of Teaching in Postmodern America* (Chicago: Open Court, 1996), 173-5.

20.   Melody Burton, "The Knee-bone is Connected to the Thigh Bone: Postmodernism, Critical Pedagogy, and Logic in the CD-ROM Workshop," *The Reference Librarian* 51-52 (1995): 133-4.

21.   Robert H. Kieft, "The Death of the Librarian in the (Post) Modern Electronic Age," in *Information for a New Age: Redefining the Librarian*, comp. Fifteenth Anniversary Task Force, Library Instruction Round Table, American Library Association, 16-17 (Englewood, Colorado: Libraries Unlimited, 1995).

22.   Ibid., 17.

23.   Taylor E. Hubbard, "Bibliographic Instruction and Postmodern Pedagogy," *Library Trends* 44, no. 2 (1995). Abstract, in InfoTrac OneFile [online database], cited 18 July 2000. Available from Appalachian State University Libraries.

24.   Ibid., paragraph 3.

25.   Ibid., paragraph 31.

26.   Bruce Harley, Megan Dreger, and Patricia Knobloch, "The Postmodern Condition: Students, the Web, and Academic Library Services," *Reference Services Review* 29, no. 1 (2001): 23.

27.   Ibid., 26-27.

28.   Marcel Cornis-Pope, "Hypertextual and Networked Communication in Undergraduate Literature Classes: Strategies For an Interactive Critical Pedagogy," in *Learning Literature in an Era of Change: Innovations in Teaching*, ed. Dona J. Hickey and Donna Reiss, 153 (Sterling, VA: Stylus, 2000).

29.   Ibid., 157.

30.   Andrew Goodwyn, "'A Bringer of New Things': An English Teacher in the Computer Age?" in *English in the Digital Age: Information and Communications Technology and the Teaching of English*, ed. Andrew Goodwyn, 1-3 (London: Cassell, 2000).

31.   Ibid., 19.

32.   Donna J. Hickey and Donna Reiss, "Introduction," in *Learning Literature in an Era of Change*, ed. Donna J. Hickey and Donna Reiss, xvi-xx (Sterling, Virginia: Stylus, 2000).

33.   Marlowe A. Miller, "Figuring Literary Theory and Refiguring Teaching: Graphics in the Undergraduate Literary Theory Course," in *Learning Literature in an Era of Change: Innovations in Teaching*, ed. Dona J. Hickey and Donna Reiss, 62-64 (Sterling, VA: Stylus, 2000).

34.   Donna J. Gunter, "Breaking Barriers and Building Boundaries: Creating Better Instructional Sessions in an Environment of Change," in *Library User Education In the New Millennium: Blending Tradition, Trends, and Innovation, Papers and Session Materials Presented At the Twenty-seventh National LOEX Library Instruction Conference Held in Houston, Texas 11 to 13 MARCH 1999*, ed. Julia K. Nims and Ann Andrew, 91 (Ann Arbor, Michigan: Pierian Press, 2001).

35.   Gloria J. Leckie, "Desperately Seeking Citations: Uncovering Faculty Assumptions about the Undergraduate Research Process," *Journal of Academic Librarianship* 22, no.3 (May 1996), 203.

36.   Ibid., 205-207.

37.   Ibid., 207-209.

38.   Catherine A. Lee, "Teaching Generation X: Six Guidelines for Developing More Appropriate BI Programs," *Research Strategies* 14 (Winter 1996): 57.

39.   Lori Ricigliano, "After X comes Y: Teaching the Next Generation," in *Library User Education in the New Millennium, Papers Presented at the Twenty-Seventh National LOEX Library Instruction Conference Held in Houston, Texas, 11 to 13 March 1999*, ed. Julia K Nims and Ann Andrew, 121-122 (Ann Arbor, Mich.: Published for Learning Resources and Technologies, Eastern Michigan University by Pierian Press, 2001).

40.   Ibid., 124-26.

41.   Chris Dede, "Planning for NeoMillennial Learning Styles," in *EDUCAUSE Quarterly* 28, no. 1 (2005): 7. See also Dede's "Planning for Neomillennial Learning Styles: Implications for Investments in Technology and Faculty," in *Educating the Net Generation* "A New EDUCAUSE e-Book," ed. Diana G. Oblinger and James L. Oblinger, Chapter 15 (Boulder, CO: EDUCAUSE, 2005). (http://www.educause.edu/educatingthenetgen/5989).

42.   Robert H. McDonald and Chuck Thomas, "Disconnects Between Library Culture and Millennial Generation Values," in *EDUCAUSE Quarterly* 29 no. 4 (2006): 5.

43.   EDUCAUSE http://www.educause.edu/ See especially the Major Initiatives section on the EDUCAUSE Learning Initiative (ELI), with the link to Net Generation Learners. http://www.educause.edu/NewLearners/5515. In addition to the chapter by Dede noted above, Joan Lippincott's "Net Generation Students and Libraries," in *Educating the Net Generation* "A New EDUCAUSE e-Book," ed. Diana G. Oblinger and James L. Oblinger, Chapter 13 (Boulder, CO: EDUCAUSE, 2005). (http://www.educause.edu/educatingthenetgen/5989), is worth noting.

44.   Brent G. Wilson, "The Postmodern Paradigm," in *Instructional Development Paradigms*, ed. Charles R. Dills and Alexander J. Romiszowski, 304-307 (Englewood Cliffs, NJ: Educational Technology Publications, 1997).

45.   Richard J. Finneran, ed., *The Literary Text in the Digital Age* (Ann Arbor: University of Michigan Press, 1996), ix-xi.

46.   John Unsworth, "Electronic Scholarship: Or, Scholarly Publishing and the Public," ibid., 241. Also published in the *Journal of Scholarly Publishing* 28 (October 1996): 3-12.

47.   Simon Gatrell, "Electronic Hardy," *The Literary Text in the Digital Age*, 186-88.

48.   Jane O'Donoghue, "To Cope, to Contribute, to Control," in *English in the Digital Age: Information and Communications Technology and the Teaching of English*, ed. Andrew Goodwyn, 69-73 (London: Cassell, 2000).

49.   Ibid., 76.

50.   Harry M. Kibirige, and Lisa DePalo, "The Internet as a Source of Academic Research Information: Findings of Two Pilot Studies," *Information Technology and Libraries* 19, no.1 (2000): paragraph 1, cited 18 July 2000, (http://www.lita.org/ital/1901_kibirige.htm).

51.   Ibid., paragraph 20.

52.   Kate Manuel, "Teaching Information Literacy to Generation Y at California State University, Hayward," *Journal of Library Administration* 36, no. 1/2 (2002): 196-197.

53.   Ibid., 199-200.

54.   Robert Rubein, *Hicks, Tribes & Dirty Realists: American Fiction After Postmodernism* (Lexington: University Press of Kentucky, 2001), 2.

55.   Paula Geyh, Fred G. Leebron, and Andrew Levy, eds., "Introduction," *Postmodern American Fiction: A Norton Anthology* (New York: W. W. Norton, 1998), xi.

56.   James J. Sosnoski, *Modern Skeletons in Postmodern Closets: A Cultural Studies Alternative* (Charlottesville: University Press of Virginia, 1995), 150-2.

57.   Ibid., 179-81.

58.   Margaret K. Brady, "Problemizing the Great Divide: Teaching Orality/Literature," *Journal of Folklore Research* 33, no. 1 (1996): 44-6.

59.   David Anthony, "Students, Narrative, Historical Longing: The Stories We (Americans) Tell About Ourselves," in *Making American Literatures in High School and College*, ed. Anne Ruggles Gere and Peter Shaheen, 75-77 (Urbana, Illinois: National Council of Teachers of English, 2001).

Part Two: Literary Situations

Researching Southwestern Literature: Challenges and Strategies

Kate Manuel

The past decade has brought increasing attention to things "Southwestern." This attention is both cause and effect of recent demographic changes within the United States. Population is increasing in Texas, Arizona, Nevada, and California faster than in the historically highly populated Northeast and Midwest,[1] and the Hispanic community has seen marked growth in numbers and in political and sociocultural influence.[2] Courses on Southwestern literature can thus be found at colleges and universities throughout the United States. From Maine and Florida to Alaska and Hawaii, states geographically unconnected with the Southwest offer courses on Southwestern literature. Even when written primarily in English, though, Southwestern literature poses numerous challenges to beginning or experienced scholars attempting to understand, appreciate, research, and produce literary criticism about it. These include establishing what constitutes Southwestern literature; obtaining bibliographic access to works of and about Southwestern literature; identifying productive search terms; understanding unfamiliar cultural settings or languages; identifying and obtaining primary sources and archival materials; finding resources that employ similar interpretive approaches; and appreciating the value of serendipitous discoveries as part of a research strategy.

Few articles discuss these challenges or strategies for meeting them from the perspective of the experienced researcher, and even fewer describe how such challenges and strategies can be addressed in teaching novice researchers. Searches of relevant databases reveal that much of what has been written about teaching Southwestern literature concerns fostering appreciation for works by particular authors among students in primary and secondary schools. There is thus need for a general introduction to the challenges of and strategies for researching Southwestern literature, and to the ways in which these challenges and strategies can be successfully taught to those with various levels of experience in literary research. The author is able to make the following comments, which she hopes will be a prelude to further work in this area, from her experiences in teaching library instruction sessions for one to three sections per semester of a Southwestern

Literature class (English 394) at New Mexico State University between 2001 and 2004.

New Mexico State University is the "only land grant institution that is also classified as Hispanic-serving ... [and] Research-Extensive."[3] It enrolls 15,244 students on its main campus, where there are 654 faculty members.[4] This background information helps to situate English 394, Southwestern Literature, within the context of the university. The focus of English 394 is on the "multicultural literature of the Southwest; oral folk literature, literary fiction (classic and contemporary), nonfiction and poetry."[5] It satisfies the General Education Program's Viewing a Wider World requirement for undergraduates with majors outside the College of Arts and Sciences. Thus, while any student on campus can take English 394, its greatest appeal is to undergraduates in the Colleges of Agriculture and Home Economics, Business Administration and Economics, Education, Engineering, and Health and Human Services—most novices in literary research. The focus of English 394 informs the content of this chapter, which concentrates on the challenges of teaching Southwestern literature to beginning researchers and strategies for doing so.

This chapter also offers a librarian's perspective on these issues, rather than that of a language or literature faculty member. Much has been written about why so few humanities faculty use librarian-provided research instruction with their classes.[6] Common explanations for this phenomenon include researchers feeling that "they were the best ones to teach the next generation of scholars about information sources and research methods in the humanities"[7] and the comparatively serendipitous and less easily teachable nature of research in the humanities.[8] Whatever the reasons, this article takes the view that literary research is best taught as a union of information research and content interpretation by librarians and language or literature faculty working in partnership, each bringing their respective areas of expertise to the endeavor. As Barnhart-Park and Carpenter suggest, "[t]he roles of the librarian and the professor should ... be intertwined in the course so that students perceive that managing information is not a task reserved for the quiet space of the library, but a process affecting all aspects of their lives."[9]

DEFINING THE SOUTHWEST

Key to determining what constitutes "Southwestern literature" is a definition of "literature," as well as of "Southwestern." The term "literature" has long been recognized as problematic, as is indicated by a story told about the experiences of J. Frank Dobie, one of the pioneers in researching and teaching Southwestern literature. Dobie is said to have gone to the Budget Council at the University of Texas, asking them to approve a course titled "The Literature of the Southwest." The Council denied its approval, objecting that there was no literature of the Southwest. Dobie re-crafted his request. His revised course title was "The Life and Literature of the Southwest," and his opening comment to the Council was "You may question the existence of literature in the Southwest, but you can't deny the life."[10]

Fictional prose, poetry, and drama had certainly been authored in and about the Southwest by the early 1900s, the time of Dobie's request. The Budget Council's initial rejection was not based upon a possible definition of "literature" either as "the entire body of writings of a specific language, period, people, etc." or as "any kind of printed material."[11] Rather, they saw none of this writing as having attained the necessary stature to be termed "literature" in that sense of the word, to be seen as "writing in prose or verse regarded as having permanent worth through its intrinsic excellence."[12] This tension in the meaning of "literature" is still present, but deconstruction has helped to break down many of the artificial boundaries between "popular fiction" and "real literature."[13] Judy Reynolds notes the expansion of the *MLAIB* to include "popular culture" topics and sources,[14] one sign of the blurring of such boundaries. This is fortunate in that much Southwestern literature could be described as "popular," rather than as "great," literature.[15]

While "literature" is an imprecise term, the "Southwest" is even more undefined. Erna Fergusson has quipped, "Geographically, Southwest should be where South and West have crossed."[16] The problem with this definition is that "South" and "West" are relative terms; as Fergusson recognizes, there once was a time "when Ohio was the West, Alabama and Tennessee Southwest."[17] Arizona and New Mexico are universally recognized as part, or even the "heartland," of today's Southwest.[18] Some also include part or all of the U.S. states of California,[19] Colorado,[20] Nevada,[21] Oklahoma,[22] Texas,[23] Utah,[24] and the Mexican states of Chihuahua, Coahuila, and Sonora[25] within the Southwest. Others have recourse to the topography or the "spirit of the place"[26] in defining the Southwest. The Southwest is thus "a territory of great open spaces;"[27] the sky is its "defining feature;"[28] and one knows one is in the Southwest "[w]hen you get that first clear breath of high, dry air."[29] Yet others, given the difficulties of establishing the boundaries of the Southwest spatially, have resorted to ethnic or thematic considerations in defining the "Southwest." In such views, the Southwest is to be know by its "tricultural fusion of Indian, Hispano, and Anglo,"[30] or by its production of writings having a "elegiac strain,"[31] focused on the quest as a theme,[32] including the land as an "overarching presence,"[33] concerned with the "ongoing relationship … among the human, the plant and animal, the land, and the supernaturals,"[34] and rooted in various oral traditions.[35] Many anthologists, in fact, have given up on establishing clear boundaries for the Southwest and instead admit that any definition of the Southwest is personal[36] and that "the term 'Southwest' is an elastic one."[37]

The problem of determining what constitutes "Southwestern literature" is further complicated by the question of whether it is literature *about* the Southwest,[38] or literature produced by writers *from* the Southwest, or both. Determining whether a particular work is "about" the Southwest is not particularly difficult, once one decides the criteria used for defining the Southwest. Works by authors from the Southwest pose trickier problems. Obviously not all who write from the Southwest would characterize themselves as Southwestern writers, or be viewed as such by others. The literary periodicals *Hadrosaur Tales* and *Sin Fronteras/Writers without Borders* are both produced from Las Cruces, New Mexico, but the latter is Southwestern, while the former is not. Similarly, *Hadrosaur Tales*' editor, David Lee Summers is viewed as a science fiction/fantasy writer, not a Southwestern writer. Other authors are seen as being more fundamentally Southwestern, in the sense of writing about or from the Southwest.

The writer may either self-associate as Southwestern or be termed such by others. The fact that an author can be labeled a "Southwestern author" by others leads to some interesting contents in anthologies and critical studies, though. In addition to such clearly Southwestern writers as Rudolfo Anaya, Louis L'Amour, and Luci Tapahonso, one can also find Barbara Kingsolver,[39] Terry McMillan,[40] Ralph Ellison,[41] D.H. Lawrence,[42] and Teddy Roosevelt[43] listed as Southwestern authors in certain contexts. In practice, most anthologies and critical studies take a broad view of Southwestern literature, including authors who "merely" wrote about the Southwest or had stays of brief duration. Some editors and critics even suggest that the length of an author's residence in the Southwest is fundamentally irrelevant to their connection with the "spirit" of the Southwest. "The length of their stay is not paramount. Intensity transcends duration,"[44] says one editor, while author Rudolfo Anaya suggests "writers who are newcomers to the Southwest can convey the sense of place as they are moved by the spirit."[45]

All these difficulties in defining what constitutes "Southwestern literature" pose problems for researching it. Explaining to students, who are accustomed to treating D. H. Lawrence as a British author, or to approaching Ralph Ellison in terms of African-American identity, why these authors are also sometimes included under the rubric of Southwestern literature can be challenging. It also affords a wonderful opportunity for discussing topics key to the current construction of the humanities as a discipline and to literature as a field, as well as to methodologies and methods for literary research.[46] As Blazek and Aversa note in their *The Humanities: A Selective Guide to Information Sources*, the purview of the humanities has shifted over time and largely been defined in relation to other fields of study:

In classical and early Christian times, the scope of the humanities seemed very broad. Literature constituted the core, but virtually every discipline relating to the mind of man was considered part of the humanities. In the Renaissance period, the term *humanities* was used in opposition to the term *divinity* and seemed to embrace all areas of study outside the field of religion. In the nineteenth century, the term was used to include those disciplines that could not be considered part of the natural sciences. By the twentieth century, the fields of study that dealt with social, rather than natural, phenomena had emerged, along with "scientific" methods of investigation in the several social sciences. In the last years of the twentieth century, the humanities remain those fields of scholarship and study which are "dedicated to the disciplined development of verbal, perceptual, and imaginative skills need to understand experience."[47]

One can discuss what has constituted the proper subjects for humanities research over time, and even how the status of humanities research has shifted. What constitutes "literature" has also changed,[48] as have literary research methodologies and methods. Much of what now constitutes the corpus of "Southwestern literature" would not, previously, have been viewed as "literature."

Even with this change, though, why are today's researchers still more likely to find articles on Zane Grey in "popular culture" or historical sources than in "literature" sources?[49] This is an important question for novice literary researchers, seeking to get a sense of what information is likely to be published where. There are various methodologies and methods for studying Southwestern and other literature: reception study, symbolic interactionalism, cultural studies, textual analysis, new historicism, document examination, interviewing, and more. These approaches and techniques also influence what is published where by establishing communities of readers and writers. One can also discuss how critics, authors, and information professionals have variously defined the "Southwest" over time. Who determines the identity of an author or work as "Southwestern"? How does being labeled "Southwestern" impact an author's self-awareness and her/his reception by others?

Currently Southwestern writers, particularly Hispanic authors, are "hot commodities" in the publishing marketplace. While such writers once had to rely on regional publishers (e.g., Arte Público, Bilingual Press) or local university presses, there is now national interest in publishing their works. In Summer 2003, Northwestern University Press debuted a Latino Voices series; and HarperCollins has been proudly touting its Rayo imprint, which it has described as the "only New York-based imprint geared to a mainstream Hispanic market."[50] While, more "Chicano-Latin authors" are currently getting published,[51] literary trends change, and authors recognize dangers in being defined primarily in terms of ethnic or regional identity. "Ethnic" or regional literature is often seen as "lesser," or its works are viewed as interchangeable. Rudolfo Anaya notes that "Reflecting one's sense of place in one's stories has at times been construed as regionalism,"[52] and a work's regionalism has been used as grounds for denying its place as "universal literature."[53] Kathryn Wilder similarly voices fear of being viewed as interchangeable in her introduction to *Walking the Twilight II: Women Writers of the Southwest*, saying, "It was even implied that those of us who write about the Southwest, about redrock and slickrock country specifically, are look-alikes, our uniqueness disappearing under the hot desert sun."[54]

BIBLIOGRAPHIC ACCESS THROUGH CALL NUMBERS AND SUBJECT HEADINGS

The questions of how authors get published and marked as "Southwestern" lead directly into the questions of how writings by them can be accessed and of how the structure of literature as a field is reflected in library structures that provide access to literary research materials. Library classification numbers are the primary means used to physically group "similar" materials. Generally, it is materials on a common topic that are kept together, although authorship by the same people or organizations can also be a consideration. In Library of Congress classification system, some works of and about Southwestern literature are clustered at the call numbers of PS277 and PS566, but most are intermingled with the rest of American literature throughout the PS classification. Rudolfo Anaya furnishes an example of how Southwestern literature is subsumed within the broader class of American literature: books by and about him can be found between Cleveland Amory and various Andersons, authors unconnected to the Southwest. This arrangement suggests both the primacy of the category "American literature," as well as of the author as an interpretive principle, and it complicates researchers' access to materials about Southwestern literature, not all of which can be found in any one place.

Researchers must thus rely heavily on descriptions of books in the form of subject headings to identify the works of Southwestern literature contained within a library's collection. Library of Congress Subject Headings (LCSH) offer a number of options for designating Southwestern literature; beyond the names of individual authors, there are headings such as:

- American literature—Southwest, New
- American literature—Southwest, Old
- American literature—Southwestern states
- Tall tales—Southwest, Old
- American wit and humor—Southwest, Old
- Southwestern states—Literary collections
- Southwest, New—Literary collections.

While the categories and constructions of these subject headings are interesting in themselves, what is even more interesting is their application to particular works. Some books carry Library of Congress Subject Headings that strongly mark them as Southwestern while others do not. Denise Chávez's *Face of an Angel* typically has a number of subject headings tying it to the Southwest:

- Mexican American women—Southwestern States—Fiction
- Mexican American families—Southwestern States—Fiction
- Mexican Americans—Southwestern States—Fiction
- Restaurants—Southwestern States—Fiction
- Waitresses—Southwestern States—Fiction
- Family—Southwestern States—Fiction
- Southwestern States—Fiction.

Tony Hillerman's *Dance Hall of the Dead: A Joe Leaphorn Mystery* is similarly linked to the Southwest by the LCSH description of "Police—Southwestern States—Fiction." John Nichols' *Milagro Beanfield War*, in contrast, is not thus linked to the Southwest; it is typically described with "Mexican Americans—Fiction" and "Water rights—Fiction." Perhaps because the *Milagro Beanfield War* is seen as a "higher" work of literature, it is less tied to the Southwest in its subject headings. More specific ethnic identities similarly take precedence over generic Southwestern ones. Luci Tapahonso's works, for example, carry the headings "American literature—Indian authors;" "Navajo Indians in literature;" "Navajo Indian Reservation—poetry;" and "Indian authors"—but generally nothing marking them as Southwestern too.

Why do these differences exist? This is a question whose answer requires the knowledge of both information professionals and literary critics, as it involves both the description and organization of information resources and content interpretation. These topics are not too abstruse, even for novice researchers; rather, they are at the core of doing literary research on the Southwest. Ignoring them—failing to discuss how information about Southwestern literature is produced, by whom, and in what sources—precludes students becoming active researchers. Students told only what databases to search, what print reference sources to look at, and how to search remain un-empowered. As Barnhart-Park and Carpenter argue, "For students to become intelligent and active participants in their academic and professional communities, they must be aware of the rhetorical and political pressures that shape how discourse is created, disseminated, and stored. Information literacy initiatives can enable such participation, helping students become more conscious of disciplinary conventions, and thus more active in their experiences with disciplinary discourse."[55]

BIBLIOGRAPHIC ACCESS THROUGH REFERENCE WORKS AND DATABASES

"Bibliographic access" refers to the methods established via print and electronic tools for allowing researchers to identify works of Southwestern literature, as well as commentary or criticism about them or their authors. Bibliographic access can be provided by some types of reference sources; print abstracts and electronic indexes; webliographies; archival finding aids; and other tools that make people aware of potential resources. The previously discussed difficulties in defining the "Southwest" relate directly to some of the difficulties experienced with bibliographic access to materials from or about the Southwest. There are sources that focus directly upon the Southwest. These include a number of reference sources, such as *American Southwest Literature*[56] and *Southwestern American Literature: A Bibliography*.[57] The Southwest can also be viewed, as in the above quote

from Fergusson, as the union of the South and West, and many works of
Southwestern literature are to be accessed bibliographically through reference sources focusing on either the South or the West, sources such as a
Bibliographical Guide to the Study of Western American Literature,[58] *Companion to Southern Literature: Themes, Genres, Places, People, Movements,
and Motifs*,[59] and *Literary History of the American West*.[60]

Beyond being viewed as "Southern" or "Western" writers, though, most
Southwestern authors can also be identified and researched in terms of
their sex, sexual orientation, ethnicity, state of residence, and genre of work.
Reference tools with such foci also exist, as the following examples show:
*American Women Writers: A Critical Reference Guide from Colonial Times
to the Present*;[61] *Chicano Literature: A Reference Guide*;[62] *Hispanic Writers:
A Selection of Sketches from Contemporary Authors*;[63] *American Indian Literature and the Southwest: Contexts and Dispositions*;[64] *Oxford Companion to
African American Literature*;[65] *American Nature Writers*;[66] and *Storied New
Mexico: An Annotated Bibliography of Novels with New Mexico Settings*.[67] Yet
other Southwestern authors have entire reference works devoted to them,
such as *Fray Angélico Chávez: A Bibliography of His Published Writings,
1925-1978*[68] or *Rudolfo A. Anaya: A Critical Companion*.[69]

Such overlaps in coverage can be frustrating to researchers. Whose
works are addressed where is unpredictable, making research feel like a
hit-or-miss activity. Figure 1 illustrates how fifty well-known Southwestern authors, all included in the Cynthia Farah's widely-used anthology,
Literature and Landscape: Writers of the Southwest, variously appear (or do
not appear) in ten reference sources.

To ignore these overlaps in coverage would be to miss good, helpful
information: sometimes one source has the best leads on researching an
author; sometimes, another source does. To ignore these overlaps would
also be to miss an excellent opportunity to address why certain authors are
included in particular sources. Why do particular sources exist? Was this
type of information included in earlier sources, or does this source reflect
the emergence of a new field and needs? Were earlier sources deficient
because they were too old, or because they reflected a view of the topic no
longer prevalent? What does the existence of a source reveal about communities of writers and researchers, as well as about publication processes?
Who determines which authors and works are included where? Why are
these determinations made? Why do certain authors have reference works
devoted solely to them, while others do not? Why are certain works bought

Figure 1: Coverage of 50 Southwestern authors in 10 reference sources
Key: An "X" indicates that author is included in that source; a blank space indicates that the author is not included.

Author's Name	Sources									
	1	**2**	**3**	**4**	**5**	**6**	**7**	**8**	**9**	**10**
Abbey, Edward	X	X			X	X				X
Abbott, Lee K.										
Anaya, Rudolfo	X	X	X	X		X		X		
Baylor, Byrd		X								
Bode, Elroy	X									
Bradford, Richard	X	X				X				
Burrus, Ernest J. , S.J.										
Chávez, Fray Angélico	X	X	X							
Chávez, Denise			X							
Church, Peggy Pond	X									
Eastlake, William	X	X				X				
Evans, Max	X	X				X				
Fierman, Floyd										
Fontana, Bernard										
Frumkin, Gene										
Harjo, Joy							X		X	
Hillerman, Tony		X				X				
Hinojosa-Smith, Rolando			X	X						
Horgan, Paul	X	X				X				
Hughes, Dorothy	X									
Islas, Arturo			X							
Kelton, Elmer		X			X	X				
Lavender, David										
Lea, Tom	X					X				
Littlebird, Harold										
Medoff, Mark										
Metz, Leon C.										
Momaday, N. Scott	X	X			X	X	X	X		X
Mora, Pat			X							
Nabhan, Gary Paul										X
Nichols, John		X				X				
Noyes, Stanley	X									

Figure 1: Coverage of 50 Southwestern authors in 10 reference sources
Key: An "X" indicates that author is included in that source; a blank space indicates that the author is not included.

Author's Name	Sources									
	1	2	3	4	5	6	7	8	9	10
Powell, Lawrence Clark										
Sagel, Jim										
Sánchez, Ricardo			X	X						
Schaefer, Jack	X	X				X				
Simmons, Marc										
Sinclair, John L.										
Somoza, Joseph										
Sonnichsen, C.	X									
Steiner, Stan										
Tallent, Elizabeth										
Tapahonso, Luci							X			
Ulibarrí, Sabine		X	X	X						
Waters, Frank	X	X				X				
Weigle, Marta										
Williams, Jeanne						X				
Wilson, Keith										
Zollinger, Norman		X								
Zwinger, Ann										X

Source 1 = John Q. Anderson, Edwin W. Gaston, and James W. Lee, eds., Southwestern American Literature: A Bibliography (Chicago: Swallow Press, 1980).
Source 2 = Mary Lee Morris, Southwestern Fiction 1960-1980: A Classified Bibliography (Albuquerque, NM: University of New Mexico Press, 1986).
Source 3 = Hispanic Writers: A Selection of Sketches from Contemporary Authors, 1st and 2nd eds. (Detroit, MI: Gale Group, 1991 and 1999).
Source 4 = Julio A. Martínez and Francisco A. Lomelí, Chicano Literature: A Reference Guide (Westport, CT: Greenwood Press, 1985).
Source 5 = Richard J. Cracroft, ed., Twentieth-Century American Western Writers, 3rd series (Detroit, MI: Gale Group, 2002).
Source 6 = Geoff Sadler, ed., Twentieth-Century Western Writers, 2nd ed. (Chicago: St. James Press, 1991).
Source 7 = Janet Witalec, ed., Native North American Literature: Biographical and Critical Information on Native Writers and Orators from the United States and Canada from Historical Times to the Present (New York: Gale Research, 1994).
Source 8 = Neil Schlager and Josh Lauer, eds., Contemporary Novelists, 7th ed. (Detroit, MI: St. James Press, 2001).
Source 9 = American Women Writers: A Critical Reference Guide From Colonial Times to the Present (Detroit, MI: St. James Press, 1999).
Source 10 = John Elder, ed., American Nature Writers (New York: Charles Scribner's Sons, 1996).

by certain libraries? Getting novice students to explore the answers to these questions typically requires the collaboration of a member of the faculty in a language or literature department and of a librarian or information scientist. The person from the language or literature department brings expertise in the interpretation of literary works, including awareness of how communities of writers and researchers are constituted and of how particular authors' reputations were established. This person is typically less aware of libraries' collection development policies and procedures and of bibliometrics, or the study of the "extrinsic facts about publications" (such as the time and place of publications, the literature cited, etc.).[70] Together, these two experts in different areas can help students attain stronger understandings of why various authors can be found listed in different sources—and why this matters.

The same difficulties that were seen with bibliographic access to Southwestern literature in reference sources can also been seen with print indexes and electronic databases. The problem, again, is that there are multiple databases including Southwestern literature; each database serves different purposes and is designed for different communities of users. The *MLAIB* is probably the first source that experienced researchers think of when doing literary research. The *MLAIB* has its origins in the Modern Language Association's *American Year Book*, a current awareness tool that MLA began publishing in 1910 "for researchers in literature to use in keeping abreast of publishing by American scholars about American, British, Germanic, and Romance literatures and languages."[71] Its scope broadened over the years to include Eastern European, African, Latin American, and Asian languages and literatures, as well as linguistics, folklore, theater and film studies, cultural studies, "the visual arts, aesthetics, human behavior, communication, and information processing."[72] The *MLAIB* does, indeed, provide fairly easy access to many good resources on Southwestern literature, but it is far from the only database needed for researching this topic. In fact, novice researchers are likely to find the types of literary criticism practiced in articles listed in the *MLAIB* difficult to understand, and they will generally be better served by *Humanities Abstracts* or a general database.[73]

Even experienced literary researchers, well versed in the types of literary criticism practiced by articles listed in the *MLAIB*, should also research their topics in other databases, however. Because much Southwestern literature is "popular fiction," in the sense of appealing to audiences beyond academic researchers, helpful articles on Southwestern authors can be found in sources not indexed in *MLAIB*.[74] Solid discussions of authors such as Tony Hillerman may be found in newspaper and magazine articles. Figure 2 illustrates how different authors are differently covered in various databases. Ten authors were selected from the same source that provided the listing in Figure 1 (Cynthia Farah's anthology, *Literature and Landscape: Writers of the Southwest*) and searched in eight different databases, with the total number of results found in search database being listed. [All searches were done using the default search option and a simple phrase search with quotation marks around author's name, a strategy deliberately selected to mimic the experiences of novice searchers.[75]]

These databases differ in their coverage, the ways in which they work, and the vendors who make them available to libraries. *Arts and Humanities Search* claims to cover over 1,000 journals in the arts and humanities, while *Humanities Abstracts* covers 400 journals in the humanities. *Arts and Humanities Search* covers the years 1980 to the present; *Humanities Abstracts*, 1984 to the present; and the *MLAIB*, 1926 to the present. Each database has different search interfaces and options. These differences are indicative of wider issues in the production and use of tools for bibliographic access, and they should be discussed with and demonstrated to students. Even more interesting are the different types of resources that one can find using these various tools. Searching Paul Horgan in the *MLAIB*, for example, finds information about his literary style in itself and in relation to other authors published in book chapters, dissertations, or journals such as *Hawaiian Review* and *Western American Literature*. *Arts & Humanities Search*, interestingly, finds an article from *Western American Literature* that was not listed in *MLAIB*. *Humanities Abstracts* finds sources about the writer's personal life from sources such as *Catholic Historical Review* and *The American Scholar*, as does *WilsonSelect*, while *America: History and Life* finds articles about Horgan's view of America published in such journals as *Southwestern Historical Quarterly*. This last set of articles is especially helpful in illustrating to students that the texts which literary studies is concerned with in their own right can also serve as "evidence" for researchers in other fields (e.g., history, anthropology).

SEARCH TERMS

It has already been noted that "Southwestern" as an identity is problematic by being overly broad. Most writers identify in terms of narrower categories: female; homosexual, bisexual, or transgendered; Native American;

Figure 2: Coverage of 10 Southwestern authors in 8 different databases
The number indicates the number of results found with a keyword phrase search of the author's name using the default search option.

Author's Name	Number of Results, MLA Int'l Bibliography	Number of Results, Arts & Humanities Search	Number of Results, Humanities Index	Number of Results, America: History & Life	Number of Results, Lexis-Nexis Academic Universe	Number of Results, HAPI (Hispanic American Periodicals Index)	Number of Results, Wilson-Select	Number of Results, Alternative Press Index
Anaya, Rudolfo	33	2	3	3	6	15	4	0
Chávez, Denise	7	0	0	1	3	0	1	0
Harjo, Joy	22	2	10	3	6	0	5	1
Hillerman, Tony	14	3	3	5	116	0	1	0
Horgan, Paul	9	1	2	7	5	0	2	0
Momaday, N. Scott	50	9	17	44	5	0	7	0
Nichols, John	19	2	9	4	81	1	2	2
Tapahonso, Luci	7	0	1	0	0	0	0	0
Waters, Frank	116	4	5	27	7	0	2	0
Wilson, Keith	2	2	0	0	60	1	4	0

* Default setting of last 6 months only was used in searching Lexis-Nexis Academic Universe.

Hispanic; Texan; and so on. Many of these identities can be expressed in multiple ways, not all of which may be palatable to either the searcher or the author being researched. "Hispanic," "Chicano/a," "Latino/a," and sometimes "Mexican American" are sometimes used as if they were synonyms. Yet, many of those described by these terms have strong feelings for or against particular terms. "Each of these terms allows for variations by class, education, and generation: a single family might include parents who identify themselves as Mexican-American, children who call themselves Chicano, and grandchildren who are 'Hispanic.'"[76] Researchers need to know that their subjects' own preferred identifications may not work well as search terms. Denise Chávez, for example, is fond of "Herspanic," a term indicating both female and Hispanic identity, but Figure 3 indicates how it fares in relation to other, similar search terms in various databases. Similarly, students may need to use search terms that they personally may find distasteful. The author has seen students fail to find adequate results because, for example, they were completely committed to Chicano/a as an identity formulation and refused to try Hispanic or Latino/a.[77] Sometimes the use of certain ethnically identifying terms is understandably unpalatable to students. Multi-racial identity is expressed rather awkwardly in Library of Congress Subject Headings under "racially mixed people," suggesting there are "racially unmixed" or "pure" people. Similarly, African-Americans have the subject heading of "Blacks" in *America: History and Life*.[78] Researchers' situation here can be a difficult one: they can either search only those identifiers they "like," missing potentially vital information, or they can search using keywords or subject headings they find distasteful. This situation results from the intersection of the complexities of identity con-

Figure 3: Results of various search terms expressing ethnic identity in 4 different databases. The number indicates the number of results found with a keyword search for that term.

	Hispanic	Latino/a	Chicano/a	Mexican-American	Herspanic
Lexis-Nexis Academic Universe*	125	125	125	125	0
WilsonSelect	3018	1048	171	243	0
MLA International Bibliography	5766	3979	1197	182	0
Google	3,350,000	3,980,000	232,000	315,000	17

* Default setting of last 6 months only was used in searching Lexis-Nexis Academic Universe.

struction (identities are often defined in relation to others and in provisional terms) with those of providing bibliographic access (which seeks to "encompass all the facets of what has been printed and subsequently collected in the library to the satisfaction of the worldwide reading community"[79] but can only do so from a single perspective).[80] Many of the difficulties here are discussed at length in Berman's *Prejudices and Antipathies: A Tract on the LC Subject Heads Concerning People*, and exploration of them can have great interest for novice undergraduate students.

The problems of identifying search terms related to Southwestern authors and works of literature does not end with ethnically identifying terms, though. Some of these authors may have published anonymously, pseudonymously, or under multiple names. The latter is particularly common with Native American authors, who may be identified by tribal and non-tribal names. Gertrude Bonnin, also known as Zitkala-Sa, is a excellent example here. Authors of "pulp fiction" may also have used multiple names, as did Elmer Kelton and Jeanne Williams. Yet other problems in generating search terms also appear. In addition to authors' names, literary researchers commonly search by geographical areas and time periods.[81] The "Southwest" is obviously a problematic search term, given the previously discussed difficulties of establishing its boundaries. Time periods and literary movements are similarly problematic.[82] The 1920s and 1930s, for example, can be called the American modernist period, Jazz age, Harlem Renaissance, or "Lost Generation."

Identifying other works of Southwestern or American literature that have the same theme can be particularly problematic. Because the "aboutness" of a work of literature is hard to determine and convey, "[l]ibrary cataloging has never seriously tried to attribute subject headings to literary works."[83] The Library of Congress Subject Headings given to works of fiction only go so far toward indicating what these works are *really* about. The subject headings given to Tony Hillerman's *Coyote Waits*, for example, indicate that it concerns "Police—Southwestern States—Fiction," but do nothing to convey that is *more specifically concerned* with one policemen who is struggling to connect to others despite his suspicious nature and personal losses (Leaphorn) and another struggling to reconcile "traditional"/Navajo and "modern"/Anglo cultures (Chee). Any judgement of "aboutness" on this more detailed level, while potentially helpful, would be irredeemably subjective, though. A different person looking at the same work would find it to be about something different. The subject headings included within the

MLAIB are similarly sketchy when attempting to convey what an information resource that addresses multiple time periods, historical or literary figures, named persons, trends, topics, and methodologies is "about."[84]

Given all this richness of language surrounding Southwestern literature, novice researchers in particular often have difficulty generating productive search terms. Their lack of background knowledge relating to the topics they are researching typically hampers their searches. A novice researcher told to research the "Chicano literature of the Southwest" will often type exactly this into a database or search engine, and s/he may not know enough about what is meant by this topic to come up with alternate ways of describing either "Chicano literature" or the "Southwest" should the initial search fail. Numerous studies have found that novice researchers "often did not have sufficient knowledge of their subject to begin searching"[85] and that "the beginning of the information search process, or 'knowing where to start,' presented the most challenges."[86] It is for this reason that the use of subject-specific encyclopedias and handbooks to generate search terms is often recommended for beginning students.[87] Even experienced researchers, however, have difficulties generating multiple search terms for a topic. They too "use the 'plug-in-the-keyword' approach, and never think about possible synonyms that they could consider."[88]

UNFAMILIAR CULTURAL SETTINGS OR LANGUAGES

Much Southwestern fiction vividly depicts specific geographic or socio-cultural settings. In fact, such depictions are often key to works being identified as Southwestern. As Lawrence Clark Powell suggests, of the forces shaping Southwestern literature, "the greatest [is] the Southwest itself, the land and its climate and configurations of desert, mountains, rivers, and skies, as well as its history and cultures as they have influenced writers of sensitivity and responsiveness, of stamina and genius."[89] This factor can pose some difficulties, though, particularly for novice researchers. Those not personally familiar with football and its place in west Texas will not, for example, appreciate its role in Dan Jenkin's *Fast Copy*, while understanding John Wesley Hardin as a folk hero, rather than a criminal, is essential to Larry McMurtry's *Streets of Laredo*. Readers not sharing the backgrounds described by these works many need various multicultural and subject-specific encyclopedias for help in understanding fictional contexts.

Similarly, Southwestern literature often casually uses smatterings of Spanish, Navajo, or other languages indigenous to its cultural settings.

This shifting from one language to another within a speech unit is known as code-switching, and it is often key to the construction of "authentic" identities for characters in Southwestern literature.[90] Sometimes only a single word of another language is used in a passage where its meaning could be inferred, especially by experienced readers, from its context. The following examples from Tony *Hillerman's Coyote Waits* all illustrate this:

- "Navajo Tribal Police regulations prohibited nepotism in the chain of command. But the rules were just picked up from *biligaana* personnel regulations. The white rules didn't recognize clan connections."[91]
- "He used the map in his endless hunt for patterns, sequences, order–something that would bring a semblance of Navajo *hohzho* to the chaos of crime and violence."[92]
- The cure had been conducted by a *hataalii* who had been very tall and had seemed to him then to be incredibly ancient. The patient had been Chee's paternal grandmother …"[93]

Less experienced readers, however, may lack the verbal processing skills to supply meaning from a word's context; they do not have that familiarity with the conventions of writing that allows expert readers to anticipate meanings.[94] Novice students confronting such passages, as well as experienced readers confronting lengthier examples of code-switching in other texts, may need to access dictionaries and other translation tools.

PRIMARY SOURCES AND ARCHIVAL MATERIALS

It has been said that "[p]erhaps only historians have as much interest in primary source material as scholars of literature and the librarians who work with these scholarly groups."[95] Two of the three "types" of literary scholarship described by Stephen E. Wiberley in his "A Typology of Literary Scholarship for Academic Librarians" draw heavily on primary source materials. The first of these types, descriptive bibliography, requires "that a bibliographer study as many copies as possible of the works that are the subject of the bibliography in order to both differentiate variants and document the works' printing and publishing history."[96] Many first or early editions that a researcher would use in compiling a bibliography are located in libraries' archival or special collections units, classed with other primary source materials. The second type of literary scholarship, reconstructions or historical studies, also relies on primary sources, "those created by the persons whose activities and accomplishments the literary scholar seeks to describe and interpret."[97]

Descriptive bibliography and reconstructions or historical studies have traditionally been the sole province of expert literary researchers, and they are likely to stay that way in typical situations. However, their potential appeal to some novice researchers in certain situations should not be underestimated. The undergraduate research movement, which seeks to improve education by making undergraduates active participants in, rather than passive recipients of, the construction of disciplinary knowledge, has made only small inroads in the humanities, despite being credited with increased student learning. While 62 percent of institutions report undergraduate research programs in the laboratory sciences that involve 50 percent, or more, of the undergraduate students, only 21 percent report the same level of involvement in the humanities.[98] One of the recognized barriers to increased undergraduate research in the humanities is that faculty are largely engaged with interpretive methodologies that rely heavily on the individual's ability to make connections between texts. The opportunities for other researchers, particularly undergraduate students who may not have read widely, to get involved are minimal.[99] Descriptive bibliography furnishes greater opportunities for students to become involved with undergraduate research and the construction of knowledge in the discipline. There *are* students who will be fascinated by the variations between different editions of a work, as well as by the process of tracking these variations down and making meaning from them.[100]

Regional archival centers have not been established in or for the Southwest in the same way that they have been established in and for the South.[101] While the South has the Center for the Study of Southern Culture,[102] which serves as a focal point for things "Southern," most archival repositories in and for the Southwest are state-based, or even institution specific. Researchers need to be taught and to employ different search strategies here; instead of looking directly for desired resources, researchers must seek sites that might potentially have the resources sought. This is a difficult cognitive adjustment for most researchers; researchers have become so accustomed to the ability of full-text electronic sources to take them "directly" to content on a topic that they have difficulty searching "indirectly" or identifying resources that *might* be able to supply information on a topic.[103] Moreover, some of the states/areas involved have not been able to afford extensive digitization, so serious researchers need to work with finding aids, an unfamiliar and potentially frustrating source. One additional complication is the fact that Southwestern literature is a comparatively new category. Most scholars trace its origins to the period immediately following the Civil War or the 1920s-1930s.[104] Many of the authors writing Southwestern literature are, thus, still living. While some of these authors maintain Web sites, their personal papers have largely not yet been donated to archival repositories.[105] Moreover, many of these writers are relying upon electronic tools for composition and communication, making it less likely that their letters and drafts of their work will be available to future researchers.[106] Another set of excellent questions about Southwestern literature centers on asking whose work ends up in particular archives, how it gets there, why, and how this impacts literary research in this area. The "politics" of answering these questions are worthy of exploration with both novice and experienced researchers.

INTERPRETIVE APPROACHES

Finding other applications of an interpretive approach is always problematic, as a researcher may want to apply to modern Southwestern literature an interpretive approach another researcher has used with Medieval Latin poetry. Such activity constitutes the third of Wiberley's "types" of literary scholarship, criticism based on theory. The range of potential interpretive approaches that could be applied to a work of literature, a body of literature, or an author is enormous, so much so that M. H. Abrams has suggested, today, "[i]f one wants to study Nietzsche, Marx, Freud, Derrida, or Foucault, one must apply not to departments of philosophy, psychology, or sociology, but to departments of English or comparative literature."[107] Interpretive approaches are only most sketchily described in either Library of Congress Subject Headings or those used in the *MLAIB*. Multifile searching, or searching more than one database simultaneously, is a strategy that Mara Saule recommends[108] for dealing with the unique need for humanities researchers to access information from such varied fields as "political history, economics, philosophy, and potentially the entire range of humanities disciplines from musicology to archaeology."[109] There are distinct difficulties to multifile searches, though, as different fields and disciplines may apply the same theoretical orientation in very different ways. In fact, there are few strategies to employ for finding materials with similar interpretive approaches beyond relying upon the serendipitous browsing that literary researchers have traditionally employed. As will be seen, though, serendipitous browsing can be a difficult strategy to "sell" to novice and experienced searchers alike.

APPRECIATING SERENDIPITY

As with most literary research, checklists of things to do or of types of resources to look for can only go so far in researching Southwestern literature; they are most helpful for beginning students with broad topics and less helpful for advanced researchers who need to develop an ability to navigate by "feel," knowing what is likely to be published and where. Humanities research in general, and literary research in particular, has traditionally relied strongly upon "fortuitous discovery" as a research technique: "humanistic research may be defined as a 'method of analysis, as a *way* of looking at subject matter' ... This method generally involves a great deal of judgment and attention to nuance which excludes quantification and 'logical clarity.'"[110] Literary researchers may not know what they are looking for until they stumble across it, and determinations of whether a particular result is relevant to a search or research topic are largely subject to the researcher's viewpoint.[111] Persuading novice researchers of the value of serendipitous discoveries can be quite difficult, though, particularly when they are traditionally aged college students. They have grown up with the "see-a-box, fill-a-box" approach to research facilitated by search engines. They tend not to appreciate browsing as a strategy, even for use with electronic resources.[112] They have little patience for browsing through print materials within a library's collection.[113] Developing such an appreciation is key to their acculturation into the community of literary researchers, however.[114] Experienced researchers, in contrast, typically have acquired appreciation for the value of serendipitous discoveries in literary research and can be shown how to hook into invisible colleges working in their topic area(s) as a way to expand upon the power of serendipitous browsing of print collections.

CONCLUSION

As the previous discussion suggests, the challenges of researching Southwestern literature really represent opportunities, most of which are also common to other areas of literary studies. They represent opportunities to foster an integrated model of library and literary research instruction wherein the content (what is being researched) is completely integrated with the process (of researching). For too long instruction librarians have concerned themselves with the false dichotomy between themselves, who (supposedly) teach processes to students, and other faculty, who (supposedly) teach content to students.[115] In reality, sophisticated understandings of the research process are always informed by—and, in turn, inform—content knowledge. Knowing who produces information on a topic, where, and over what time frames is a crucial component of content knowledge, and one that strongly shapes understanding of the research process.[116] Such an approach to the fusion of content and process requires more, however, than the traditional "one shot" library instruction session. All of the issues explored in this article could not be presented in a fifty-minute library instruction session, nor should they be. They should be explored over multiple sessions, throughout a student's academic career, by both disciplinary faculty and librarians working in concert and individually.

NOTES

1.   Missouri Economic Research and Information Center, *The First Numbers of the 2000 Census*, No Date, http://www.missourieconomy.org/indicators/population/popl-dec2000.stm (15 June 2008)

2.   Patrick Reddy, "The Hispanic Factor: As They Become an Ever-Larger Percentage of the U.S. Population, Hispanic Americans Are Gaining Political Clout and Reshaping Policy," *The Buffalo News*, 12 January 2003, H1.

3.   Regents of New Mexico State University, *NMSU at a Glance*, 2002, July 28 http://www.nmsu.edu/General/NMSU_At_a_Glance.html (31 July 2003).

4.   Ibid.

5.   New Mexico State University, *Undergraduate Catalog 2003-2004* (Las Cruces, NM: NMSU, 2003), 137.

6.   Martha Fleming, "Bibliographic Instruction on Electronic Resources: The Humanities," *LIBRES: Library and Information Science Research Electronic Journal* (1993), http://dhsws1.humanities.curtin.edu.au/libres/LIBRES3N5/featurearticle.txt (15 Jun 2008).

7.   Mara R. Saule, "User Instruction Issues for Databases in the Humanities," *Library Trends* 40 (1992): 596. See also Judy Reynolds, "The *MLA International Bibliography* and Library Instruction in Literature and the Humanities," in *Literature in English: A Guide for Librarians in the Digital Age*, ed. Betty H. Day and William A. Wortman, 226 (Chicago: Association of College and Research Libraries, 2000).

8.   Ron Blazek and Elizabeth Aversa, *The Humanities: A Selective Guide to Information Sources*, 4th ed. (Englewood, CO: Libraries Unlimited, 1994), 3.

9.   Anne C. Barnhart-Park and William J. Carpenter, "Information Literacy and Literary Questions," *Academic Exchange Quarterly* 6 (2002): 10-16.

10.   C.L. Sonnichsen, "The Fabulous Southwest: An Introduction," in *The Southwest in Life and Literature: A Pageant in Seven Parts*, ed. C. L. Sonnichsen (New York: Devin-Adair, 1962), 3.

11.   "Literature," in *Random House Webster's College Dictionary* (New York: Random House, 1991), 792, meanings 2 and 6.

12.   Ibid., meaning 1.

13.   "Deconstruction," in J.A. Cuddon, *A Dictionary of Literary Terms and Literary Theory*, 4th ed. (Malden, MA: Blackwell Publishers, 1998), 209-212. See also W. James Potter, *An Analysis of Thinking and Research about Qualitative Methods* (Mahwah, NJ: Lawrence Erlbaum Associates, 1996), 149.

14.   Reynolds, "The *MLA International Bibliography* and Library Instruction," 215.

15. Coverage and criticism of literature produced in electronic instead of print format are still largely lacking in the *MLAIB*, however. The writers publishing in "Southwestern" zines such as *Border Beat* (http://www.borderbeat.com) still tend to be those whose works are not discussed in the sources indexed in the *MLAIB*.

16. Erna Fergusson, "What Is Southwest?" in *The Southwest in Life and Literature: A Pageant in Seven Parts*, ed. C. L. Sonnichsen, 9 (New York: Devin-Adair, 1962).

17. Ibid.

18. Lawrence Clark Powell, *Southwest Classics: The Creative Literature of the Arid Lands: Essays on the Books and Their Writers* (Los Angeles, CA: W. Ritchie Pr., 1974), 3. See also, Sonnichsen, "The Fabulous Southwest," 4; Fergusson, "What Is Southwest?" 12; Paula Gunn Allen, "Preface," in *Writing the Southwest*, ed. David King Dunaway and Sara L. Spurgeon, xix (New York: Plume, 1995); and David James Harkness, *Southwest and West Coast in Literature* (Knoxville: University of Tennessee, 1954).

19. Fergusson, "What Is Southwest?" 10; Allen, "Preface," xix; Harkness.

20. Allen, "Preface," xix.

21. Fergusson, "What Is Southwest?" 11.

22. Fergusson, "What Is Southwest?" 11; Harkness; Sonnichsen, "The Fabulous Southwest," 4.

23. Fergusson, "What Is Southwest?" 10; Harkness; Sonnichsen, "The Fabulous Southwest," 4.

24. Fergusson, "What Is Southwest?" 11.

25. Ibid.

26. Rudolfo Anaya, "Foreword: The Spirit of the Place," in *Writing the Southwest*, ed. David King Dunaway and Sara L. Spurgeon, ix-xvi (New York: Plume, 1995).

27. Max Apple, "Introduction," in *Southwest Fiction* (New York: Bantam Books, 1981), ix-x.

28. Powell, Southwest Classics, 9.

29. Fergusson, "What Is Southwest?" 11.

30. Powell, *Southwest Classics*, 4. See also, Apple, "Introduction," xvi and Allen, "Preface," xviii.

31. Ibid., xv.

32. Ibid., xvii.

33. Allen, "Preface," xviii.

34. Ibid., xxi.

35. David King Dunaway and Sara L. Spurgeon, "Introduction," in *Writing the Southwest*, ed. David King Dunaway and Sara L. Spurgeon (New York: Plume, 1995), xxx.

36. Powell, Southwest Classics, 4.

37. Sonnichsen, "The Fabulous Southwest," 4.

38. Kathryn Wilder, "Introduction," *Walking the Twilight II: Women Writers of the Southwest* (Flagstaff, AZ: Northland Pub., 1996), ix.

39. Included in Dunaway and Spurgeon, *Writing the Southwest*.

40. Ibid.

41. Included in Apple, *Southwest Fiction*.

42. Included in Powell, *Southwest Classics*.

43. Ibid.

44. Ibid., 5.

45. Anaya, "Foreword," xiii.

46. Potter, *Analysis of Thinking and Research*, 50, notes that "Methodologies are perspectives on research; they set out a vision for what research is and how it should be conducted.

They are the connection between axioms and methods; methods are tools—techniques of data gathering, techniques of analysis, and techniques of writing. Because it is a tool, a particular method can be used by many different methodologies."

47.   Blazek and Aversa, *Humanities: A Selective Guide*, 1.

48.   Ibid., 330-331.

49.   A search for articles about Zane Grey in the *MLAIB*, for example, finds articles in such journals as: *Brigham Young University Studies*, *Aethlon: The Journal of Sport Literature*, and *Journal of American Culture*.

50.   Rigoberto González, "Latino Literature: Publishing Houses Hungry for Up-and-coming Writers," *El Paso Times*, 29 June 2003, 2F.

51.   Ibid.

52.   Anaya, "Foreword," x.

53.   Ibid.

54.   Wilder, "Introduction," ix.

55.   Barnhart-Park and Carpenter, "Information Literary and Literary Questions," 10.

56.   Available at http://uassowestlit.users3.50megs.com/.

57.   (Chicago: Swallow Press, 1980).

58.   (Albuquerque, NM: University of New Mexico Press, 1995).

59.   (Baton Rouge, LA: Louisiana State University Press, 2002).

60.   (Fort Worth, TX: Texas Christian University Press, 1987; also available at http://www2.tcu.edu/depts/prs/amwest/).

61.   (Detroit, MI: St. James Press, 1999).

62.   (Westport, CT; Greenwood Press, 1985).

63.   (Detroit, MI: Gale Group, 1999).

64.   (Austin, TX: University of Texas Press, 1999).

65.   (New York: Oxford University Press, 1997).

66.   (New York: Charles Scribner's Sons, 1996).

67.   (Albuquerque, NM: University of New Mexico Press, 1991).

68.   (Santa Fe, NM: Lightning Tree, 1980).

69.   (Westport, CT: Greenwood Press, 1999).

70.   William Paisley, "Bibliometrics, Scholarly Communication, and Communication Research," *Communication Research* 16 (1989): 707.

71.   Reynolds, "The *MLA International Bibliography* and Library Instruction," 215.

72.   Ibid., 216-217.

73.   See also, Ibid., 218, who notes that "advanced research tools such as the *MLAIB* should be introduced at the point in a student's career when their use is essential for successful completion of course work."

74.   Ibid., 227.

75.   Studies have repeatedly shown that novice researchers do not make effective use of Boolean logic or advanced search options. See A. G. Sutcliffe, M. Ennis, and S. J. Watkinson, "Empirical Studies of End-User Information Searching," *Journal of the American Society for Information Science* 51 (2000): 1216.

76.   Dunaway and Spurgeon, "Introduction," xl.

77.   This is actually a very complicated question, as these different ways to express ethnic identity are not completely synonymous. Uses of different ethnically identifying terms can represent different communities of discourse and meaning.

78.   Obsolete terms for expressing ethnic identity are sometimes preserved, as separately searchable terms, within databases as a way of allowing more precise access to historical material.

79. Sanford Berman, *Prejudices and Antipathies: A Tract on the LC Subject Heads Concerning People* (Metuchen, NJ: Scarecrow Press, 1971), ix.

80. See Theodor H. Nelson, *Literary Machines* (Swarthmore, PA: Self-published, 1981), 2/49, who notes "there is nothing wrong with categorization. It is, however, by its nature transient. Category systems have a half-life, and categorizations begin to look fairly stupid after a few years."

81. Reynolds, "The *MLA International Bibliography* and Library Instruction," 223.

82. See Saule, "User Instruction Issues," 606.

83. Ibid., 223.

84. As Reynolds, "The *MLA International Bibliography* and Library Instruction," 216, notes, "detailed subject headings" were first used in the *MLA International Bibliography* in 1981.

85. Debora J. Shaw, "Undergraduate Use of CD-ROM Databases: Observations of Human-Computer Interaction and Relevance Judgments," *Library and Information Science Research* 18 (1996): 264.

86. Nancy J. Young and Marilyn Von Seggern, "General Information Seeking in Changing Times," *Reference and User Services Quarterly* 41 (2001): 163.

87. Reynolds, "The *MLA International Bibliography* and Library Instruction," 242.

88. Rita Vine, "Real People Don't Do Boolean: How to Teach End Users to Find High-Quality Information on the Internet," *Information Outlook* 5 (2001): 18.

89. Powell, Southwest Classics, 3.

90. See Dunaway and Spurgeon, "Introduction," xxxix.

91. Tony Hillerman, *Coyote Waits* (New York: HarperPaperbacks, 1992), 34.

92. Ibid., 150.

93. Ibid., 191.

94. Michael Pressley and Peter Afflerbach, *The Verbal Protocols of Reading: The Nature of Constructively Responsive Reading* (Hillsdale, NJ: Lawrence Erlbaum Associates, 1995), 39.

95. Susan L. Peters, "Primary Source Material: Responsibilities and Realities," in *Literature in English: A Guide for Librarians in the Digital Age*, ed. Betty H. Day and William A. Wortman, 108 (Chicago: Association of College and Research Libraries, 2000). See also Stephen E. Wiberley, "A Typology of Literary Scholarship for Academic Librarians," in *Literature in English: A Guide for Librarians in the Digital Age*, ed. Betty H. Day and William A. Wortman, 301 (Chicago: Association of College and Research Libraries, 2000).

96. Wiberley, "Typology of Literary Scholarship," 303. See also Peters, "Primary Source Material," 109.

97. Wiberley, "Typology of Literary Scholarship," 307. See also Peters, "Primary Source Material," 109.

98. Boyer Commission on Educating Undergraduates in the Research University, *Reinventing Undergraduate Education: Three Years after the Boyer Report*, 2002 <http://www.sunysb.edu/pres/0210066-Boyer%20Report%20Final.pdf> (31 July 2003).

99. The Reinvention Center at Stony Brook, "Breakout Session: Humanities and Humanistic Social Sciences," in *Undergraduate Research and Scholarship and the Mission of the Research University*, 29-33 (Stony Brook, NY: Reinvention Center, 2003).

100. As Laurie Lounsberry McFadden, "Making History Live: How to Get Students Interested in University Archives," *College and Research Libraries News* 59 (1998): 423-425 suggests, "College students can get excited about archives and all the riches found within. And they don't have to be history majors."

101. Many of the national archival repositories, such as the Electronic Text Center, the Humanities Text Initiative, and the On-Line Books Page, either focus on texts earlier than

those of Southwestern literature or are based outside the Southwest and give little attention to this body of literature.

102.   Available at http://www.olemiss.edu/depts/south.

103.   As Chris Sherman and Gary Price, *The Invisible Web: Uncovering Information the Search Engines Can't See* (Medford, NJ: CyberAge Books, 2001), 91-113, note, many searchers experience similar difficulties in finding "invisible Web" sources.

104.   Dunaway and Spurgeon, "Introduction," xxvii and xxxi.

105.   Michelle Mach and Cynthia D. Shirkey, "Twentieth-Century Authors: Biographic and Bibliographic Information Is Just a Click Away," *College and Research Libraries News* 60 (1999): 904.

106.   George P. Landow, *Hypertext: The Convergence of Contemporary Literary Theory and Technology* (Baltimore, MD: Johns Hopkins University Press, 1992), 33 and 64.

107.   M.H. Abrams, "The Transformation of English Studies: 1930-1995," *Daedalus* 126 (1997): 124. See also Wiberley, "Typology of Literary Scholarship," 311-314.

108.   Saule, "User Instruction Issues for Databases," 607.

109.   Ibid., 598.

110.   Ibid., 600.

111.   Marcia J. Bates, "The Design of Databases and Other Information Resources for Humanities Scholars: The Getty Online Searching Project Report No. 4," *Online and CD-ROM Review* 18 (1994): 338.

112.   Susan Augustine and Courtney Greene, "Discovering How Students Search a Library Web Site: A Usability Case Study," *College and Research Libraries* 63 (2002): 363.

113.   See Lorna Peterson, "From Literate to Scholar: Teaching Library Research Skills to Sixth Graders Using Primary Documents," *Urban Education* 32 (1997) who discusses the difficulties of fostering an appreciation of print sources among students used to searching. She suggests that librarians' focus upon teaching students how to access books often works at cross-purposes with fostering a love of books.

114.   Blazek and Aversa, *The Humanities: A Selective Guide*, 3.

115.   Larry Hardesty, *Faculty and the Library: The Undergraduate Experience* (Norwood, NJ: Ablex Publishing, 1991), 128, for example, writes, "Faculty members emphasize content. Librarians emphasize process." Faculty members, however, would not necessarily agree with this split between content/faculty and process/librarians. Many faculty see themselves as actively engaged in teaching students processes—although these processes are typically communicating orally or in writing, thinking like an historian, reading critically, etc., rather than using library research. See Kate Manuel, Susan E. Beck, and Molly Molloy, "An Ethnographic Study of Attitudes Influencing Faculty Collaboration in Library Instruction," *The Reference Librarian* 43, (89/90) [2005]: 139-161.

116.   This approach is fundamentally similar to that advocated by Ann Grafstein, "A Discipline-Based Approach to Information Literacy," *Journal of Academic Librarianship* 28, no. 4 (2002): 201.

Literary Research in a Bilingual Environment: Information Literacy as a Language-Learning Tool

Miriam Laskin and José Díaz

INTRODUCTION

Like research in any discipline, literary research calls upon the teaching and learning of a sophisticated set of cognitive, critical and analytical skills. At Hostos Community College, City University of New York (Hostos, CUNY),[1] library faculty believe that Information Literacy (IL) is a foundation upon which to build these research abilities. All students, but particularly English as a Second Language (ESL) and Low English Proficiency (LEP) students, benefit from IL instruction as a language-learning tool and, more broadly, as a set of skills and abilities that support reading comprehension, critical and analytical thinking, and problem solving.

This chapter addresses several interlocking issues. After a brief overview of Hostos Community College, its student body, and a description of the Library's IL program, we address the importance of librarian/disciplinary faculty collaboration and suggest Writing Across the Curriculum (WAC) programs as a successful model for collaborations and as a means of avoiding the undue impact on librarians' workloads that can occur when librarian/disciplinary faculty collaboration becomes "too successful." We then offer an example of a course-integrated research workshop for an English course that demonstrates how IL instruction can be a language-learning tool and a way to support language awareness as well as student retention efforts. Finally, we suggest a role for academic librarians as information literacy mentors to faculty, and possibly as initiators of "teach the teachers" programs, wherein librarians teach disciplinary faculty about electronic resources and information technologies that they may not be familiar with. Librarians also have a role in working with disciplinary faculty on ways to successfully integrate IL into their course syllabi.

A substantial proportion of Hostos students have language deficiencies affecting their reading comprehension, writing, critical/analytical and other cognitive skills—all of which are needed for inquiry and content-based research. Today, educators advocate the integration of IL, critical thinking, and writing intensive curricula (WIC) at all levels of the college experience and these academic literacies are now required by many regional accrediting agencies.[2] Student-centered learning that is content and inquiry-based is fast becoming the educational strategy of choice, but this challenges both students and faculty. Retention of Bilingual, ESL and LEP students demands as full an array as possible of support services and opportunities for these students to practice those practical and cognitive skills that will enable them to succeed. Our faculty—including library faculty—have a mission and a mandate to teach these skills, and provide the support necessary for their success in community college and beyond.

LITERATURE REVIEW: IL FOR ESL STUDENTS

While the literature on library services to Hispanics and other minorities is well developed, Ormsby and Tobin[3] note in their annotated bibliography, *Information Literacy: Reaching Diverse Populations* (2001) that there are relatively few articles published about Hispanic-Americans and library instruction in academic settings. Of the available literature, we find contributions about the role of the librarian, and general perspectives on academic library use by, and services to, Hispanic populations.[4] Other contributions focus on specific issues such as Hispanic learning styles, the impact of cultural values on the learning process in teaching new information technologies, and innovations in the bilingual teaching-learning environment to support academic readiness skills.[5]

Of particular interest to us is literature pertaining to ESL/LEP students and information literacy. There are a number of publications exploring ways IL instructors can understand and work with the special needs of this population, but there is, as yet, virtually nothing on information literacy as a language-learning tool. Karen Bordonaro's 2006 article, "Language Learning in the Library: An Exploratory Study of ESL Students," describes a research study about how ESL students use a college library in a self-directed manner in order to improve their English, but the study does not include IL instruction or any faculty-directed work. Bowley and Meng's 1994 article, "Library Skills for ESL Students" may well represent one of the earliest attempts to address specific needs of ESL students by promoting a framework upon which to develop a successful IL program. One of the crucial elements cited by the authors is library-faculty collaborations. Miriam Conteh-Morgan proposes innovative collaborations between library faculty and ESL instructors to create a library instruction model that emphasizes the cross-applicability of ESL objectives and IL concepts and skills. Conteh-Morgan also describes the connection between second language acquisition and information literacy.[6] The challenge before Hostos, then, was to design a program which would integrate the goals of IL with effective service to an ESL/LEP student population.

INFORMATION LITERACY IN THE HOSTOS-CUNY ENVIRONMENT

At Hostos, library faculty all teach in the IL program and play a vital role in college initiative focused on retaining its linguistically and culturally diverse students. The Library's still-evolving, curriculum-integrated, multi-level IL program was created and implemented in 2001. The IL program is among the reasons the Association of College and Research Libraries honored Hostos Library with its 2007 ACRL Excellence in Academic Libraries Award for a community college library.[7]

The IL curriculum includes six interlocking foundational ("Basic") workshops, described in the Appendix. The Basic workshops are offered 4-6 times a week and students can sign up for as many workshops as they like, according to their own schedules. In this way, teachers do not have to give up a class session in order to ensure that their students are receiving IL instruction. Typically, students are assigned to take one to two workshops by faculty, though some assign more. An average of 800 students attend approximately eighty Basic IL workshops each semester. These workshops are separate from the course-integrated research workshops, one of which is the research session described below.

The Library's IL curriculum supports a number of campus student retention and academic literacy programs and initiatives. The Counseling department's College Orientation course, which all Liberal Arts majors must take, includes attendance in three of the Basic IL workshops as a course requirement. Since 2004, the English department's two-semester Freshman English sequence includes required attendance in at least two of the Basic workshops and students in all English courses, including at the remedial level, must attend our "Plagiarism & How to Avoid It" workshop. Spanish-language IL workshops are provided for students enrolled in courses given in Spanish. We also offer CUNY's online Information Competency Tutorial modules in a bilingual format. These tutorials function as a language-learning tool, since students read the English and Spanish texts next to each other. The IL program also supports students and faculty who take or teach Writing Intensive (WI) courses. Library faculty work with WI faculty to incorporate inquiry-based assignments into their syllabi and then work with their students in course-integrated research workshops.

Information Literacy, Standardized Testing and Student Retention

The trend throughout U.S. educational systems to test student performance outcomes using standardized exams is one of the reasons we offer IL to students via a variety of avenues, since the professional literature points to the added value of IL instruction for students who will eventually have to pass these exams. Another reason is to support Hostos' student retention efforts. Approximately 25% of Hostos students take at least one ESL course and a majority take one or more remedial courses in writing, reading or mathematics. Our students must pass the CUNY-wide ACT placement exams before enrolling in credit-bearing English or Math courses. The CUNY Proficiency Exam (CPE) is a fairly recent addition to CUNY standardized performance outcomes. A passing score is required for graduation from all of the CUNY community and senior colleges. The CPE is meant to test academic literacy through analytical reading, analysis, comparison, and integration of information from a diverse range of subjects and graphs.[8] If students are to pass the ACT and the CPE exit exams and continue successfully in further college studies and in their chosen careers, then all academic departments and the entire institution must continue to find vehicles to reinforce classroom learning. The Library's IL program and other collaborations with faculty play a reinforcing role in the college's remedial and ESL/LEP programs and in the college's retention efforts. IL is a tool to increase language-learning, critical thinking and problem-solving skills. In fact, a review of the literature increasingly indicates that IL competencies support acquisition of critical thinking, analytical and language skills and that IL in a variety of delivery modes supports colleges' efforts at student retention.[9] In relation to the retention of Hispanic college students, research conducted over the past 15-20 years demonstrates that the integration of Hispanic perspectives, culture and history into the curriculum improves retention rates.[10] Thus, we have developed programs to improve the teaching and learning experience by working closely with faculty to include more Hispanic perspectives into the classroom and more Hispanic resources and materials such as our Eugenio Mariá de Hostos Bilingual Digital Archives, and our Web-based IL and language-learning tool, the CUNY Bilingual Information Competency Tutorials.

The concepts and skills we teach in the six Basic IL workshops are transferable "generic" research and information technology skills not directed at any specific discipline. As one of our IL curricular innovations, disciplinary faculty who request a course-integrated workshop are asked to require their students to take two of our Basic IL workshops before the course-integrated session is scheduled. In this way, less time is spent in the course-integrated workshop bringing students "up to speed" on basic information technology and transferable research skills; instead, the focus can be kept on the research topic and students can apply and practice the IL skills they learned in the Basic IL workshops.

LIBRARIAN-FACULTY COLLABORATION: UNDERLYING RATIONALES

The importance of teaching collaborations between librarians and disciplinary faculty is well represented in the literature.[11] While no consensus has been formed yet about the type and extent of such collaboration, there are many who believe as Gloria Leckie does, that "at some point in the student's educational experience, there must be a convergence of both information and disciplinary literacy if true learning is to be facilitated. It seems clear that both academic librarians and faculty have to be actively involved in this process together."[12]

Even without recent mandates by regional accreditation agencies calling for joint librarian/faculty responsibility in teaching information literacy across the curriculum and at all levels, there are good reasons for academic librarians and disciplinary faculty to work together when students are assigned research papers.[13] The literature on librarian/disciplinary faculty collaborations to teach IL and, more specifically, discipline-specific methodologies, has grown in recent years, as the significance of IL has grown.[14]

One of the most important proponents of librarian-faculty (and Library-Writing Center) collaboration is James Elmborg. In *Centers for Learning: Writing Centers and Libraries in Collaboration* he notes that "the writing process and the research process are so intimately intertwined in the academic work of students that any effort to separate the two compromises the effort to create an accurate model for working with students."[15] Elmborg, Norgaard, Leckie, Fister and other experts in the writing/research process advocate collaborations with disciplinary faculty to teach the incremental, integrative processes by which students learn.[16]

One type of collaboration increasingly utilized is that of librarians working with disciplinary faculty to craft or revise research assignments that allow students to move through the process so that each stage prepares them for the next. Students benefit from librarian/disciplinary faculty collaboration to guide them through incremental acquisition of the complex set of cognitive and developmental skills that lead to information and disciplinary literacy. As Ann Grafstein puts it, we must be aware that "being information literate crucially involves being literate *about something* [emphasis in original]."[17] Because of lingering difficulties academic librarians encounter in creating working partnerships with disciplinary faculty, library instruction programs tend to offer "one-size-fits-all" IL workshops that are not tailored to a specific discipline. Even the most inclusive IL workshops can not address the diverse modes of professional discourse and the constellation of research approaches needed by students in a variety of academic majors. Disciplinary faculty have the discipline-specific expertise, and collaboration between librarians and disciplinary faculty will enrich and facilitate students' research experiences.

In "Desperately Seeking Citations," Gloria Leckie uses the phrase "expert researcher model" to describe disciplinary faculty's approach to research in their fields, and she compares the expert model to the "novice researcher" model that undergraduates employ.[18] Some faculty may have forgotten their own undergraduate novice research experiences; or they completed their graduate research prior to the revolutionary changes that digital technology and the Internet have wrought on the research landscape, and so are more or less at sea in a world of online catalogs and licensed databases—to say nothing of the World Wide Web's pleasures and pitfalls.[19]

Enough has now been published on specific difficulties novice researchers have for there to be a consensus. Sonia Bodi lists students' top three problem areas: 1. choosing and narrowing a topic; 2. understanding and using subject headings for searches; and 3. evaluating sources, especially web sites.[20] There are more of these troublesome areas, including students' inability to identify scholarly works in a particular discipline; and having enough time to read, reflect, and integrate new information, or explore new avenues of inquiry. Students are as yet unfamiliar with the body of knowledge within a field; they do not know who the major scholars are; and they have not yet learned to follow citation trails. The nature of education, of course, is that through the incremental, interactive acquisition of skills and knowledge, the experts guide novices through the processes that lead to higher level thinking skills.[21]

Librarians and disciplinary faculty should collaborate to support ESL/ LEP and bilingual students, reinforcing their language studies across the disciplines through IL instruction. Learning how to navigate the digital landscape and find materials for coursework and research involves a focus on vocabulary, as well as critical thinking. Students need to formulate search queries, understand and use keywords, find synonyms and related terms, use broader or narrower terms, and controlled vocabulary (i.e., Library of Congress Subject Headings, or Descriptors). All of these IL activities provide an additional learning arena for students still grappling with English. When students are motivated by problem or inquiry-based assignments, language-learning can come more consciously into focus for these students. Coming up with relevant results by using successful search strategies reinforces language comprehension and helps develop vocabulary. Though more published data on student outcomes are needed, Deborah Moore, a librarian, and several of her disciplinary faculty colleagues at Glendale Community College published the results of a study that shows higher student retention rates and higher levels of success in English courses for ESL students who have taken IL workshops, as opposed to ESL students who have not.[22]

As we work with disciplinary faculty to introduce students to discipline-specific resources and research techniques in course-integrated IL sessions, we continue to look for ways to make faculty more conscious of the need to create assignments that, while challenging, are structured to incorporate the learning processes of novice researchers.

A LIBRARIAN-ENGLISH FACULTY COLLABORATION: "LANGUAGE, CULTURE AND SOCIETY"

The Hostos Library's Instructional Services coordinator, an author of this chapter, was approached by a colleague in the English department to discuss a student research project for her course "Language, Culture and Society." The course content reflects the professor's interest in sociolinguistics. It introduces students to the sociological, anthropological and political aspects of language use. Her students' culturally and linguistically diverse backgrounds were an advantage and the professor wanted the assignment to include explorations of language as used by their families or in their neighborhoods (their "speech community"). Part of the project was to design a survey/questionnaire. There would also be a library-based research component, and the professor wanted a course-integrated IL workshop to help her students with their research. There was enough lead time before the course-integrated session for the English professor to require that her students take two Basic IL workshops outside of their class meetings and thus the Library instructor would be able to move faster in applying keyword and search strategies to the research topics.

Preparing for the Course-Integrated Research Workshop

The Library instructor and English professor discussed the specific research assignment. The paper was to be ten pages, including the results of students' "speech community" surveys. It would include citations and a bibliography in MLA format. The English professor structured the research and writing process so that she could supervise the students individually and as a group at each step. She distributed a "Research Timetable" with deadline dates for the introduction and an outline, draft of the bibliography, and the research design for the questionnaire and survey.

After this discussion, the Library instructor did some exploratory searches for potential information sources. It became apparent that the Library's print resources should be supplemented by full-text periodical databases and web resources. Three of the Library's licensed full-text databases were identified as having the most promise for fruitful research: *Academic Search Premier, Ethnic NewsWatch,* and *Literature Research Center.* A search for appropriate web resources revealed high quality web sites that the students would find helpful and the Library instructor created a collection of annotated Internet pathfinder with links to the sites to the Library's web pages.

The Research Session

The course-integrated research session began with a review of keyword searching techniques, using one of the full-text databases. As the students examined the citation records, the Library instructor pointed out that the words and phrases included as subject descriptors can be helpful in finding more (and sometimes more relevant) articles; she reminded the students of the importance of writing down any newly-discovered terms that the students could use in subsequent searches on their specific topics. In fact, by discussing subject descriptors and helping students understand that there are often several ways to describe the same thing, students were already becoming more aware of the advantage of expanding their vocabulary.

The students then did some searches on their topics. During this process, they discovered that different writers use different terms to describe the same subject. The solution, they discovered, is to use what they had learned about how to expand the retrieval possibilities using the Boolean connector "OR" between synonyms or related terms. For example, a number of terms are used by linguists to describe African-American Vernacular English, including "Ebonics," "Black English," and "African-American English." One student whose research focused on Ebonics retrieved only seven records using that term, but when she expanded the search using "Ebonics OR Black English OR African-American English" she retrieved over thirty. The Library instructor also showed the students examples of how combining two or more terms with "AND" can focus the results so they would not be caught in an avalanche of results. For example, a student was looking for material in Literary Research Center using "Latino fiction." He retrieved a huge number of results. But after narrowing his topic to fiction by Hispanics about the immigrant experience and reformulating the search query to "fiction AND immigrant AND (Hispanic-American OR Latino)" the student retrieved a reasonable number of relevant articles. In addition, it was a chance to reinforce the importance of using vocabulary that is both precise and inclusive. In the course of practicing search strategies on their topics in electronic databases and on the Web, students who are still learning English become more aware of the importance of thinking about their word choices, expanding their own possibilities for describing what they are looking for, and, becoming more aware of the subtleties and intricacies of English (or any language).

Some of the students were interested in exploring how the way a person speaks English can affect how he or she is treated by others. The Library instructor encouraged these students to think of related terms. For example, their results were better when a search combined "language AND society" with "prejudice OR racism" rather than using just "prejudice" or "racism." Other students were interested in how language background informs identity and they found that "language" combined with the related terms "ethnicity OR identity" worked well.

After working with the databases, the students turned to the Internet pathfinder. The Library instructor was able to use this part of the session to point out ways the students could apply some basic evaluation criteria to discover: Who is responsible for the web site? What are some ways to determine whether the information on the web page or web site is authoritative enough to be trustworthy? What is the currency of the information? Who is the intended audience? Going over how to evaluate web sites in this research session served to reinforce what the students had learned when they attended Surf Smart I, one of the Library's Basic IL workshops that addresses web site evaluation, and, hopefully, to show them that a "generic" IL skill (evaluation of resources) has a very real and practical application once they apply it to their own research about their speech community.

The course-integrated research workshop just described was successful from the points of view of the English professor, her students, and from the Library instructor's perspective as well. The students were able to apply what they had learned in the Basic IL workshops about the relative reliability of web sites maintained by educational institutions and nonprofit organizations as one aid in evaluating authority and bias in web documents. They were able to engage in inquiry-based active learning by doing searches on their own research topics and in the process, got help with, and practice in, the other two major problems of novice researchers as noted by Bodi.[23] This time, the skills they had been introduced to in our Basic workshops were being used to fulfill a specific assignment and the students were motivated by their interest in their topics.

In the days following this research session Hostos librarians noticed the students in the "Language, Culture and Society" course working at the reference area computers and were able to offer them further one-on-one help when needed. These students, so many of whom had entered college with the challenges posed by their ESL/LEP status, had become involved through the research assignment in exploring their own speech communities, turning what can often feel like a social and educational liability into a source of intellectual interest and cultural pride. As previously discussed, retention efforts for our large Hispanic student population is supported when these students can see their perspectives, cultures and history integrated into the curriculum and campus life in general.

ACADEMIC LIBRARIANS AS INFORMATION LITERACY MENTORS FOR DISCIPLINARY FACULTY

Any discussion of librarian/faculty collaboration in discipline-specific research workshops brings up a range of assertions and critiques about the best way to 'combine forces' with disciplinary faculty to teach IL competencies. The diverse collaboration strategies librarians have been using include: helping an instructor create a better research assignment; creating a pathfinder, subject guide, or interactive online tutorial; teaching a research module in the professor's classroom during the semester; or providing course-integrated

IL sessions. Often, a successful partnership with one faculty member leads to requests by other faculty members as word spreads about how helpful librarians can be in helping students meet their learning objectives.

While it seems safe to assert that more librarian/disciplinary faculty collaboration to teach IL and the research process is a worthy goal, library faculty sometimes discover that they need to manage their success carefully. As more disciplinary faculty ask for collaborations with their library colleagues, the additional work load on already busy library faculty can become overwhelming.[24] The Hostos Library IL program was designed, in part, to minimize the potentially sizable number of course-integrated IL sessions requested by individual disciplinary faculty for their classes. Four to seven basic IL workshops are offered per week throughout the semester in a variety of time slots, which faculty can require their students to attend outside of class time. This eliminates the need to schedule sessions for twenty sections of Freshman English or College Orientation and other multi-section courses and leaves more time for library faculty to work on course-integrated, discipline-specific IL sessions, reference duties, collection development, or other responsibilities.

Library faculty can look to Writing Across the Curriculum programs as a successful model for integrating IL across the curriculum without librarians shouldering the major burden for IL. WAC provides a structure and support for faculty involved in revising curricula and learning to use writing more effectively in their courses. It is essentially a faculty development program; and it takes the sole responsibility for teaching writing off the shoulders of English department faculty and places it across all academic departments. As James Elmborg cautions, "information literacy librarians may want to consider their desire to 'own' information literacy as a subject."[25] Gloria Leckie suggests that, ideally, academic librarians become "bibliographic instruction mentors, assisting and encouraging faculty with respect to integrating information literacy into their courses."[26] This idea is attractive and practicable, although we might update it by replacing "bibliographic instruction" with the more current expression of "information literacy." Being an information literacy mentor implies that the responsibility to teach IL does not fall solely on librarians; librarians can mentor their faculty colleagues, and this could prove to be more effective and permanent than trying to do it all ourselves.

One promising approach being taken by library departments to help fulfill accrediting agency mandates for all faculty to share responsibility for teaching IL is to create opportunities for "teaching the teachers" programs. One of the colleges where this seems to have found success is at the University of Montana, according to Samson and Granath,[27] whose study in 2004 documented the effectiveness of a "teach the teachers" collaborative model to integrate IL into Freshman Composition courses.

CONCLUSION

We began the Hostos Library IL program in the fall of 2001. Since then, we have seen our reference room transformed into the Information/Learning Commons (ILC) and its computers go from being used mainly for email, online chatting and playing online games, to being used for the purpose of research, discovery, acquiring and communicating new knowledge. Just as heartening, where we had become used to seeing students begin their searches by zooming onto the web to use Google or Yahoo, we now see many making other choices, including the Library's web site, licensed subscription databases or online subject guides. We see literature students turning to Gale's *Literature Resource Center* or other appropriate databases when they need literary criticism. And we see ESL and LEP students using the research workstations to connect with tutorials and other language materials we have provided. With its recent redesign, our ILC offers students the extra space and ability to study in groups and collaborate on projects. More disciplinary faculty are asking library faculty to provide course-integrated research sessions for their classes.

We have anecdotal evidence that IL instruction and faculty collaborations are making a difference. Beyond the anecdotal, we are in the process of applying outcomes assessment tools to our IL program and other services to students and faculty. Every workshop ends with students filling out online evaluations of the session. These forms also collect data on the students' backgrounds, including their native language, what courses required the workshop (if any), what kinds of information software and technology they use. The data is tied to their ID's and when the analysis is completed, we will be in a position to know much more about our students' strengths and needs, and whether taking our IL workshops has had a measurable effect on their academic success, measured by passing the CPE, CUNY's exit exam.

In focusing on the Hostos Library's Information Literacy program and some of the work our faculty have been doing with students and disciplinary faculty, we suggest some of the ways librarians who work with similar bilingual or ESL/LEP populations can use IL instruction not only to teach information-seeking skills and research processes, but also how these techniques and concepts can be used as a language-learning tool.

WAC proponents have been markedly successful in delivering the message that there is a great need for writing to be integrated into all academic disciplines and that the responsibility for teaching writing be partially lifted from the shoulders of English department faculty. The students are the real winners in this movement. At Hostos and many other CUNY Colleges, the WAC initiative has resulted in Writing Intensive (WI) courses offered in every academic department and making WI courses a requirement for every student. The Hostos Library faculty, like library faculty elsewhere, have embarked on collaborations with disciplinary faculty, especially those teaching WI courses, to integrate IL and research skills into their curricula, and to create rubrics measuring student research outcomes. The movement for IL Across the Curriculum (ILAC) is much more recent, but it appears to be gaining momentum.

As library faculty continue to teach IL workshops or offer credit-bearing Information Studies courses and as they continue to contribute to best teaching practices and other academic literature, students will benefit. To paraphrase Gloria Leckie, students need both information *and* disciplinary literacy in order to truly learn.[28] Further, when librarians teach, collaborate with disciplinary faculty, and communicate through academic publications, in conferences and other forums, valuable relationships are formed. Faculty and librarians begin to see one another as academic equals.

Collaboration between librarians and disciplinary faculty to accomplish the goals of IL is an idea that has developed slowly and fitfully, but, as previously mentioned, the Middle States Commission on Higher Education, our accrediting agency, has published *Developing Research & Communications Skills: Guidelines for Information Literacy in the Curriculum*.[29] The *Guidelines* make it clear that Middle States and other accrediting agencies are mandating IL throughout the curriculum and at all levels. It *must* be addressed by faculty and by administration, not just by librarians.

In this Information Age of ever-changing and expanding digital resources, technologies and new challenges in understanding the social, legal and ethical use of information, our students deserve faculty who can teach and support their efforts to find, understand, evaluate and use the plethora of resources available to them—not only for their college studies, but for their continuing success as independent, savvy critical thinkers and lifelong learners.

APPENDIX: Hostos Library's Basic Workshop Program

Note: All six workshops include hands-on exercises and are 75 minutes long. Each session ends with student feedback via online evaluations. The workshop instructors' materials include a "Design & Goals" sheet which, among other things, notes which ACRL IL Standards the workshop addresses. The students don't see this, but here, we include a reference to the Standards in each description below. To see the complete ACRL document, go to: http://www.ala.org/ala/mgrps/divs/acrl/standards/informationliteracycompetency.cfm

INFOLIT 101

Lighten your study hours by taking this workshop and upgrading your information retrieval skills. You will tour the Library's Web site, discover why information users need to evaluate sources of information, especially Web pages. Learn about the role of libraries in society. Learn how to select and use appropriate databases and Internet resources to find up-to-date materials for your coursework.

ACRL Standards 2, 3, 5. This workshop covers:
+ An introduction to the Library's Web site and a Virtual Library Tour
+ Information literacy basics
+ How to access CUNY's licensed subscription databases from on-campus or off
+ Library databases vs. World Wide Web
+ Tour of selected Resources

SURF SMART! USING THE WEB FOR INFORMATION AND RESEARCH

Did you know that the Internet and the World Wide Web are not the same thing? Do you understand how to look at a URL (WWW address) and be able to tell who sponsored or created the site? Are you tired of getting over a million hits every time you try to do a search? You will learn tips and techniques to help you make the most of what the Web has to offer, including when to avoid using it to do research. ACRL Standards 3, 5. This workshop covers:
+ Where and How to access the Web on campus
+ Features of the MS Explorer browser

- Good starting places for research
- Searching techniques in the web environment.
- Evaluating Web documents for their usefulness and authority.
- The Web vs. Subscription Databases: when to use one or the other for your particular needs.

GOOGLEMANIA: SECRETS OF THE WEB

Google is today's most popular and sophisticated search engine. Its constantly updated search tools and features are both fun and useful to explore. You may be missing out on some of the ways that Google can help you do high quality research, including easy ways to find that definition, free reference material, books or articles you long for, consumer trends, Web 2.0 collaborations and much more – unless you take this workshop. ACRL Standards 2, 4, 5. This workshop covers:

- Basic vs. Advanced searching
- Special features: definitions, vocabulary building and ready reference
- Google Images to find charts, graphs, photos and other images
- Google Books and Google Scholar for research
- Google News, Archives and Timelines

KEYS TO DATABASE SEARCHING

Learn simple and effective database search techniques. This workshop introduces you to transferable skills that can be used to find books or articles in any database! Learn how use how our online catalog of library holdings and tour a few key research databases. ACRL Standards 1, 2, 3. This workshop covers:

- Searching the Library's online catalog of holdings, on-campus or off and CUNY Libraries' new book delivery service called CLICS – get a book you need sent to you at your campus
- Academic Search Premier, our popular database for articles on virtually any subject
- Basic database search techniques: keyword & subject searching, Boolean operators
- Topic development and refining research questions for best results

FINDING ARTICLES

Build on keyword searching skills you learned in our "Keys to Database

Searching" workshop. Find full text articles in electronic databases on any subject - from the most recent political controversy or social issue, to medical research and case studies, to literary criticism on your favorite author. Do you need expert information to put into your speech? Or the "pros and cons" of the death penalty? Professional and academic articles are the basis for many assignments, and understanding citations for periodical literature is a key to finding the articles you need. ACRL Standards 1, 2, 5. This workshop covers:

- What is a database and how does it organize information for searching
- What is a record and how are they different from citations in a research paper
- Database selection for periodical literature in different academic disciplines
- Citation analysis. What's in a citation
- Using Information Responsibly- Citing Sources

RESEARCH SURVIVAL SKILLS: PLAGIARISM & HOW TO AVOID IT

Academic integrity includes understanding how to respectfully use the intellectual property of others. Plagiarism is using someone else's words, ideas, or creations without proper acknowledgment of the source. In to-day's world of digital technology and the Internet, it is important to know what the penalties for plagiarizing are, and how to avoid unintentionally committing plagiarism. ACRL Standards 4, 5. In this workshop, you will learn about how to:

- Quote a source correctly, using MLA and APA styles
- Use parenthetical (in-text) citations in your research paper
- Create a list of references (bibliography) at the end of your research paper
- How summarizing and paraphrasing strengthen your writing
- Use our online Plagiarism resources guide, with tutorials, online style guides for MLA, APA and other citation formats, and much more, to help you hand in a better research paper.

NOTES

1. Hostos Community College of the City University of New York lies in the heart of the South Bronx, the poorest congressional district in the nation, whose population is 62%

Hispanic. This urban, bilingual institution is the only CUNY campus whose mission is specifically bilingual, allowing Spanish-dominant students to begin courses in their native language while enrolled in our English as a Second Language (ESL) program. The college is named after the Puerto Rican educator, writer and patriot, Eugenio María de Hostos (1839-1903). His educational vision is reflected in our college's mission, "to meet the higher educational needs of people from this and similar communities who historically have been excluded from higher education…." Hostos offers "higher education leading to intellectual growth and socio-economic mobility… to students from diverse ethnic, racial, cultural and linguistic backgrounds, particularly Hispanics and African Americans." For the complete Hostos Community College Mission Statement, see http://www.hostos.cuny.edu/about/.

2.   See Lana W. Jackman, "Information Literacy: Whose Job Is It?" *Academic Exchange Quarterly* 6, no. 4 (2002): 29-33; Karen L. Michaelsen, "Integrating Information Literacy into the Curriculum," in *Programs that Work*, ed. Linda Shirato, 101-104 (Ann Arbor: Pieran Press, 1997); Middle States Commission on Higher Education, *Developing Research & Communication Skills: Guidelines for Information Literacy in the Curriculum* (Philadelphia: Middle States Commission on Higher Education, 2003); Gary B. Thompson, "Information Literacy Accreditation Mandates: What They Mean for Faculty and Librarians," *Library Trends* 51, no. 2 (2002): 218-241.

3.   Rita Ormsby and Tess Tobin, "Information Literacy: Reaching Diverse Populations: Annotated Bibliography" (published for the LACUNY Institute 2001, by the Library Association of the City University of New York). Available at: http://lacuny.cuny.edu/institute/.

4.   See John Ayala, Luis Chaparro, and Ana Maria Cobos, "Serving the Hispanic Student in the Community College Library," in *Library Services to Latinos: An Anthology*, ed. Salvador Güereña (Jefferson, NC: McFarland, 2000); Susan Hinojosa, "Libraries in the New Millennium- and What About the Students?" loc. cit.

5.   See Shirley Griggs and Rita Dunn, "Hispanic-American Students and Learning Style," *Emergency Librarian* 23, no.2 (1995): 11-16; Donna L. Gilton, "A World of Difference: Preparing for Information Literacy Instruction for Diverse Groups," *MultiCultural Review* 3, no. 3 (1994): 54-62; Lori S. Mestre, "Designing Internet Instruction for Latinos," *Internet Reference Services Quarterly* 2, no. 4 (1997): 185-199; and Anne C. Moore and Gary Ivory, "Do Hispanic-Serving Institutions Have What It Takes to Foster Information Literacy? One Case," *Journal of Latinos & Education* 24 (2003): 217-231.

6.   Karen Bordonaro, "Language Learning in the Library: An Exploratory Study of ESL Students," *The Journal of Academic Librarianship* 32, no. 5 (2006): 518-526; Barbara Bowley and Lynn Meng, "Library Skills for ESL Students," *Community College Journal* 64 (1994): 13-14; Miriam Conteh-Morgan, "Connecting the Dots: Limited English Proficiency, Second Language Learning Theories, and Information Literacy Instruction," *The Journal of Academic Librarianship* 28, no. 4 (2002): 191-196; _____, "Empowering ESL Students: A New Model for Information Literacy Instruction," *Research Strategies* 18, no.1 (2001): 29-38. See also Gina Macdonald and Elizabeth Sarkodie-Mensah, "ESL Students and American Libraries," *College & Research Libraries* 49 (1988): 425-431; Diane DiMartino, William J. Ferns and Sharon Swacker, "CDROM Search Techniques of Novice End-Users: Is the English-as-a-Second-Language Student at a Disadvantage?" *College & Research Libraries* 56 (1995): 49-59.

7.   The ACRL award panel noted, "Hostos Community College Library demonstrates exemplary partnership and leadership by working with faculty to develop new courses on information literacy, critical thinking and computer literacy…. and to create an inviting and bilingual student-focused environment in the library…." The complete press release is at our website: http://www.hostos.cuny.edu/library.

8.   See "CUNY Testing Programs" at the City University of New York's web site, http://portal.cuny.edu.

9.   For discussions of IL's role in supporting student retention, see, for example, Barry Beyer, "Critical Thinking: What is it?" *Social Education* 49, no. 4 (1985): 270-276; Patricia S. Breivik, "Information Literacy for the Skeptical Library Director," paper presented at the 21st Annual Conference of IATUL, Brisbane, Queensland, Australia (2000), http://www.iatul.org/conference/proceedings/vol10/papers/breivik_full.html; Miriam Laskin, "Bilingual Information Literacy and Academic Readiness: Reading, Writing, and Retention," *Academic Exchange Quarterly* 6, no. 4 (2002): 41-51; Jeremy J. Shapiro and Shelley K. Hughes, "Information Literacy as a Liberal Art," *Educom Review* 31, no. 2 (1996), http://www.educause.edu/pub/er/review/reviewarticles/31231.html.

10.   *New Directions for Community Colleges*, no. 112 (Winter 2000) is devoted to issues of minority student retention, learning styles and problems with standardized testing of minority students. See especially Romero Jalomo, Jr., "Beyond Access: Methods and Models for Increasing Retention and Learning Success Among Minority Students," 7-18; and Irene M. Sanchez, "Motivating and Maximizing Learning in Minority Classrooms," 35-44. Sanchez discusses the relationship of learning preferences to motivation and retention of Hispanics and Native Americans. For other relevant discussions, see J.C. Hernandez, "Understanding the Retention of Latino College Students. *Journal of College Student Development*, 41, no. 6 (2000): 575-588; and L. I Rendon and M.T. Taylor, "Hispanic Students: Action for Access," *Community, Technical, and Junior College Journal*, 60 no.3 (Dec.-Jan.1989):18-23.

11.   Many articles and monographs present overviews, research or analysis that support the importance of librarian-faculty collaborations in teaching research methods to undergraduates. See, for example: Christine Black, Sarah Crest and Mary Volland, "Building a Successful Information Literacy Infrastructure on the Foundation of Librarian-Faculty Collaboration," *Research Strategies*, 18 no.3 (2001): 215-225; Evelyn B. Haynes, "Librarian-Faculty Partnerships in Instruction," *Advances in Librarianship*, 20 (San Diego: Academic Press, 1996): 191-223; Patricia Iannuzzi, "Faculty Development and Information Literacy: Establishing Campus Partnerships," *Reference Services Review* 26, nos. 3-4 (1998): 97-102, 116; Thomas G. Kirk, Jr., "Course-Related Bibliographic Instruction in the 1990's," *Reference Services Review* 27, no. 3 (1999): 235-241; Marian C. Winner, "Librarians as Partners in the Classroom: An Increasing Imperative," *Reference Services Review* 26, no. 1 (Spring 1998): 25-30; and Rosemary M. Young and Stephena Harmony, *Working with Faculty to Design Undergraduate Information Literacy Programs: A How-To-Do-It Manual for Librarians* (New York: Neal-Schuman, 1999). For descriptions of actual librarian-disciplinary faculty collaborations, see Dennis Isbell and Dottie Broaddus, "Teaching Writing and Research as Inseparable: A Faculty-Librarian Teaching Team," *Reference Services Review* 23, no. 4 (1995): 51-62; Colleen Bell and Juanita Benedicto, "The Companion Course: A Pilot Project to Teach Discipline-Specific Library Research Skills," *Reference Services Review* 26, no. 3 (1998): 117-24; and Linda L. Stein and Jane M. Lamb, "Not Just Another BI: Faculty Librarian Collaboration to Guide Students Through the Research Process," *Research Strategies* 16, no. 1 (1998): 29-39.

12.   Gloria J. Leckie, "Desperately Seeking Citations: Uncovering Faculty Assumptions about the Undergraduate Research Process," *The Journal of Academic Librarianship* 22 (1996): 201-8; quote on 206-7.

13.   For an excellent analytical review of the current accreditation mandates, see Gary B. Thompson, "Information Literacy Accreditation Mandates: What They Mean for Faculty and Librarians," *Library Trends* 51, no. 2 (2002): 218-41. For an extensive discussion and detailed presentation on IL across the curriculum and IL assessment, see the Middle States

Commission's 2003 *Guidelines* cited in Note 2, above.

14.   For an inclusive starting point in understanding the importance of librarian-faculty collaborations, IL's contributions to student retention, as well as its pedagogic connection to Reading and Writing Across the Curriculum, see Sue Samson and Kim Granath, "Reading, Writing and Research: Added Value to University First-Year Experience Programs," *Reference Services Review* 32, no. 2 (2004): 149-156. Other relevant publications are: Sonia Bodi, "How Do We Bridge the Gap between What We Teach and What They Do? Some Thoughts on the Place of Questions in the Process of Research," *The Journal of Academic Librarianship* 28, no. 3 (May 2002): 109-114; Cheryl Jones, Carla Reichard, and Kouider Mokhtari. "Are Students' Learning Styles Discipline Specific?" *Community College Journal of Research & Practice* 27, no. 5 (2003): 363-76. Ann Grafstein also articulates the argument and places it in an historical perspective in her article, "A Discipline-Based Approach to Information Literacy," *The Journal of Academic Librarianship* 28, no. 4 (2002):197-204.

15.   James K. Elmborg and Sheril Hook, *Centers for Learning: Writing Centers and Libraries in Collaboration* (Chicago: Association of College and Research Libraries, 2005), 9.

16.   In addition to Elmborg and Hook, cited above, see: James K. Elmborg, "Information Literacy and Writing Across the Curriculum: Sharing the Vision," *Reference Services Review* 31, no. 1 (2003): 68-80. For a compelling discussion of the goals and methodologies shared by writing and information literacy instructors by an instructor of writing and rhetoric, see Rolf Norgaard's "Writing Information Literacy in the Classroom: Pedagogical Enactments and Implications," *Reference & User Services Quarterly* 43, no. 3 (Spring 2004): 220-26; and his preceding article, "Writing Information Literacy: Contributions to a Concept," *Reference & User Services Quarterly* 43 no. 2 (Winter 2003):124-130. Gloria J. Leckie, "Desperately Seeking Citations" (see Note 12 for full citation); Barbara Fister, "The Research Processes of Undergraduate Students," *The Journal of Academic Librarianship* 18, no. 3 (1992): 163-169. See also Isbell and Broaddus, "Teaching Writing and Research as Inseparable: A Faculty Librarian Teaching Team," cited above in Note 11. For an excellent and provocative review/ discussion of publications by librarians, composition experts and disciplinary faculty on students' experiences with the research process and a clear-eyed argument for more collaboration among these three academic groups, see Celia Rabinowitz, "Working in a Vacuum: A Study of the Literature of Student Research and Writing," *Research Strategies* 17, no. 4 (2000): 337-346.

17.   Ann Grafstein, "A Discipline-Based Approach to Information Literacy," 202.

18.   Gloria Leckie, "Desperately Seeking Citations," 202.

19.   For an account of problems arising when disciplinary faculty with little experience with Internet resources assign research on the Web, see Deborah J. Grimes, and Carl H. Boening, "Worries with the Web: A Look at Student Use of Web Resources Among Students in a Junior-College English Class," *College & Research Libraries* 62, no.1 (2001): 11-23.

20.   Bodi, "How Do We Bridge the Gap between What We Teach and What They Do?" 109.

21.   In addition to Leckie, "Desperately Seeking Citations," see also Sonia Bodi, "Critical Thinking and Bibliographic Instruction: The Relationship," *The Journal of Academic Librarianship* 14, no. 3 (1988): 150-153; Carol Collier Kuhlthau, *Seeking Meaning: A Process Approach to Library and Information Services* (Norwood, N.J.: Ablex, 1993); and Kuhlthau, "Developing A Model of the Library Search Process: Investigation of Cognitive and Affective Aspects," *Reference Quarterly* 28, no.2 (1988): 232-242; Patricia Senn Breivik and Dan L. Jones, "Information Literacy: Liberal Education for the Information Age Discourse," *Liberal Education* 79, no. 1 (1993): 24-29; and Howard B. Tinberg and Ronald Weisberger, "In Over Our Heads: Applying Kegan's Theory of Development to Community College Students,"

Community College Review 26, no. 2 (Fall 1998): 43-56.

22.   Deborah Moore, Steve Brewster, Cynthia Dorroh, and Michael Moreau, "Information Competency Instruction in a Two-Year College: One Size Does Not Fit All," *Reference Services Review* 30, no. 4 (2002): 300-306.

23.   Sonia Bodi, "How Do We Bridge the Gap between What We Teach and What They Do? (See Note 14 for full citation.)

24.   In "Desperately Seeking Citations," 207, Leckie observes that "Academic librarians seem to be taking on an inordinate amount of the work load" in library-disciplinary faculty collaborations. See also Carla List, "Branching Out: A Required Library Research Course Targets Disciplines and Programs," *The Reference Librarian*, no. 51-52 (1995): 385-98.

25.   James K. Elmborg, "Information Literacy and Writing across the Curriculum," 77.

26.   Gloria Leckie, "Desperately Seeking Citations," 207.

27.   Samson and Granath, "Reading, Writing and Research" (See Note 14 for citation.)

28.   Gloria Leckie, "Desperately Seeking Citations," 206.

29.   Middle States Commission on Higher Education, *Developing Research & Communication Skills: Guidelines for Information Literacy in the Curriculum*, (Philadelphia: Middle States Commission on Higher Education, 2003).

Ways of Knowing: Integrating Folklore Studies with Composition and Information Literacy through a Learning Community

Vickery Lebbin and Kristin M. McAndrews

INTRODUCTION

At the University of Hawaii at Manoa (UH-Manoa), learning communities create opportunities for faculty to combine interests and to offer students a well-rounded curriculum that enhances academic proficiency. The focus on both analytical skills and research methodology make English composition and library science courses well-suited partners for learning communities. English instructors and librarians have similar challenges when teaching the research process. More often than not, students are unfamiliar with the dynamics of a university library, despite the fact that research papers are necessary components of many college English courses. In this context, English composition and library science are exceptional academic partners. Add to this partnership a folklore theme that comprises information literacy skills and students are immersed in a rich learning environment, featuring both traditional and non-traditional approaches to reading, writing, and research.

Linking information literacy to the study of folklore provides an opportunity for students to concentrate on evaluating material critically. On one hand, familiarity with oral narratives, folktales, and urban legends enables students to see themselves as part of a larger cultural story as well as to recognize and validate the particular stories that give meaning to their community and personal lives. Through the study of folklore students often discover archetypal images that echo through literature and popular culture. For example, most students have extensive knowledge of email legends as well as of local legends prevalent in culturally diverse Hawaii. On the other hand, often, students tend uncritically to accept the truth of an urban legend and are quite adamant that some legends are true despite the fact that they have been debunked (Snopes.com). Two examples are the urban legend regarding aspartame that was claimed to have been responsible for a number of diseases from cancer to multiple sclerosis and the one that

129

cell phone users must register with a national database to avoid telemarket-ers. In class, students are quite surprised that the local legend of Morgan's Corner (in Nuuanu Valley on the island of Oahu) has roots in the story "The Boyfriends Death." In the legend, a teenage couple parks in a secluded area to make out. The girl is often nervous. When she hears something outside the car, the boy steps out to investigate. When he doesn't return, the girl begins to worry. Then, she hears a dripping noise (or hair swish-ing) on the roof top of the car. She gets out and sees her boyfriend either beheaded or hanging upside down from a tree near the car. Throughout the United States there are many variations of this cautionary tale about teenage sexuality. Urban legends often impart a moral—in this particular tale the lesson is clear—teens should not have sex.

An examination of a folktale and folklore scholarship in relation to popular cultural trends encourages students to go beyond a hasty, superfi-cial reading, which leans on accepted wisdom, and to gain a critical perspec-tive that enables them to question. This exercise validates a student's way of knowing, while imparting useful tools and functional skills that help him or her become less gullible and more critically literate.

Information literacy incorporates both traditional library material and new technologies. Traditionally, evaluative criteria have focused on print resources and included such elements as currency, coverage, author-ity, accuracy, and objectivity. Each of these elements is still necessary, but today's technological environment also necessitates the use of new evalu-ative criteria.[1] Examining the Internet and electronic communication in terms of function, type, and the social/political structure (including access, language, and use), allows students to challenge their ways of knowing.

FOLKLORE STUDIES

While sometimes characterized as "elusive, flowing along separately from the mainstream," folklore studies offers numerous ways to consider cul-ture, especially "social attitudes and psychological insights."[2] Folklore is one of the oldest forms of human creativity and includes many traditional genres such as riddles, proverbs, myths, and fairy tales as well as children's games, urban legends, and graffiti, to name a few. Alan Dundes writes, "Folklore always tells it like it is or at least tells it as some people think it is or as they would like it to be. Folklore is a kind of popular pulse, ever indicating what is going on in a people's minds and in a people's heart."[3] Folklore, in particular scholarship on the folktale, is an excellent way to introduce English composition students to a variety of disciplines and to encourage critical thinking. The study of folklore and its influence on literature and popular culture is necessarily conservative, insofar as folklore is tied to notions of tradition, a pivotal criterion considered in academic and classroom studies. William Bascom claims that folklore authenticates a culture by explaining "its rituals and institutions."[4] Folklore "is a diversified and complex subject," Brunvand notes, "because it reflects the whole intricate mosaic of the rest of human culture."[5] Yet, the study of folklore and its influence on literature and popular culture is also dynamic. Although early folklore scholarship and research critiqued primitive versus modern cultures, and, as Richard Bauman points out, nineteenth-century notions of folklore imposed a "distorted conception of folklore as folly, superstition, and falsehood, anachronistic leftovers from an earlier stage of human social development since transcended by the scientific rationalism of modern civilization,"[6] since the mid-nineteen sixties, folklore studies have burgeoned as scholars consider folk traditions in terms of popular culture. Literature, anthropology, psychology, sociology, and many other fields of study use folklore to understand "how, why, and which traditional cultural mentifacts, sociofacts, and artifacts developed, varied, and were passed on."[7] Through the study of folklore imagery students often discover ideas that reverberate through the literature they read, which gives them a deeper understanding of the text and consequently the culture they live in.

While sometimes acquainted with Greek or Roman mythology and fables, students often have difficulty in making any connection between themselves and the elements of the tales.[8] But they are frequently surprised and horrified at how folklore informs their lives on a daily basis through television, music, the Internet, and advertising. To know the folklore of our country, ethnicity, community, family, childhood, and age group is to know ourselves and others in new and more significant ways. Through the following assignment, students find "a human involvement and genuineness ... that is not found in public expressions of national life."[9] Students discover the connection between their own lives and personal history to the multidimensional world beyond them. This type of literacy "challenges the status quo in an effort to discover alternative paths for self and social development."[10]

LEARNING COMMUNITIES

As stated above, English composition and library science make excellent partners in teaching students critical information literacy skills. Although at many colleges and universities, librarians and English faculty members or teaching assistants collaborate in teaching students about information resources and research skills, frequently this is limited to one or two class meetings. Extended collaboration, with a focus on a topic such as folklore, however, is greatly enhanced through creation of a learning community.

A useful definition and explanation of learning communities is offered by Faith Gabelnick and others: the purposeful restructuring of "curriculum to link together courses or course work so that students find greater coherence in what they are learning as well as increased intellectual interaction with faculty and fellow students."[11] There are generally five major models of learning communities: linked courses, learning clusters, freshmen interest groups, federated learning communities, and coordinated studies.[12]

Each model varies in terms of the number of courses that comprise the community and the coordination between the instructors. Additionally, each design typically has one element that makes it unique. The most basic learning community model and the one described in this chapter is that of the "linked course." This learning community model consists of two courses with the same students enrolled in each course. Instructor coordination in this model can vary from simply knowing the name of the other instructor to designing assignments and course lectures together. The unique element of the linked course model is that one of the courses is often a skills course. This enables students to apply the theories and content learned from one course into practical application in the skills course.

Writing and research are both proficiencies utilized when applying theory and content from numerous subjects. In this respect, English composition or library science would be appropriate as the skills course in the linked course model. Instead of following the generic model of linking skills with content, the authors decided to link two skills courses and selected folklore as the content. The rationale for this decision was to provide students with the knowledge and practice of the entire research process. The learning community was aptly named *Writing and Research: the Whole Process*.[13] This connection between research and writing is recognized in other librarian and English instructor teams. James Ford, in describing course-related instruction explains, "English teachers are most likely to occupy one end of what is rightly viewed as one continuous research process, the other being occupied by librarians." Ford goes on to say, "that neither the English teacher nor the librarian is knowledgeable enough about the whole process."[14] Dennis Isbell describes this relationship by stating that research and writing, "exist on a continuum, and that perceived distinctions between the two are artificial."[15]

After reaching the decision to link a library science course and English composition course, the authors needed to decide what types of connections to make between the two courses, which is one of the benefits of creating a learning community. There are usually three levels of connections: student, instructor, and discipline. Student connections are generally the easiest to create. Simply by having two courses together students have the opportunity for greater interaction. Student connections are considered especially valuable on commuter campuses where students may not feel part of the university community. The second level of connection is between instructors. Learning communities can exist where instructors do not create connections. This however, seems to miss the point of establishing a learning community. There are a variety of ways instructors can connect. In the learning community described here, the instructors attended each others' courses, met regularly to discuss the courses, shared textbooks, assignments, and handouts, and received copies of student assignments for both courses. The discipline or subject area is the third connection. In this learning community, the discipline connection was created through the use of a combined schedule and the culminating assignment of a Research Portfolio and a Writing Portfolio.

INFORMATION LITERACY AND ENGLISH COMPOSITION

The learning community *Writing and Research: the Whole Process* combines the skill sets of information literacy and English composition. Information literacy is a set of skills needed to find, retrieve, analyze, and use information. English composition is the acquisition of communication skills through reading and writing practice. Students discover voice and audience, learn to analyze, and utilize information and literature in a comprehensive way.

In the learning community *Writing and Research: the Whole Process*, information literacy skills are emphasized through the course LIS 100. At UH-Manoa, librarians teach information literacy through a variety of methods including online tutorials, one-time lectures, and semester-long courses. In 1998, librarians designed a three-credit, semester-long information literacy course to form learning communities with other university courses.[16] The first course offered was for honors students through a linkage with an honors English composition course. The honors program promotes the learning community course as advantageous for future college work. The course titled *Libraries, Scholarship and Technology* (LIS 100) is designed as an undergraduate, writing intensive course to provide students with the knowledge and skills required to perform library research in an academic environment. As a writing-intensive course, class size is limited to twenty students. LIS 100 introduces students to the major elements of scholarship and to the nature of investigation, discussion, and creation of knowledge in a university setting, emphasizing the role of libraries. In addition, students learn to perform research using a variety of library resources, including electronic databases and the Internet, and to evaluate critically information resources.

The second linked course in *Writing and Research: the Whole Process* is ENG 100, a semester-long, three-credit course. This is where English composition skills are emphasized; English composition courses teach students to write clear, evocative, and focused prose in an assortment of forms and genres. A required course at UH-Manoa, students usually take *English Composition* (ENG 100) as freshmen. Typically, composition instructors assign six to ten essays focusing on a variety of forms such as narrative, description, summary, comparison/contrast, cause and effect, and argument. Although a research/argument paper is recommended but not mandatory, instructors usually require one.

Folklore and the role of storytelling, especially as it relates to issues of cultural politics, is an academic interest of one of the authors. Throughout the semester, this English instructor emphasizes writing exercises that incorporate these topics into assignments. In addition to teaching students how to master the basics of essay writing and grasp the importance of reading well in order to write well, this instructor aims for students to comprehend their roles as writers and readers within culture, and to appreciate the influence of cultural norms, particularly those imparted by the folktale, on their notions of reading and writing.

THE ASSIGNMENT

The culminating assignments for each of the courses are portfolios that connect the two components of the learning community. For LIS 100 it is a Research Portfolio. For ENG 100 the assignment is a Writing Portfolio. Drafts of all sections of each portfolio are submitted to allow for feedback from the librarian, English instructor, and student peers.

The Research Portfolio enables students to synthesize and employ the library research knowledge acquired throughout LIS 100. The Research

Portfolio is a three-part assignment that helps students to actively think about the research they conduct for their Writing Portfolio. Students are asked, 1) to create a research plan (three pages), 2) record a research log (five pages), and 3) present a research analysis (three pages).

Like the Research Portfolio, the Writing Portfolio is a three-part assignment. In order to become more fluent writers, students need plenty of material. The topics must honestly engage them, while at the same time drawing on their personal experiences. When a research component is added through LIS 100, the following writing assignment becomes even more productive. The combination helps students achieve full personal involvement with their selected topic, and a growing intellectual understanding of the discipline. With the Writing and Research Portfolios, students refine their writing skills through several complementary tasks. For the Writing Portfolio, students have three writing tasks that focus on four variations of a specific folktale, and two essays that reflect on pertinent folkloric issues revealed in the stories. These works are discussed and analyzed in class. Students are asked, 1) to create their own revision of a folktale (250 words maximum) based on the narrative elements of the story we have studied, 2) to write a short summary and a personal opinion based on one of two essays they read for class regarding this tale (in total, no more than 250 words), and 3) to compose a researched and persuasive essay based on a topic of interest generated from the folktales, the creative writing, the criticism, and the class discussions (a minimum of five to seven pages, with an additional Works Cited page).

Research Plan and Revision of Folktale

In both courses, it is important that students discover the power of their opinions and develop academic or research interests. The Research Plan and the Revision of a Folktale involve a number of intellectual processes which diverge yet reinforce the final portfolios.

The first part of the Research Portfolio assignment includes an analysis of a *research question* related to folklore and a *description of the proposed research* approach. The *research question* analysis requires students to create a sentence that names their topic, identifies the research question, and states the reason for the question (why this research is important).

The *description of the proposed research* (Research Plan) requires students to think about their research. Many times students will simply begin research without any forethought. This haphazard approach can be time consuming, frustrating, and lead the student in the wrong direction. To avoid these problems, in the description of the research approach, students must identify the disciplines from which they plan to approach the topic, name the types of resources they think will cover their topic, indicate the steps they plan to take in their research, and specify sources they plan to consult. The approach is designed to be an outline for their upcoming research.

Both the librarian and English instructor review the Research Plan before the student proceeds to next section of the Research Portfolio. The librarian generally focuses on the research sources while the English instructor focuses on the folklore topic. A common dilemma encountered by students is that they are too specific about sources they hope to locate through their research. They expect to find many articles on their specific tale analyzed from the same approach they have selected. For example, a student working on the role of the stepmother in "Hansel and Gretel" will search for an article that addresses both these concepts. Students must be encouraged to look for information on a single concept and make the connection in their analysis. In this example, a student could search for psychology articles on the roles of stepmothers and in her paper discuss how these relate to "Hansel and Gretel." This approach results in more productive research and enables students to write their own analysis rather than simply to restate several other authorities.

In the English course, the instructor teaches writing as an expressive, cognitive, and social process, as well as teaching the structure of writing. The student's personal vision is as important as traditional conventions or codes of composition, especially in the drafting stage. Emphasis on pre-writing and free-writing empowers the student writer as it stimulates originality or invention. Goldberg gives some excellent ideas on how to generate text she calls "First Thoughts." "First thoughts have tremendous energy," she says, "It is a way the mind first flashes on something. The internal censor usually squelches them, so we live in the realm of second and third thoughts, thoughts on thoughts, twice and three times removed from the direct connection with the first fresh flash."[17] Also, students discover a control over the subject matter after having written about a topic from their own point of view. While some critics argue this theory tends to create an inclusive rather than exclusive intellectual environment, pre-writing and re-envisioning a folktale allow students to reconsider the subject matter at hand and develop honest and meaningful ideas. Students spend so much time on the Writing Portfolio partly because they must have a comprehensive knowledge of the material. Through pre-writing, drafting, and making oral presentations, students observe the subject matter in relationship to individuality, variability, and how it relates to a larger cultural system. By revising a tale from another point of view, students gain understanding of the social dynamics that drive the story and the influence of social norms on popular culture. For example, when considering the story "Hansel and Gretel" students have taken the point of view of the witch or the duck. Or in "Cinderella," a student wrote from the perspective of one of the wicked stepsisters. In "Little Red Riding Hood" several students assumed the voice of the wolf, or have told the story of the mother. At UH-Manoa, there is a diverse multi-ethnic student body. In the revision of the folktale, students are encouraged to bring their ethnic heritage to the writing. The study of folklore is a positive and supportive way of conveying ethnicity into the curriculum; it honors ethnic heritage and allows students to connect the personal with the seemingly impersonal world beyond them. In addition, this exercise allows students to discover their creativity and to utilize descriptive language. As appropriate to the tales folkloric imagery, the students choose the language, style and organization of the story.

Students are encouraged to write twice as much is required for the final assignment. They need plenty of material to find a creative dynamic and to edit. Peter Elbow argues "writing requires two mental abilities that are so different that they usually conflict with each other: the ability to create an abundance of words and ideas: and the ability to criticize and discard words and ideas. To write well we need to be both generative and cutthroat."[18] Students who freely discuss a subject matter will have a tendency to respond more honestly to issues and arguments that develop and become better writers and critical thinkers.

Composition and folklore studies are a powerful combination. They help students achieve full personal involvement and intellectual understanding of the discipline, and at the same time improve writing skills and elevate confidence.

Research Log, Summary and Personal Opinion

In the Research Portfolio assignment, student writing and focus are further developed by the Research Log in the form of annotations. Students must cite eight of the sources they locate and analyze through their research. Generally students will find more than eight sources but only eight, and not necessarily the first eight, are annotated. Additionally, the student is not required to use all of the eight sources in their English portfolio. Each annotation is approximately 200 words in length and explains the search strategy and sources used to find the cited material. Next the annotation must include an evaluation of the source content. The author's argument, evidence, conclusion, and credentials must be addressed in this evaluation. Finally, the annotation must describe how the source contributed to their research. Was the content relevant? Did it lead to other research? Having students annotate their research requires them to be more actively engaged in the process and to think about it more systematically.

The point of the next part of the Writing Portfolio is to remind students of the power of summary writing with a focus on the argumentation of the essay. Students have already read and summarized an essay by Emily Martin entitled "The Egg and the Sperm: How Science Has Constructed a Romance based on Stereotypical Male-Female Roles."[19] Students find this essay challenging because they are unfamiliar with the issues and, there are a number of lengthy footnotes. Students also question popular notions of scientific objectivity and how "facts" are utilized.[20] Students learn to summarize the argument of an essay, rather than merely summarizing the text.

After students have discovered a personal "relationship" with the folktale, they read two pieces of academic criticism that examine the specific folktale being studied. Obviously, since the study of folklore is such a diverse academic field, folklore criticism is varied and complex. Noted scholars Jack Zipes and Bruno Bettelheim hold diverse views on the function of folktales. Neither expert's language is overburdened with jargon and thus is accessible to introductory composition students.[21] While they are responsible for their own work, students discuss and decipher the authors' arguments in peer groups of four to five students presenting the issues to the class. After presentations, and feedback from peers and the instructor, students are asked to identify the key points of the essays and write short summaries on either Zipes' or Bettelheim's arguments. They are reminded not to impose their opinion into the summary.

Separately, they also write a short personal response to one issue evoked from the essays by Zipes or Bettelheim. For this personal response, students are required to write about something that provoked or bothered them, and provide evidence in the form of a sentence or two from the article to explain why.

Research Analysis and Persuasive Essay

In LIS 100, the last part of the Research Portfolio is a reflective piece analyzing the entire research process. Students evaluate their research plan, the research usefulness of the sources consulted, and the effectiveness of the research techniques they used. In this process, students move towards their persuasive essay for English.

In traditional ENG 100 courses, writing instructors typically ask for a formulaic research paper usually on some popular topic. In the Writing Portfolio students are asked to consider and discuss the cultural parameters of an issue or theme evoked from the folktale they have studied in order to illuminate those influences on popular culture. The goal of the essay is to discuss a question, persuade an audience of a point of view, and to propose a solution to the problem.

By the time the students in this learning community get to this part of the assignment, they are fairly clear about their interests. The essay should have a clear thesis and several body paragraphs that offer enough sensible reasons and persuasive evidence to convince an audience to agree with the argument. Students are required to demonstrate the use of summary, paraphrase, and quotation as well as personal opinion. They utilize a structural device called 'paragraph as unit of argument'.[22]

The student's voice is critical in this essay. Traditionally, argument papers were taught in terms of eliminating the author's voice in order to make the argument seem more rational and logical. For this assignment, students are required to use their own voice: "I" is not only acceptable, but mandatory. How else can students assume the responsibility of their opinions? In addition, students must have at least five "Works Cited" in their text, two from journals, one from a book, and two from the open Internet. Of course, they are welcome to use more sources. Internet use is encouraged but the point of this exercise is for students to understand the many ways in which knowledge can be accessed.

For structure, students are introduced to a traditional schematic for organizing argumentative papers as well as variations on that model. Students test the essay's structure in class by giving an oral presentation and receiving verbal and written feedback from peers. Based on peer evaluations, students revise their drafts. Before they submit the final essay, students meet with the English instructor to discuss the effectiveness of their argument.

CONCLUSION

The learning community environment offers rewards for the university, instructors and students. For UH-Manoa, the learning community links logically connected but separate academic courses, resulting in a well-rounded curriculum and diverse course offerings. For instructors, the learning community enhances the teaching experience, imparts knowledge of another academic field, provides a support system for critiquing student work, and nurtures a rich environment for collaboration and creativity.[23]

For students, the learning community offers insight into how they can access raw, unfiltered and even contradictory information and present it in such a way that gives them confidence in their own experience as well as enhancing their research, writing, and critical thinking.[24] The use of a folklore theme in the learning community environment provides the added benefit of connecting the lives of students with contemporary issues, resulting in greater self-knowledge and stronger understanding of diverse people.

NOTES

1.   Jan Alexander and Marsha Tate of Wolfram Memorial Library, Widener University, offer web evaluation materials at http://www3.widener.edu/Academics/Libraries/Wolfgram_Memorial_Library/Evaluate_Web_Pages/Original_Web_Evaluation_Materials/6160/ (access as of 14 November 2006)

2.   Jan Harold Brunvand, "The Study of Folklore," in *The Study of American Folklore: An Introduction* (New York: W. W. Norton, 1978), 10.

3.   Alan Dundes, "What is Folklore," in *The Study of Folklore*, ed. Alan Dundes (Englewood Cliffs, New Jersey: University of California at Berkeley, 1965), 2.

4.   Ibid., 291.

5.   Brunvand, 11.

6.   Richard Bauman, "Folklore." in *Folklore, Cultural Performances, and Popular Entertainments: A Communications-Centered Handbook*, ed. Richard Bauman, 31 (New York: Oxford University Press, 1992).

7.   Brunvand, 12. Mentifacts, artifacts and sociofacts focus on ways in which to analyze culture in terms of ideas, material objects and interpersonal relationships. See Http://fog.ccsf.cc.ca.us/~aforsber/ccsf/culture_defined.html.

8.   In Hawaii, public and private school students are also familiar with Hawaiian myths and legends but they are not usually taught Hawaiian folklore with much reflection. In addition, Hawaii has diverse ethnic groups whose folktales or legends do not usually emerge in the classroom.

9.   Simon J. Bronner, *Following Tradition: Folklore in the Discourse of American Culture* (Logan, Utah: Utah State University Press, 1998), 123.

10.   Ira Shor, "What is Critical Literacy?" *Journal for Pedagogy, Pluralism and Practice* (College of Staten Island, CUNY), paragraph 2. http://www.lesley.edu/journals/jppp/4/shor.html

11.   Faith Gabelnick and others, *Learning Communities: Creating Connections among Students, Faculty and Disciplines*, New Directions for Teaching and Learning, no. 41 (San Francisco: Jossey-Bass, 1990), 5.

12. To read more about the various learning community models, see Faith Gabelnick and others, *Learning Communities*; Oscar T. Lenning and Larry H. Ebbers, *The Powerful Potential of Learning Communities: Improving Education for the Future*, ASHE-ERIC Higher Education Report, vol. 26, no.6 (Washington, D.C.: The George Washington University, Graduate School of Education and Human Development, 1999); and Nancy S. Shapiro and Jodi H. Levine, *Creating Learning Communities: A Practical Guide to Winning Support, Organizing for Change, and Implementing Programs* (San Francisco: Jossey-Bass, 1999). The following works also are valuable. Aaron M. Brower and Karen M. Dettinger, "What IS a Learning Community? Toward a Comprehensive Model," *About Campus* 3, no. 5 (1998): 15-21; K. Patricia Cross, "Why Learning Communities? Why Now?" *About Campus* 3, no.3 (1998): 4-11; Elizabeth K. DeMulder and Kimberly K. Eby, "Bridging Troubled Waters: Learning Communities for the 21st Century," *American Behavioral Scientist* 42 (1999): 892-901; Jean-Paul Orgeron, "Learning Communities: A Selective Overview of Academic Library Involvement," *Journal of Southern Academic and Special Librarianship* 1, no.2 (1999). http://southernlibrarianship.icaap.org/content/v01n02/orgeron_j01.html; and Vincent Tinto, "Enhancing Learning Via Community," *Thought & Action, The NEA Higher Education Journal* 8 (1993): 53-58.

13. Both instructors taught in the learning community for six semesters to approximately seventy-five students. The courses began development in fall 1998. In the early stages, instructors meet weekly to plan the curriculum. As the course progressed instructors continued meeting regularly every two weeks.

14. James Ford, "The Natural Alliance between Librarians and English Teachers in Course-Related Library Use Instruction," *College & Research Libraries* 43 (1982): 380.

15. Dennis Isbell, "Teaching Writing and Research as Inseparable: A Faculty-Librarian Teaching Team," *Reference Services Review* 23 (1995): 52.

16. This course received the 2001 Innovation in Instruction award from the Instruction Section of ACRL. This annual award recognized librarians who have developed and implemented best practices in education at their institutions or in their communities.

17. Natalie Goldberg, *Writing Down the Bones: Freeing the Writer Within* (Boston, Massachusetts: Shambhala Publications, 1986), 9.

18. Peter Elbow and Pat Belanoff, *A Community of Writers: A Workshop Course in Writing*, 2d ed. (New York: McGraw-Hill, 1995), 6.

19. Emily Martin, "The Egg and the Sperm: How Science Has Constructed a Romance Based on Stereotypical Male-Female Roles," in *Fields of Reading: Motives for Writing*, 5th ed., ed. Nancy R. Comley, et al. (New York: St. Martin's Press, 1998), 701-716.

20. This particular essay is an excellent way to demonstrate how stereotypic images specific to culture and the folktale are pervasive.

21. See Jack Zipes, *Breaking the Magic Spell: Radical Theories of Folk and Fairytales* (New York: Methuen, 1984) and Bruno Bettelheim, *The Uses of Enchantment: The Meaning and Importance of Fairy Tales* (New York: Knopf, 1976).

22. 1. What is the thesis? Or what does the paragraph cover? 2. Where is the Proof? A quote, summary or paraphrase, please. 3. What is the analysis and opinion on the information? Or So What?

23. In terms of collaboration, the instructors have also presented a sixteen-hour workshop for Hawaii Department of Education credit to elementary and high school teachers on using folklore, critically literacy, and information literacy. Also instructors presented a panel entitled, "Pond Stew, Chocolate and Cat Manapua: Teaching Folklore and Critical Literacy in a Learning Community" at the 2001 American Folklore Society Meeting in Anchorage, Alaska.

24.   Qualitative research in the form of focus groups has been completed on students who enrolled in LIS 100 from fall 1999 through fall 2002. The research findings include benefits students found in linking LIS 100 and ENG 100. Lebbin authored an article reporting on this research: "Students Perceptions on the Long-Range Value of Information Literacy Instruction through a Learning Community." *Research Strategies* 20, no.3 (2005): 204-218.

The Changing Nature of the Book: Literary Research, Cultural Studies, and the Digital Age

Austin Booth and Laura Taddeo

INTRODUCTION

The emergence of cultural studies as a theoretical and political framework for literary studies and the wealth of digital technologies available to humanities scholars have changed how we conduct and teach literary research in the twenty-first century. Alternative research methods that can stimulate students within this framework include examining the production, distribution and consumption of literary texts in their sociohistorical contexts; studying canon formation and genre definition; and examining a wider array of material, including popular texts and non-written material such as film and hypertext productions. This chapter describes approaches to teaching literary research that explore the significance of cultural studies as well as the relationships among cultural studies, digital texts and information literacy standards. Descriptions of classes and assignments are included as representative examples.

CULTURAL STUDIES

In *Culture and Society: 1780-1950*, Raymond Williams argues that studying culture requires studying not just part but the whole of cultural production.[1] Literary studies has traditionally been largely focused on the literary canon, while cultural studies has generally paid attention to what remains: newspapers, magazines, radio, film, television, advertising, popular music, movies, art, architecture, urban folklore, fashion, photography, music, youth subcultures, theater, working-class literature, and popular literary genres (thrillers, romances, Westerns, science fiction). Cultural studies focuses on the products and discourses of mass and popular culture rather than (solely) on canonical works of art. By examining how culture is defined, used, and transformed by a wide range of social groups, cultural studies conceives of readers not simply as consumers, but also as potential producers of new cultural meanings and values.

Cultural studies has had a tremendous influence on the English curriculum. The attention in cultural studies to the production and consumption of literary texts poses challenges for the ways in which humanities scholars do literary research, not the least of which is the inclusion of a whole other set of materials beyond critical or biographical histories. Scholars must examine non-fictional texts; mechanisms of production, distribution and consumption; historical and cultural contexts; and the physical layout of texts.

The whole array of practices and texts that constitute a culture potentially provide the subject of cultural studies. The original focus of cultural studies was popular or mass culture, but in the 1970s and 1980s, cultural studies shifted towards challenging the opposition between high and popular culture; in the last two decades it has taken both high and mass culture together as its purview.[2] Examining belletristic literature from this "new" perspective of cultural studies, scholars have focused on literature as a cultural event or document with social, historical, and political roots and ramifications. As such, some critics have seen cultural studies as a methodological break from traditional literary criticism, from treating literature as an autonomous entity whose aesthetic rank raises it above conditions of production, distribution and consumption. For example, Robert Scholes argues that "we must stop 'teaching literature' and start 'studying texts.' Our rebuilt apparatus must be devoted to textual studies.... Our favorite works of literature need not be lost in this new enterprise, but the exclusivity of literature as a category must be discarded."[3] Non-canonical texts are routinely included in literature courses, which now frequently pay attention to the canon debate and the process of canonization along with other cultural processes such as genre definitions, production of taste, reading practices, and the historical production and consumption of books as literary products. It is this last aspect of the influence of cultural studies—an attention to the production and consumption of literary and non-literary texts—that has influenced the way that faculty and librarians teach literary research at the State University of New York at Buffalo.

In many undergraduate and graduate English programs the introduction to theory class has replaced the introduction to research class.[4] Both faculty and librarians find that these introductory theory classes make an excellent starting place for integrating cultural studies methods into the curriculum. In fact, many introductory theory classes address the question of what literary research consists of quite directly, since classroom debates about theory turn out frequently to be debates about what constitutes literary scholarship. This is not so say that "literature" itself as a category has not always been under scrutiny. As William Cain points out in his introduction to *Teaching Contemporary Theory to Undergraduates*, "[I]t is inaccurate to claim that current theory has led to unprecedented, radical changes in the canon. Nearly all the major figures in the history of criticism—Johnson, Coleridge, Arnold, Eliot, Lawrence, Pound, Leavis—reorganized the canon, and they did so with an uncompromising boldness that alarmed their contemporaries."[5] Indeed, examining literary critics' challenges to various canons can be an effective way of engaging students in the processes of literary research. Many of the faculty with whom librarians collaborate purposefully design their syllabi in order to juxtapose canonical and marginal, literary and non-literary texts in order to highlight the ways in which the canon (and its margins) are constructed.

RETHINKING LITERARY HISTORY

Introductory theory and literary criticism classes ask why we read what we do in the ways that we do. Simply because of their introductory nature, these classes emphasize debates within canon and curriculum formation. A simple way to engage students in these debates is to have them examine the anthologies, course packs and introductory texts used in their own classes. Both faculty and librarians at the University at Buffalo explain to students that the texts selected for literary anthologies, like all textbooks, reflect historically and culturally-located beliefs.

Many of the introductory theory, criticism, and genre or period courses taught use anthologies and readers.[6] Even in courses that do not rely on anthologies and readers, librarians often use casebooks in library research sessions. It is best to use an example of a particular literary text in a theory class, showing students how different approaches they have studied can be applied to a specific text. Students can be introduced to casebooks that include contemporary criticism or reviews, biographical and historical readings, as well as a sampling of diverse critical approaches. The Bedford series *Case Studies in Contemporary Criticism*, for example, provides texts of frequently-taught literary works along with representative readings from a range of schools of critical theory.[7] These casebooks not only provide useful historical background, but also emphasize the central tenet of most introductory literary theory classes: that there is no single correct or true reading of a literary text, but rather that a literary text may elicit multiple, equally-valid readings.

Casebooks also lend themselves to a variety of useful assignments. As part of the library component of a course, students may, for example, create their own casebooks based on texts read in the class. Students may create an annotated bibliography of relevant historical documents or critical readings of the text that demonstrate a range of critical, theoretical and methodical approaches. These assignments teach students to locate documents and criticism as well as to create a bibliography. Casebook creation can be easily expanded to a group project: the class can compile a casebook in which each student locates an historical document or example of a critical approach. In more advanced classes, students locate a critical essay on one of the texts read for class and then attempt to refute the critic's argument (or find arguments that refute it) or write the critical essays that make up the class casebook themselves.

WORKING WITH THE CURRICULUM

Outlined below are ways in which librarians at the University at Buffalo specifically integrate cultural studies approaches into undergraduate and graduate English classes that focus on eighteenth-, nineteenth-, and twentieth-century English and American Literature. Many literary history and literary theory courses now focus on the production and consumption of literary texts. Courses on the eighteenth- and early nineteenth-century novel, for example, examine the emergence of distinctively modern forms of subjectivity by looking at what types of oppositions emerge with the advent of capitalism and the rise of the middle class. Many courses explore how class, gender and ethnic distinctions are used to divide the public and the private, production and consumption, and the socioeconomic and the aesthetic into separate realms. In addition to reading texts and understanding the historical milieus in which they are embedded, students are frequently presented with the central issues that have come up in literary historians' explorations of the genre or subgenres in question. Eighteenth-century novel courses, for example, typically examine the rise of the novel in relation to capitalism, the novel's role in producing the bourgeois public sphere, and the change from a society organized around status to one organized around socioeconomic class. Many twentieth-century literature courses also focus on consumption, specifically on the rise of mass consumer culture. These courses typically include both "high" and "low" artifacts and examine the production and contestation of the boundaries between high, middle and lowbrow culture.

Course: 18th-Century Novel (Graduate)

Librarians work with faculty who teach a variety of graduate courses on the eighteenth-century novel, including courses focused on the rise of the novel, gender and eighteenth-century fiction, sentimental fiction and epistolary fiction. We are invited to visit these classes several times during the semester and we also work with students independently throughout the semester. In-class workshops focus on the consumption, distribution and production of books as commodities in the eighteenth century. Library assignments are given at regular intervals, and frequently form the basis of students' longer seminar-paper work. In addition to readings assigned in classes, students are asked to read selections on consumption and eighteenth-century England, such as Ann Bermingham and John Brewer, eds., *The Consumption of Culture, 1600-1800: Image, Object, Text*.[8]

After introducing the conditions of production, distribution and consumption of books in the eighteenth century, librarians give assignments requiring the use of research tools and eighteenth-century sources. Students are asked to examine the reference and bibliographical tools from the periods they are studying in order to explore the relationship between ideology and the way that information is organized, in order to learn how knowledge was structured in the periods they are studying. Students explore topics that have emerged in their reading of eighteenth-century literature in a range of eighteenth-century reference tools such as *Chambers' Cyclopedia* and the *Encyclopaedia Britannica*. They compare the organization and style of these encyclopedias and detail ways in which that organization and style compare to the eighteenth-century literature they have read.

Librarians also use the case-study method to teach advanced research skills. In an eighteenth-century novel class, for example, we show students the actual volumes of Sterne's *Tristram Shandy* as they appeared to the contemporary audience—it is important for students to see how the serials worked, that the volumes were slight and pocket-sized (in contrast to the dense 500-page edition that they are reading for class). Students are usually struck by the page itself: the low word count per page, the amount of white space, and Sterne's favorite punctuation mark, the dash. We use facsimile editions of eighteenth-century novels that are now available in Garland's reprint collection, *Foundations of the Novel: Representative Early Eighteenth-Century Fiction*. Of particular interest is Sterne's signature on the first page of volumes 5, 7, and 9, protection against the imitations that his work inspired. Students then enjoy seeing the many imitations of *Tristram Shandy* (examples of which have been reprinted in Garland's series *Sterneiana*).

Students also analyze reviews,[9] looking at the history of the critical reception of their novels as well as implicit arguments being made about the genre, the status of literature and literary criticism, and the role of the reader throughout different time periods.[10] We often use reviews of Sterne's eighteenth century *Tristram Shandy* as an example because the critical reception of Sterne's novel demonstrates relatively easily the ways in which critical responses are frequently dictated by moral or political reactions to the author. The critical history of reactions to Sterne often provokes classroom discussions of the relationships among literary "merit," reputation and social norms as well.

We encourage students to use non-fictional primary sources in order to better understand the cultural context within fiction is created. Students use the *Short-title Catalogue* to identify books useful for their research. In the case of *Tristram Shandy*, for instance, we teach students how to find eighteenth-century books on military strategy or obstetrics. Students select one or two non-fictional texts relevant to their own research and detail the style, organization and relationship to audience as well as general social attitudes towards a topic they have discussed in class. Using the literature database *Literature Online (LION)* or the searchable texts available via *Eighteenth Century Collections Online (ECCO)*, they select several words or phrases that they have noted and see how those same terms are defined and used in eighteenth-century literature, as well as in eighteenth-century reference tools such as in Johnson's *Dictionary of the English Language* (1755) and Hester Lynch Piozzi's *British Synonymy* (1794). (*Tristram Shandy* is again a useful model for this assignment, because of the novel's bawdy terminology—a discussion of bawdiness can also lead to more general discussions of the malleability of language itself and the relationship between definitions and ideology.)

Using secondary sources, students discover which essays have been the most influential on a particular author or text. Essential resources include handbooks, casebooks, critical editions, collections of criticism, Routledge's *Critical Heritage Series*, and the *Dictionary of Literary Biography*. Using bibliographies and the *Arts and Humanities Citation Index*, students trace the critical reception of an idea they have studied in class, such as the debates around the rise of the novel. They begin with Ian Watt's *The Rise of the Novel: Studies in Defoe, Richardson and Fielding* and Watt's identification of individualism with the middle classes, for instance, and then move to those critics who have attacked Watt's views on the socioeconomic foundations of the novel, defenses of Watt, and alternative approaches to the rise of the novel.[11]

Course: 19th-Century Novel (Graduate)

Librarians at the University at Buffalo take a similar approach to teaching literary research to graduate students studying the nineteenth century. Students receive an overview of book production and marketing in the nineteenth century, including assigned readings on the book trade and reading audiences.[12] As part of the library component, students must locate (if possible) original editions of the novels they are reading in class, especially if they first appeared in serial form. Students discover the transformation that the novel underwent as a result of new mechanisms for producing and distributing literature. The serialization of novels as well as the three-decker format had a large influence on the fiction of the nineteenth century.[13] Dickens' *David Copperfield* is an excellent case study for examining the serialization of nineteenth-century fiction. Students learn how the original publication pattern emphasizes the unfolding of the narrative from installment to installment, and how the use of recurring phrases, images and themes builds over the length of the novel's original nineteen-month serialization. We ask that students read the book in serial form so that they can experience the way that nineteenth-century readers' understanding of the novel changed as the book progressed. Through experiencing the length of (including gaps in) the reading process, students start to see how the serial structure of *David Copperfield* mirrors or highlights David's development, and even the reader's own development in understanding the story. Drawing attention to the conclusions of the monthly numbers, in which David's progress towards adulthood is measured, helps students not only see that David's growth is slow and painful, but also that the serial structure itself helps to create meaning.

Locating novels in their original serial form also introduces students to Victorian periodicals. During class-time, we demonstrate how students can use bibliographies and *Poole's Index* to trace contemporary reviews of the novels they are studying. Students then describe the subject focus and organization of the Victorian periodicals in which the reviews were published. They analyze the cultural assumptions behind the magazines' layouts, such as the relationship between text and image, or between fiction and other literary and non-literary writing. We also ask students to interpret Victorian periodicals' construction of their audiences as well as the relationship between editor and reader.

An interesting way to present the periodical literature of the nineteenth century is to show students how to find periodical literature by the authors they are reading. Students learn how to find Dickens's work in *Household Words*, for example, and then how such essays can be used to gain insight into his views on topics mentioned in his novels, such as the post office, the Great Exhibition, forgeries, slums, insane asylums, arctic exploration, the London Foundling Hospital etc. If students are reading social- problem novels, we introduce them to nineteenth-century newspaper literature. Using *Palmer's Index to the Times Newspaper* students can locate material on topics in their novels, from the "servant" problem to immigration, from prostitution to labor strikes. Another useful way to introduce students to nineteenth-century politics or social views is to have students compare the representation of the same event or topic in establishment and radical papers. More advanced students may also be introduced to the illustrated journalism of the period in order to explore questions of images and the creation of meaning.

Librarians work with faculty to develop assignments that ask students to locate relevant non-fictional nineteenth-century material. Professional handbooks, Parliamentary papers, tour books, medical texts, textbooks, childrearing manuals, etiquette books, and servant manuals are part of class reading assignments. Many of these materials may now be found in online text collections as well as the large microfilm collections that many libraries own—*The Nineteenth Century* collection, for example, or the *History of Women* microfilm collection. Just browsing the subject indexes of these collections (online, print or microfilm) frequently inspires students to choose original, diverse research topics. Once students have picked a topic, they can locate two or three non-fictional texts using the library resources and compare the treatment of the topic in question in the non-fictional works they have chosen with a novel's treatment of the identical topic.

In addition to teaching students how to locate contemporary reviews of their novels and current criticism, librarians teach students how to find overviews of the most influential schools of thought on their novel; if they are reading *David Copperfield*, for example, we show students George H. Ford, *Dickens and His Readers: Aspects of Novel-Criticism since 1836* and Philip Collins, *Dickens: The Critical Heritage*.[14] Students can then create annotated bibliographies of criticism, with a special emphasis on exploring how alternative approaches to literature represent alternative beliefs about the role of the text, the author and the reader.

Course: 20th-Century Novel (Undergraduate) Best Sellers

While we continue to design engaging case studies and assignments for our graduate students, we cannot ignore demands of undergraduate English majors who are expected to become proficient researchers and writers by the end of their college careers. Librarians and professors often work together to construct productive upper-level English assignments that utilize a rich array of writing and research tools.

A perfect venue for examining twentieth-century texts in terms of their cultural contexts is a class that examines the production and consumption of the American bestseller. In his advanced undergraduate English class entitled *Best Sellers*, David Willbern aligns popular novels with major movements or political happenings in history. A survey of literature and popular culture after World War II to the early 1990s, this class introduces students not only to influential authors and literary genres, but also to social, political, and economic movements. The students examine the novels' artistic, cultural, ideological, and social significance and their relationships to commercial, pop, and high art standards. Willbern has created his own web site tailored to this course, providing a separate section for each novel, which includes interactive links, slide shows, book jacket covers, interviews, film adaptations reviews, and audio clips.[15]

Students read a variety of novels throughout the course. An attempt has been made to include female as well as male authors and to cover a range of issues, such as class division, gender roles, racial discrimination, and the aftermath of war. The majority of the novels chosen are non-canonical, forcing students to explore the cultural and historical significance of the novels' place in the literary world. The novels studied include: J.D. Salinger, *The Catcher in the Rye*; Grace Metalious, *Peyton Place*; Harper Lee, *To Kill a Mockingbird*; Judith Rossner, *Looking for Mr. Goodbar*; Peter Benchley, *Jaws*; Tim O'Brien, *The Things They Carried*; Toni Morrison, *Beloved*; Stephen King, *Misery*; John Grisham, *The Street Lawyer*.

For this specific course, the professor asked the literature librarian to create a research guide which could be posted as part of the online class materials. The online tool, *20th-Century American Best Sellers Research Guide*, designed to help students with their research topics and comprehension of the novels, outlines what databases and print resources to use to locate information such as biographies, book reviews, and literary criticism. It also includes tips on writing and composition, using MLA citation-style guidelines, and determining if web sites contain authoritative and reliable data on a specific authors or novels.[16]

Since this pathfinder is online, it is very easy to demonstrate the resources to the students in a large group. During regular class time, the librarian walks the students through databases tailored for undergraduates, including *Literature Resource Center* and *InfoTrac* (*MLA International Bibliography* [*MLAIB*] and *Annual Bibliography of English Language and Literature* [*ABELL*] are usually shown last, depending on time constraints).[17] Before the workshop, the professor assigns students writing topics or at least requires them to come to class with topic ideas. In class, the librarian reviews how to narrow topics, using the subject heading fields in the library catalog and online databases, and how to construct Boolean searches. During the second half of the class, students work in groups looking for answers to questions that have been prepared ahead of time in a worksheet format. Questions revolve around the publication history of the novels, the composition of the book, both as written and as read, and the representation of gender roles, family relations, and cultural stereotypes such as racism and sexism.[18]

We also emphasize the importance of reading a variety of secondary resources such as Janice Radway's book *A Feeling for Books: the Book-of-the-Month Club, Literary Taste, and Middle-Class Desire* and Andrew Ross's *No Respect: Intellectuals and Popular Culture*. Both of these texts explore the cultural impact of books on the middle class.[19] For example, Radway discusses how events in her own childhood influenced her interpretation of Harper Lee's novel *To Kill a Mockingbird* and how the book dissects the middlebrow subjects of race, racism, and the fight for individuality.

Course: Literary Criticism (Undergraduate) Detective and Mystery Novels

Upper-level English courses are also intended to teach students how to construct good critical essays. Such classes introduce the craft of literary criticism, including techniques of close reading, two or more types of literary theory, and strategies for writing and revising critical papers. The genre of choice for this course at the University at Buffalo often is detective and mystery fiction. Using a combination of novels, films, and critical essays, the instructor strives to teach students how to read texts, interpret and use literary theory, do original research, and identify relevant literary criticism.

Why choose detective and crime novels? According to David Schmid, associate professor of English at the University at Buffalo and an expert in popular literature and culture, pulp fiction is a primary source for information on the American zeitgeist from the 1930s through the 1970s. Whether sci-fi, westerns, erotic stories, horror, action-adventure or detective fiction, this material is written quickly and according to a formula. Some of the authors are hacks, but many are quite talented and their work has held up over time. Crime fiction remains a genre amenable to a wide range of critical approaches.[20]

Thus, by reading and analyzing hardboiled and pulp fiction, students are introduced to specific times and places in history and at the same time entertained.

In Schmid's class students are expected to read novels and critical theory essays, and to analyze films, reflecting a combination of conventional and postmodern teaching. Conventional readings usually "focus on the literary meanings, textual significance, and other book related aspects of the novel."[21] However, effective postmodern literacy focuses on intertextual interpretation. In other words, the reader has to identify the network of texts, media, and discourses and interpret by juxtaposing the many discourses. Students are required to read novels, critical essays, and view two films.[22]

Similar to the Best Seller class, the librarian creates a research guide[23] that supplements the course syllabus and assignments. By the end of the first half of the course, the students receive library instruction during regular class time and are introduced to applicable databases, reference books such as mystery and crime fiction encyclopedias and bibliographies, and biographical resources. Using these tools as well as reading contemporary and scholarly reviews, students learn about the development of the detective novel, its historical reception, and the cultural significance of its genre.[24] Introducing students to special collections, such as the *George Kelley Paperback and Pulp Fiction Collection*[25] housed at University at Buffalo, is another way to encourage students to look beyond the obvious interpretations of a novel in order to focus on historical impact and the development of literary themes and audiences. By examining the novels inside and out, students unravel the relationship among this specific genre, the construction of the reader, and the consumption of the text. The vivid covers, for instance, often do not reflect the content or plot of the books but rather were used as advertising ploys to catch a reader's attention, revealing certain assumptions about the working class reader.[26]

Additional assignments using films are used if time allows. Films complement the assigned readings and also capture the students' interest in the chosen subject matter. The films can be viewed and analyzed much like the novels, and students learn about the production of non-print genres and subgenres. For instance, *Double Indemnity* illustrates the changing attitudes of a post World War II culture. *Memento*, a product of the twenty-first century, uses classic film noir techniques such as voice-over narration, flashbacks, and black and white sequences, reflecting similar moods captured in films like *Double Indemnity*.[27]

TECHNOLOGY, RESEARCH, AND CULTURAL STUDIES

Whether in an undergraduate or graduate course, librarians at the University at Buffalo encourage the use of digital resources to support class assignments and to teach literary research within the context of cultural studies.[28] Students explore the production and consumption of digital texts, examining the ways in which electronic production, distribution and consumption of texts change the relationships among the reader, text, canon, and margin. We teach our students the value and uses of online formats including online anthologies, hypermedia, electronic texts, and electronic editions. Below is a discussion of these formats and how they can be incorporated into the classroom. We are interested in using electronic texts in order to engage students with primary texts as well as to foster the ability to access and manipulate historical and cultural resources electronically. Hypermedia materials can enable complex approaches to cultural materials and encourage interdisciplinary ways of thinking through representing multiple points of access to materials, and relationships between archival record and explanatory materials. While we do not have the room here to discuss the use of electronic resources in cultural studies extensively, below we offer a few examples of the ways in which we use electronic texts to complement the cultural studies approaches to literature outlined above.

Hypertext

In his discussion in *Hypertext: the Convergence of Contemporary Critical Theory and Technology*, George Landow provides an in-depth look at the significance of hypertext and how scholars and students can utilize this virtual technology. Unlike print technology, hypertext creates and requires an active reader:

Both an author's tool and a reader's medium, a hypertext document system allows authors or groups of authors to link information together, create paths through a corpus of related material, annotate existing texts, and create notes that point readers to either bibliographic data or the body of the referenced text… . Readers can browse through linked, cross-referenced, annotated texts in an orderly but nonsequential manner."[29]

In his article "What's All this Hype About Hypertext?: Teaching Literature with George P. Landow's 'The Dickens Web'" Jonathan Smith discusses how he used Landow's hypertext The Dickens Web (which is now part of the Victorian Web, described below) in an advanced under-graduate literature course. While he considered the class a success, Smith concluded that a hypertext should be used as a reference tool and not solely as a pedagogical one.[30] Based on his students' responses and actual assign-ment outcomes, Smith concluded that active learning was not a guaranteed outcome of using hypertext sites. While Landow "argues that hypertext enables a novice reader to learn the habit of nonsequential reading, to quickly and easily learn the culture of a discipline," Smith goes further and asserts that educators must actually teach students how to understand the intellectual connection between links. Indeed, through assignments librarians can explain the significance of these links to students.

Students gain a richer understanding of a particular time period and the development of genres and reading audiences within that time period when they are guided through links by study questions. At the University at Buffalo, librarians have successfully used questions (as the basis for in-class discussions and short writing assignments) to guide students through rich web sites such as The Victorian Web and Romantic Circles.[31] The Victorian Web not only provides contextual information for courses taught at Brown University, but also acts as a virtual encyclopedia of nineteenth-century Britain. It is also an invaluable tool for both undergraduate and graduate students;[32] the critical essays are helpful and for the most part are written by advanced graduate students. The best feature, however, remains the hyperlinks to primary resources, which provide insight into public health, race, class, gender, education, and parliamentary issues. Links to excerpts from Punch, Cornhill Magazine, Blackwood's Edinburgh Magazine, as well as book illustrations are among the many special features of this web site. We ask students to use this site to discover authors' positions on social issues and to locate significant legislative acts or publications that might have influenced authors' conceptions of social or literary issues. Students also read contemporary reviews to explore issues of canonization and definitions of literary movements.

Romantic Circles is "devoted to the study of Lord Byron, Mary Wollstonecraft Shelley, Percy Bysshe Shelley, John Keats, their contemporaries and historical contexts."[33] Edited by Laura Mandell, the pedagogy section offers teachers ways to design and utilize online resources, including sample syllabi and a guide to studying Romanticism on the World Wide Web. The Electronic Editions section is comprised of a searchable archive of texts such as *The Last Man* by Mary Shelley and *The Wanderings of Cain* by Samuel Taylor Coleridge. By examining the editors' comments, introductions to the texts, and authors' personal letters, students discover details about a text's production and its relationship to the author. For example, reading "John Keats: A Rediscovered Letter by John Keats," students are not only exposed to the earliest dated copy of a poem by Keats later titled *Lines on the Mermaid Tavern*, but learn of Keats' personal worries over his financial security which depended heavily on his success as a poet.

Rita Raley and Laura Mandell's Anthologies and Miscellanies Web page further address issues of canon formation.[34] The goal of this site is to provide cultural context for examinations of the canonization of English poetry. It contains tables of contents for anthologies, miscellanies and beauties of English poetry. The site is based on the principle that "a discussion of the canonization of literary texts can never be separated from a discussion of the ways in which they were published, circulated and put to use in the schools."[35] Students can use the site to track reception of poetry and the production of poetic canons since the eighteenth century.

Students' examination of the differences between the poems collected in miscellanies and beauties, and those selected for inclusion in anthologies give rise to provocative discussions about the processes that deem particular works suitable for inclusion in poetic canons. The site itself provides potential study questions we have used successfully in our teaching. At the University at Buffalo, we have also asked students to compare the contents of anthologies currently used in classrooms, such as the Norton anthologies or Blackwell anthologies of Romantic or Victorian poetry, to older anthologies in order to understand how different eras or critical schools frame the distinctions between major and minor authors, the Romantic canon, or even definitions of the period itself.

In a library workshop, we use these web sites to direct students' attention to the relationships among historical forms (such as the anthology), academic culture, and the canon. Students examine the ways in which their own concepts of the literary have been shaped by the textbooks used in their literature classes. We usually end the class by moving towards electronic anthologies or hypertext productions and asking how the Internet intersects with or changes productions of texts and canons we have been examined thus far. After teaching students how to locate online text archives, we ask them what the relationship is between electronic text archives and the print anthologies they use in their classes. For more advanced classes, we may ask students to make up their own online anthologies, focused on a period or a theme.

Editions/Manuscripts

Traditionally, librarians teach students how to find editions and manuscripts, using tools such as *Index of English Literary Manuscripts*, *American Literary Manuscripts*, *National Union Catalog of Manuscript Collections*, and WorldCat. In the majority of our classes, students now learn how to locate electronic editions of the texts they are studying as well (if such editions exist). In more advanced classes, we give an overview of editorial theory and history, including practices around the creation of both print and electronic editions. The readings assigned for the library sessions range from W. W. Greg's classic "The Rationale of Copy Text" to Jerome McGann's response "The Rationale of Hypertext."[36] Current editorial theory attempts to demystify material texts by revealing them as neither transparent nor problematic but rather highly constructed and contingent. We emphasize that the texts we study and teach never come to us unmediated, but are always the product of individual and social forces. Students attempt to examine both theoretical positions and their practical applications for the construction of texts, and to explore the relation between contemporary textual theory on the one hand and contemporary literary theory and interpretation on the other. We emphasize manuscripts not to assert the primacy of the book, but conversely to stress the recognition that "the" book does not exist; in other words, what we must study—whether from a background of editorial theory or cultural studies—is the creation, production and consumption of texts, including the production of the "standard" text. Together, we examine the status of "the" text, the implications of multiple versions of literary works, and the importance of material features of the text within the context of both print and electronic media, moving through examples of editorial theory and practice such as Shakespeare's *King Lear*, Joyce's *Ulysses*, Dickinson's poems, and Yeats' poems.

McGann's own The Complete Writings and Pictures of Dante Gabriel Rossetti: A Hypermedia Research Archive is a good example of a hypermedia research archive that integrates a variety of texts.[37] Hypermedia editions that contain links to multiple versions of a text allow the user to compare variants without asserting a primary text, as well as facilitating the creation of a network of relative documents such as those found in the Dickens Web mentioned above. Hypereditions consisting of multiple texts or hyperlinks to annotations or other texts are extremely valuable, but hypermedia editions that integrate visual and audio sources are even more useful in a classroom setting, allowing students to return to an understanding of "the book" itself as a potentially multimedia product. Audio and visual resources may also be included in hypertext editions. McGann points out, for example, that Robert Burns's ballad "Tam Glen" is best studied with contemporary and older versions of performances. He argues that we need to interrelate audio materials the way that critical editions interrelate textual materials. Hypereditions allow us to return to original layouts of text and illustrations. The Blake Archive is a good example of a site that incorporates images into electronic editions.[38] At the University at Buffalo, our next step is to offer a workshop that treats electronic texts just as we treat print texts in our workshops for eighteenth-, nineteenth-, and twentieth-century classes described above; that is, we need to examine the production, distribution and consumption of electronic texts themselves, not just how they help us to understand other kinds of texts. We are beginning to work with faculty who teach digital literature, emphasizing the relationships among the reader, digital media, surface and "code."

INFORMATION LITERACY AND LITERARY RESEARCH

Transforming students into savvy and responsible researchers requires a clear understanding of the relationship between the English curriculum and the national information literacy standards. Cultural studies has not only changed what is taught in our English courses (the texts and discourses examined) but also has changed how these texts and discourses are taught (assignments as well as course context). These changes have in turn influenced what we see as routine literary research tasks and how we teach literary research.

Dissecting works within their cultural and historical context introduces a student not just to a story, but to new ways of thinking. Classes that closely examine both primary and secondary texts and use traditional and online sources tend to be the most successful at teaching students how to be critical readers and thinkers. Ideally, librarians and course instructors should work together to help their students achieve the highest standard of information literacy. In fact, ACRL's *Information Literacy Competency Standards for Higher Education* stress the importance of collaboration among faculty and librarians and outline the steps needed to gather, analyze, and use information successfully.[39] As we incorporate the ACRL literacy competency standards in the classroom, the goal should be to strike a balance between what some poststructuralists might call the "static and fluid approach" to reading and teaching: using printed and electronic text side by side.

Students can learn how print and digital sources complement one another. For example, the *Dictionary of Literary Biography* (DLB) is an invaluable resource for librarians, beginning students, and scholars.[40] Not only does the online version allow simultaneous searching across the print volumes, it provides access to contemporary reviews that are essential to understanding the sociohistorical context of an author's work. Illustrations, photos, and excerpts from manuscripts, however, are only available in the print editions. Being able to see pictures of an author, manuscript notes, or the photographs of an author's estate adds another layer of substance to the laundry list of critical essays and biographical sketches on the authors. In addition, as we noted earlier, hands-on access to special collections such as the *George Kelley Paperback and Pulp Fiction* material provides invaluable insight on how a particular genre reflects assumptions about class, gender, and sexuality.

Knowing how to "differentiate between primary and secondary sources and to recognize how their use and importance vary with each discipline"[41] is a key element in the information literacy standards. A good example of a rich collection of primary resources is *Early English Books*. In microfilm format *Early English Books* is often an underutilized source.[42] The online version *Early English Books Online* (EEBO) provides access to photographic images of the texts of over 125,000 works printed in Britain and its colonies from 1473 to 1700.[43] The collection not only includes English literature, but also history, philosophy, linguistics, and the fine arts, featuring works by Newton and Galileo, musical exercises by Henry Purcell, and novels by

Aphra Behn. Prayer books, pamphlets, almanacs, calendars, and many other primary sources are easily accessible. The database can be used in library instruction for students of various levels. No longer hindered by having to use microfilm, undergraduates will readily use it and will be exposed to new areas of research. *EEBO* introduces students to the cultural and historical contexts within which much of the fiction they are reading existed. Instructors can certainly use it to identify and explain "characteristics of information that make an item a primary or secondary source in a given field."[44]

The competency standards stress the need for students to recognize "the cultural, physical, or other context within which information was created and understand the impact of context on interpreting the information."[45] Attention to the cultural contexts within literature and non-literary texts, as well as the definitions of "literature" and "non-literary" is the basic tenet of cultural studies. In other words, any research course that uses cultural studies as its theoretical starting point by necessity will stress students' recognition of a variety of contexts within which information is created and understood. Librarians attempt to incorporate the basic philosophy of the standards into the English curriculum. For instance, at the University at Buffalo, Honors students were encouraged to research *Early English Books Online* (*EEBO*) for their final theses. One paper in particular received international recognition by winning first prize in the 2004 essay competition sponsored by *EEBO*. The student used facsimiles of 17th century execution pamphlets in the *EEBO* collection to produce her award-winning essay, "Reason through the Unreasonable," which addresses the last words of condemned women prior to being put to death in England. Her paper examines actual testaments of women "felons" and religious pamphlets that described in detail happenings surrounding specific executions. The essay introduces readers to the social, cultural and political context of seventeenth century England. The use of first- hand accounts provide a contextual framework for an examination of a distinct genre of execution accounts.[46] The extent of the student's research and the recognition she has received illustrate the advanced scholarly capability of a digital collection of this magnitude. *EEBO* clearly supports the intellectual rewards of integrating library resources into course assignments that revolve around the cultural and political studies of a specific era.

NEXT STEPS

Librarians need to be proactive in relating information literacy standards to developments in literary theory and the English curriculum, showing administrators and faculty how furthering information literacy goals will advance their own goals and agendas as well. In order to create an effective information literacy program, it is essential to introduce the information literacy lexicon to departmental administrators and faculty in terms relevant to their goals. A review of both external and internal documents such as accreditation standards, mission/vision statements, curricular guidelines, the course catalog, long- and short-term planning documents, general education requirements, major requirements, and honors requirements provides informative sources for learning about national standards, institute goals, and disciplinary criteria. Librarians at the University at Buffalo, for example, have looked for specific mention of "cultural studies," "cultural context," "sociohistorical context" and "genre definition" in course descriptions, program goals and department mission statements. We look for any required skills to be targeted to programmatic groups or particular learning experiences—honors programs, first year programs, residential colleges, or required courses. Such programs typically reveal commitments to student learning that can serve as a springboard for advancing the library information literacy agendas and serve as a backdrop for collaboration with key faculty. Librarians need to keep abreast of the professional literature and trends monitored and promoted by departmental administrators. Regular review of articles in the *Chronicle of Higher Education* or *Profession*, for example, can give librarians insight into key trends in teaching and learning within English departments. The terms we use to describe information literacy are frequently the same terms that faculty use to describe critical thinking, for example, or historical understanding. Librarians need to demonstrate the close alignment of information literacy goals and the goals of departmental administrators in order to justify and gain support for information literacy instruction. We can often demonstrate this alignment in one of three ways: (1) through describing the parallels between specific administrative goals and specific information literacy standards; (2) through demonstrating the ways in which students will need to master information literacy skills in order to meet national and local teaching/learning goals; and (3) through revealing the alignment of instructional methods used to achieve local teaching/learning goals and the instructional methods used to achieve information literacy goals. Above, we have outlined how librarians at the University at Buffalo align the teaching of information literacy skills with their English department's commitment to cultural studies.

NOTES

The authors would like to express their thanks to William McPheron, whose research course at Stanford University inspired their own teaching.

1.   Raymond Williams, *Culture and Society, 1780-1950* (New York: Columbia University Press, 1960).

2.   For a history of cultural studies see Antony Easthope, *Literary into Cultural Studies* (New York: Routledge, 1991).

3.   Robert Scholes, *Textual Power: Literary Theory and the Teaching of English* (New Haven: Yale University Press, 1985), 16.

4.   For discussions of introductory theory classes and the curriculum see the essays gathered in Dianne F. Sadoff and William E. Cain, eds., *Teaching Contemporary Theory to Undergraduates* (New York: Modern Language Association of America, 1994).

5.   William E. Cain, "Contemporary Theory, the Academy, and Pedagogy," in *Teaching Contemporary Theory to Undergraduates*, 10.

6.   For a useful list of theory anthologies, casebooks and readers see Donald G. Marshall, *Contemporary Critical Theory: A Selective Bibliography* (New York: MLA, 1993).

7.   Representative titles in this series include Naomi Ritter, ed., *Death in Venice: Complete, Authoritative Text with Biographical and Historical Contexts, Critical History, and Essays from Five Contemporary Critical Perspectives* (Boston: Bedford Books, 1998) and Janice Carlisle, ed., *Great Expectations: Complete, Authoritative Text with Biographical and Historical Contexts, Critical History, and Essays from Five Contemporary Critical Perspectives* (Boston: Bedford Books, 1996).

8.   Additional Readings include: Neil McKendrick, John Brewer, and J. H. Plumb eds., *The Birth of a Consumer Society: The Commercialization of Eighteenth-Century England* (Bloomington: Indiana University Press, 1982); and students are introduced to the growth of books as commodities by lectures and readings including Richard Altick, *The English Common Reader: A Social History of the Mass Reading Public 1800-1900* ([Chicago]: University of Chicago Press, 1957); Isabel Rivers, ed., *Books and Their Readers in Eighteenth-Century England* ([Leicester, Leicestershire]: Leicester University Press, 1982); Jon P. Klancher, *The Making of English Reading Audiences, 1790-1832* (Madison: University of Wisconsin Press, 1987); and William B. Warner, *Licensing Entertainment: the Elevation of Novel Reading in Britain, 1684-1750* (Berkeley: University of California Press, 1998).

9.   Students use Antonia Forster, *Index to Book Reviews in England 1749-1774* (Carbondale: Southern Illinois University Press, 1990); Antonia Forster, *Index to Book Reviews in England 1775-1800* (London: British Library, 1997); *Literature Criticism from 1400-1800* (Detroit, Mich.: Gale Research Co., 1984-); and Routledge's *Critical Heritage Series* to locate reviews of a novel of their choosing in a variety of eighteenth-century periodicals such as *The Monthly Review* or *The Critical Review*.

10.   For background information, we may show students sources on periodicals such as Alvin Sullivan, ed., *British Literary Magazines: 1698-1984* (Westport, Conn.: Greenwood Press, 1983-).

11.   Ian Watt, *The Rise of the Novel: Studies in Defoe, Richardson and Fielding* (Berkeley: University of California Press, 2001). Texts we frequently discuss during this session include: John Richetti, *The English Novel in History, 1700-1780* (New York: Routledge, 1999); Nancy Armstrong, *Desire and Domestic Fiction: A Political History of the Novel* (New York: Oxford University Press, 1987); Michael McKeon, *The Origins of the English Novel, 1600-1740* (Baltimore: Johns Hopkins University Press, 1987); and Catherine Gallagher, *Nobody's Story: the Vanishing acts of Women Writers in the Marketplace, 1670-1820* (Berkeley: University of California Press, 1994).

12.   Recommended readings include: Richard Altick, *The English Common Reader: A Social History of the Mass Reading Public, 1800-1900*; N. N. Feltes, *Modes of Production of Victorian Novels* (Chicago: University of Chicago Press, 1986); John O. Jordan and Robert L. Patten, eds. *Literature in the Marketplace: Nineteenth-Century British Publishing and Reading Practice* (Cambridge: Cambridge University Press, 1995); Patrick Brantlinger, *The Reading Lesson: the Threat of Mass Literacy in Nineteenth-Century British Fiction* (Bloomington: Indiana University Press, 1998); Gaye Tuchman with Nina E. Fortin, *Edging Women Out: Victorian Novelists Publishers and Social Change* (New Haven: Yale University Press, 1989); and Gerard Curtis, *Visual Words: Art and the Material Book in Victorian England* (Aldershot, Hants, England: Ashgate, 2002).

13.   See Graham Law, *Serializing Fiction in the Victorian Press* (New York: Palgrave, 2000).

14.   George H. Ford, *Dickens and His Readers; Aspects of Novel-Criticism since 1836* (Princeton, N.J.: Princeton University Press, 1955); Phillip Collins, ed., *Dickens: The Critical Heritage* (London, Routledge & K. Paul, 1971).

15.   To access to Professor Willbern's Best Sellers syllabus and lecture notes, see http://www.cas.buffalo.edu/classes/eng/willbern/BestSellers/index.htm

16.   Laura Taddeo, *Best Sellers: 20th Century American Best Sellers Research Guide*, http://ublib.buffalo.edu/libraries/asl/guides/best_sellers.html (accessed 17 July 2003).

17.   The Gale Group. *Literature Resource Center* <electronic resource>. (Detroit, MI: Gale Research); *InfoTrac OneFile* <electronic resource>. (S.l.: Gale Group); *MLA International Bibliography*, Modern Language Association <electronic resource>. (S.l.: MLA, 1999); *Annual Bibliography of English Language and Literature* <electronic resource>: (ABELL. Alexandria, Va.: Chadwyck-Healey, 1998-).

18.   Some study questions that Willbern uses are as follows:
Peyton Place: Read the section on Rodney Harrington and Betty Anderson. To many 1950s readers, this was a "meat and potatoes" section of the book. Paying attention to all the moments—not just the sensationally sexual—what conclusions can you derive about the intentions and assumptions of the novel? *The Things They Carried*: On the title page, what is the *full* title of the novel? What do you make of it? Examine the reverse side of the title page, specifically the publication history of the stories in the book. What does this information tell you about the writing of the book? How did O'Brien assemble his novel? This question is about the *composition* of the book, both as written and as read.

19.   Janice A. Radway, *A Feeling for Books: the Book-of-the-Month Club, Literary Taste, and Middle-class Desire* (Chapel Hill: University of North Carolina Press, 1997); Andrew Ross, *No Respect: Intellectuals & Popular Culture* (New York: Routledge, 1989). For a detailed discussion of the position of the bestseller and the shaping of the canon, see Richard Ohmann, *Politics of Letters* (Middletown, Conn.: Wesleyan University Press, 1987), 68-91.

20.   David Schmid, "Pulp Fiction," *UBToday*, Winter 2000, http://www.buffalo.edu/UBT/UBT-archives/13_ubtw00/features/feature3.html (accessed 27 June 2003).

21.   Shuaib J. Meacham and Edward Buendia, "Focus on Research: Modernism, Postmodernism, and Post-structuralism and their Impact on Literacy," *Language Arts* 76 (1999): 510-516.

22.   The novels of choice often are: Edgar Allan Poe, *Tales of Terror and Detection*; Sir Arthur Conan Doyle, *Six Great Sherlock Holmes Stories*; Agatha Christie, *The ABC Murders*; Dashiell Hammett, *The Maltese Falcon*; Chester Himes, *Cotton Comes to Harlem*; Barbara Wilson, *Murder in the Collective*. Films include *Double Indemnity* and *Memento* and can be viewed either during or outside of class time.

23.   Laura Taddeo, *Mystery and Crime Fiction: Guide to Literary Theory and Criticism Sources*, 1 August 2002, http://ublib.buffalo.edu/libraries/asl/guides/mysterycrime.html (accessed 31 March 2003).

24.   Secondary sources that can enhance class discussion are: Marc Lits, "The Classical Origins and the Development of the Detective Novel Genre," *Paradoxa* 1, no. 2 (1995): 126-144; Donald Hall, "From Aesthetics to Cultural Studies: The Many Productive Forms of Critical Analysis," in *Literary and Cultural Theory from Basic Principles to Advanced Applications* (Boston: Houghton Mifflin, 2001), 1-12; Julian Symons, "What They Are and Why We Read Them," in *Mortal Consequences: A History from the Detective Story to the Crime Novel* (New York: Harper & Row, 1972), 1-16; Michael Denning, *Mechanic Accents: Dime Novels and Working-Class Culture in America* (New York: Verso, 1998); Erin A. Smith, *Hard-Boiled: Working-Class Readers and Pulp Magazines* (Philadelphia: Temple University Press, 2000).

25.   *The George Kelley paperback and Pulp Fiction Collection.* http://ublib.buffalo.edu/libraries/units/lml/kelley/collection.html (accessed 26 July 2006).

26.   Sample study questions/assignments include: Using the database Dictionary of Literary Biography (DLB), determine what pulp fiction magazine Dashiell Hammett's *Maltese Falcon* appeared in and in how many installments. In what year and by what publishing company was the story released in novel format? A more advanced library workshop might involve using a school's special collection. The following questions require on-site access to the University at Buffalo's *George Kelley Paperback and Pulp Fiction Collection*; instructors can use different pulp fiction paperbacks or magazines to answer similar questions. The idea is to get a sense of the range of subject and style of pulp fiction published in the early 20th century. Provide the professor with the following assignments, which s/he in turn can give to his students to prepare for a library workshop/discussion on detective and crime fiction: 1. Select issues of *Hardboiled Detectives, Detective Story Magazine, A Matter of Crime.* Outline the plots and themes that routinely appear in these magazines. Describe the design of the magazines' covers. What understanding of gender, race and class emerge in the stories in these magazines? 2. Read chapter 2 of Erin Smith's book on pulp fiction (referenced above), entitled "The Adam on the Shop Floor: Workers, Consumer Culture, and the Pulps." Prepare for a class discussion on pulp advertisements and the working-class reader. 3. Visual Vocabulary: Examine the book jackets of a few novels from the *George Kelley Paperback and Pulp Fiction Collection.* What can you determine about twentieth-century culture from the covers? Do the covers reflect the content in the books or are they simply used as an advertising ploy to catch a reader's attention? A few sample covers and plot summaries can be found on the web site for the *George Kelley Paperback and Pulp Fiction Collection.*

27.   For a class discussion of the film genre "film noir," have students view *Double Indemnity* and *Memento.* Find a thorough explanation of the term "film noir." After watching both films, have a class discussion; compare both films, and identify some techniques used in each film that represents this genre. Comment on the representations of man as a "lone figure" and his role in a corrupt urban world.

28.   For a more detailed discussion of the role of technology in literary research, see *Literature in English: A Guide for Librarians in the Digital Age* (Chicago: Association of College and Research Libraries, 2000). This book not only examines digital collections of English and American literature, but also describes the opportunities and challenges involved in selecting, purchasing, providing access to, and preserving digital materials. A comprehensive list of electronic texts and selected web sites for English and American Literature can be found in *Literature in English: A Guide for Librarians in the Digital Age.*

29.   George Landow, *Hypertext: The Convergence of Contemporary Critical Theory and Technology* (Baltimore: The John Hopkins University Press, 1992), 6.

30.   Jonathan Smith, "What's All this Hype About Hypertext?: Teaching Literature with George P. Landow's 'The Dickens Web,'" *Computers and the Humanities* 30 (2) (1996): 121-129.

31.   Sample Study Questions/Assignments include: Use the section on the author Christina Rossetti to learn about her life, writing styles, and literary themes. Under the section entitled "Literary, Artistic, Religious, and Other Cultural Contexts," click on the heading "Gender Matters." Using the information embedded within this section, answer the following questions: What was Rossetti's position on women's suffrage? What significant legislative acts and publications might have influenced Rossetti's works? Based on contemporary reviews of her work and the description of the Pre-Raphaelite Brotherhood, how does Rossetti fit into the description of this movement?

32.   Victorian Web, http://www.victorianweb.org (accessed 27 June 2003).

33.   Romantic Circles, http://www.rc.umd.edu (accessed 27 June 2003).

34.   Rita Raley and Laura Mandell, Anthologies and Miscellanies, http://www.english. ucsb.edu/faculty/rraley/research/anthologies/ (accessed 1 July 2003).

35.   Ibid.

36.   W. W. Greg, "The Rationale of Copy-text," *Studies in Bibliography* 3 (1950-51): 19-36; Jerome J. McGann, "The Rationale of Hypertext," in *Electronic Text: Investigations in Method and Theory*, ed. Kathryn Sutherland, 19-46 (Oxford: Oxford University Press, 1997).

37.   Jerome McGann, ed. *The Rossetti Archive, http://www.rossettiarchive.org/* (accessed 1 July 2003).

38.   Morris Eaves, Robert Essick and Joseph Viscomi, eds. *The William Blake Archive*, http://www.blakearchive.org/ (accessed 1 July 2003).

39.   Association of College and Research Libraries (ACRL), *Information Literacy Competency Standards for Higher Education*, 2000, http://www.ala.org/ala/mgrps/divs/acrl/standards/informationliteracycompetency.cfm (accessed 14 May 2003).

40.   *Dictionary of Literary Biography (DLB)* <electronic resource>. (Detroit, MI: Gale Research, 2002).

41.   Association of College and Research Libraries (ACRL), *Objectives for Information Literacy Instruction: A Model Statement for Academic Librarians*, January 2001, http://www.ala.org/ala/mgrps/divs/acrl/standards/objectivesinformation.cfm (accessed 14 May 2003).

42.   *Early English books, 1475-1640*, (Ann Arbor, Michigan: University Microfilms, 1937-), and *Early English Books, 1641-1700* (Ann Arbor, Michigan: University Microfilms1966-).

43.   *Early English Books Online (EEBO)* <electronic resource>. (Ann Arbor, Michigan: Bell & Howell Information and Learning, 1999-).

44.   Association of College and Research Libraries (ACRL), *Objectives for Information Literacy Instruction: A Model Statement for Academic Librarians*, January 2001, http://www.ala.org/ala/mgrps/divs/acrl/standards/objectivesinformation.cfm (accessed 14 May 2003).

45.   Association of College and Research Libraries (ACRL), *Information Literacy Competency Standards for Higher Education*, 2000, http://www.ala.org/ala/mgrps/divs/acrl/standards/informationliteracycompetency.cfm (accessed 14 May 2003).

46.   University at Buffalo News, *UB Student Receives First Prize in International Essay Competition*, 22 March 2005, http://www.buffalo.edu/news/fast-execute.cgi/article-page.html?article=71380009&hilite=eebo.

Part Three: Literary Librarians

Through the Eyes of Picasso: Literary Research from the Best of Both Worlds

Meg Meiman

For years, the defining characteristic of my research as an undergraduate English major was serendipity. Naturally I would begin with the card catalog or print version of the *Reader's Guide to Periodical Literature*, dutifully jotting down each title in my notebook. But once I got into the stacks and began looking for my required books (for they were almost always books), the list of titles often became signposts pointing to other books that I would pluck from the shelves in the hope that *this* was what I needed. Chance, pure and simple, operated as the force behind much of my research.

Given my moderate success in finding sources, it was no wonder I continued to rely on chance all through graduate school, this time consulting the online catalog and a few specialized databases. When I entered library school, however, I was stunned to discover more sources and organized methods of research. Why hadn't anyone told me (or why hadn't I asked) about the *Arts and Humanities Citation Index*? Or Library of Congress subject headings? Of course, I had used those subject headings without knowing their organization for quite a while, clicking on what looked like relevant "links" to other records within the catalog, after entering keywords and trawling through dozens of entries that didn't seem quite on target. My database searching as an English graduate student followed a similar pattern, in which I would enter keywords and click on whatever terms seemed promising within the records I'd retrieved. Yet library school was the place where I learned more nuanced and expedient forms of searching: how to truncate words, cross search sets, and use a combination of keywords and controlled vocabulary (those relevant "links" I'd unwittingly used as an English student). What was once my sometimes muddled approach to research became an infinitely more informed and conscious endeavor.

And this realization seemed like a revelation, as though I'd experienced a sort of Cubist blessing, suddenly able to see literary research from more than one angle at the same time, and also gain a greater sense of the breadth of literature. The sources I discovered in library school introduced a discipline that was vaster and more multi-faceted than the time period and country I had been compelled to stay within as an English graduate student. And whereas my previous method of literary research consisted of browsing the stacks and scanning bibliographies to find sources and prominent scholars in my field, my research after library school allowed me to better understand the organization of, and use more efficiently, a wider selection of literary sources, particularly online ones. In light of this knowledge, my days of serendipitous research initially seemed foolish, although I now realize my research style—slow, solitary, and grounded firmly in print—was a direct result of the field in which I specialized, and continues to inform much of my research.

ENTER THE LIBRARIANS

Thus the continual need for a "librarian intervention" among English graduate education, particularly within the realm of research methods classes, because academic librarians, particularly subject-specialist librarians, are the ideal agents for introducing this multi-perspective approach to literary research. Just as Picasso's Cubist images render more than one perspective of an object simultaneously, so graduate students should ideally approach literary research from several angles, using a variety of sources in order to "see" their topic from more than one viewpoint, to effectively navigate various sources to find relevant information, and, most importantly, to better understand the context of their research. And librarians, in conjunction with teaching faculty, are precisely the people to show students these multiple perspectives. In the course of this essay, I will briefly describe other models of subject-specific instruction, along with my own "Cubist" attempt at teaching literary research to graduate students in English, and the possible implications this approach has for future librarian-faculty collaborations.

A METHOD TO THE MODEL

Anita Kay Lowry, Pamela Bradigan, Susan Kroll, Sally Sims, and Judy Reynolds have all developed various models of teaching literary research designed to address its complexities, and these models can be roughly classified into what Helene Williams categorizes as general workshops, course-related instruction (in which library sessions are integrated into a discipline-specific research methods class) and librarian-taught, for-credit courses tailored to a specific discipline.[1] Anita Kay Lowry's approach to research was of the lattermost; at Columbia University, she developed a stand-alone, for-credit class entitled Research in the Humanities, comprised of eight two-hours sessions designed to teach humanities students about traditional and electronic resources, not only searching them, but also learning to "place specific sources and methods in the broader context of scholarly inquiry."[2] While this seems an ideal class for any student within the field of humanities, in that it thoroughly addresses both the practical matter of using various sources and their theoretical framework within the field of humanities, I believe a modified version of this for graduate students in English would be even more ideal, if only because they have an assignment (or assignments) to give them a more immediate context from which to work.

Another model similar to Lowry's is one developed by Pamela Bradigan, Susan Kroll, and Sally Sims, and centers upon a workshop conducted at the Ohio State University Libraries. Led by a subject-specialist librarian and a librarian from the user-education office, the workshop consists of choosing an interdisciplinary topic and leading students through the process of researching it, using a number of sources and search techniques, and supplementing the library demonstration with a twelve-page handout while emphasizing the pertinence of the demonstration to students' own research.[3] As another promising approach to teaching literary research, this method demonstrates for students the number and kinds of sources applicable to the wide-ranging nature of research in English literature. The only potential drawbacks, however, are its brevity (each workshop is a one-shot session) and the possible pedagogical clash with research methods in English, unless a professor were willing to adopt an interdisciplinary approach within her own class, allowing students to choose a literary theme and research it for the entire semester. Nevertheless, Bradigan, Kroll, and Sims have developed a model that does not threaten to compete with research methods classes (or other graduate courses) in the way that a stand-alone, for-credit course such as Lowry's might. Of course, getting an English professor to cede one or two classes of his or her course may also be seen as a competition for territory and/or time, but perhaps it may be easier for librarians to make inroads this way first, then gradually propose a semester-long model.

Like Bradigan, Kroll, and Sims, Judy Reynolds advocates a variation of this interdisciplinary method in the audience-specific ways she developed to teach the *Modern Language Association International Bibliography (MLAIB)* database. Graduate students, she asserts, are the ones who need to know some of the *MLAIB's* history of its structure in order to understand the bibliography's "pliable vocabulary" and lack of standardized, easily-indexed terms.[4] Moreover, in showing students the numerous access points provided by the *MLAIB*, including author, country, literary period and genre, Reynolds creates the model of a spiral in which the perspective of a topic changes according to one's approach; as she states, "[the model] is especially useful for graduate students as a graphical demonstration of the importance of approaching a subject from different angles."[5] Included within the spiral model are the goals of understanding the limits of subject headings and variant spellings, and the use of multiple search sets in combining terms.[6]

Upon first encountering Reynolds' model while researching this essay, and well after my own first attempt at teaching English graduate students, I experienced a moment of "Eureka!" since I was once one of those students in need of understanding research within a spiral context, and of controlling my view of the spiral with carefully crafted search strategies. Given my training as a graduate student, I knew precisely what to do once I got my hands on a particular source (analyze it, review the bibliography, align the source and its references with certain literary theories), but my subsequent awakening to other research methods in library school compelled me to learn—and later, as a subject-specialist librarian, to teach other graduate students in English—how to expeditiously obtain those sources, and re-envision discipline-specific library sessions as exploring part of a spiral. More importantly, my experiences in both English and library science graduate programs compelled me to discover ways of mentally reconciling and teaching what became my "Cubist" perspective of research: the process-driven nature of finding sources (especially online sources), the conceptual frameworks of those sources (especially the *MLAIB*) and the recursive, context-dependent nature of literary research.

THE CUBIST APPROACH (PART ONE)

Fortunately, I had the chance to put my money where my mouth was, by conducting four library instructional sessions for an English graduate research methods class. Originally, the professor wanted only one or two sessions, but after looking at his assignments for the semester and mentioning my background in graduate English coursework, I convinced him that four sessions would allow his students to learn what they needed for the assignment, and (in my mind) introduce them to resources that might help them in future classes. This initial interaction with the professor was fortunate, because of his flexibility with his syllabus, his already-engaged relationship with library resources, and his openness to the idea of a semester-long collaboration, although that aspect unfortunately did not work out. Nevertheless, his assignment was graduate school déjà vu for me: his students had to choose a text before 1800, describe its historical context, provide a bibliographic description of the text, compare it with two later versions, and discuss the significance of the differences among the texts. Ultimately, the goal of the assignment mirrored the goal of the class: to give his students a greater understanding of bibliography as a fundamental part of literary studies, and to learn something about books as objects in order to critique and analyze them as texts.

I was in heaven and hell at once, eager to convey what I had learned as a graduate student in two disciplines and to help lead his students further into the Promised Land of Research, but in a quandary as how best to do it. I did not want to teach solely to the assignment for fear of reinforcing the boundaries of the discipline, yet knew I could not possibly cover every resource I had learned about in the language and literature section of my reference class in humanities. I also wanted to tie each class not only to a particular part of the assignment, but also to the larger concepts underpinning each of the sources I would cover, and in turn tie those sources to the context of students' individual projects. Not surprisingly, my reach exceeded my grasp. Although I carefully tailored sessions to address relationships as well as mechanics—e.g., the relation between the print and online *Modern Language Association International Bibliography* and the conceptual differences in searching each—and although I allowed ample time within each session for students to search both online databases and the stacks, my overall approach to teaching literary research was ultimately an elaborate "how-to" session.

On the first day I focused on the Library of Congress subject headings and the classification system (which was, interestingly, a revelation to many of the students) in order to give them a starting point for the historical part of the assignment. The second session was "computer day," in which I re-introduced subject-specific databases that would help them find criticism about their text, showing them advanced search techniques, such as combining key words with subject headings, truncating terms, and using Boolean operators. The third session, "book day," introduced them to several print catalogs in which they could find more than one version of their text and see what a bibliographic description looked like, and the fourth session focused on general handbooks and research guides pertinent to their field of interest within English, as well as on databases which initially seemed outside the field of English but might prove relevant later on in their graduate careers. All of this was accompanied, of course, by a three-page handout of the sources I had covered, each with brief annotations and suggestions for use (see Appendix I for the handout).

Even after four sessions in the library, as well as two classes that I attended in the department to offer research advice, the professor and I agreed this was not enough: he wanted his students to learn how to do what I had done. Part of my work, I reminded him, was a result of my training as a librarian, but part of it was my experience as a graduate research assistant, repeatedly assigned to find and contextualize sources for literature professors, *combined* with my experience in library school (and my subsequent experience as a full-time librarian). Ironically, what I remembered as a researcher was what I had failed to adequately emphasize as a literature librarian: the importance of context.

CONTEXT IS EVERYTHING—THE CUBIST APPROACH (PART TWO)

Establishing a background for particular sources (e.g., the complexity of subject terms in the *MLAIB*), emphasizing Reynolds' "spiral" approach to a topic, and connecting each of these approaches to an individual graduate student's work are important forms of contextualization. Yet another, equally significant approach to teaching students is to ground the entire process of searching, online or in the stacks, within the greater scholarly community. That is, re-casting the research process as joining a scholarly cocktail party (or keg party, depending on the audience) helps students see a bibliography at the end of an article, or the list of hits from a database as fragments of a conversation, from which, after much reading, writing, and more research, they can begin to see which scholars are friends, which ones disagree with each other and to what extent, and which ones will always be standing next to, or across the room from each other. Barbara Fister echoes this idea when she encourages librarians to "describe [the search process] as a way of tapping into the scholarly communication network"[7] without sacrificing the "how-to" aspect of library sessions (an important component, given the complexity and profusion of subject-specific resources in English). For graduate students in English already familiar with the metaphor of scholarly conversation, emphasizing the use of citation mining (exploring bibliographies) and citation indexes to gain a clearer picture of the scholarly conversation surrounding their ideas, and to determine the influence of a particular work or author may prove helpful. Finally, emphasizing for students the recursive nature of the research process is crucial. Barbara Fister's directive to "convince students that searching, reading, and writing are non-consecutive activities"[8] bears particular relevance for English literature students, and the librarian subject-specialists teaching them, since much of their research ideally happens not when they locate a list of results in a database, but later when they read and interpret what they find, when they situate their sources within the larger context of the scholarly cocktail party that surrounds their topic, and when they incorporate all these ideas into their already-existing knowledge of their subject.

Of course, this recursiveness often clashes with the reality of an assignment due in a few hours, and is unwelcome news for students hoping to make a one-stop shopping trip to the library. It also presents a challenge for librarians hoping (as I did) to cover "the basic sources for graduate students" in four library sessions, or six, or even one semester. As C. Paul Vincent asserts,

> Instructors should never imply that a session with the librarian has provided students with all the keys to their research problems…Research…in the humanities, is not an exact science. It tolerates—indeed, it encourages—the subjective impression. And this adds a certain poignance to [Constance] McCarthy's claim that 'there is no such thing as *sufficient* library instruction.'"[9]

Research, in all its glory, requires time, reflection, and a continual return to what one has found, in order to make meaning from it; thus the necessity for librarians to teach literary research in ways that promote these aspects of it, without neglecting the equally essential "how to" components of searching print and online sources. Herein lies the need to teach a "Cubist vision" of literary research.

BACK TO THE STACKS

Given the varying approaches to teaching literary research as (for example) textual scholarship, historical scholarship, literary criticism, and/or literary theory,[10] depending upon the teacher's goals for the class, and given the various meanings of what literary research encompasses,[11][12][1] course-integrated instruction emphasizing the contextual elements of literature sources seems like one of the more flexible models in which librarians can collaborate with professors to teach literary research. And if today's graduate students, who include distance learners, adults with full-time jobs, Millennials, and many others, are to engage in this admittedly idealized portrait of literary research, I believe their opportunities to learn must not only be situated within the context of their ideas, their discipline, and the scholarly community as a whole, but that these opportunities occur within the context of the library, either literally (within the building), or virtually (through remote access), but preferably the former. Literary research in the library is essential for researchers, not merely because most literature sources still reside in books, but also because the library serves as a powerful visual reminder that literary research does not happen only in one or two databases from a student's dorm room: it also happens in the stacks, at the reference desk, sitting alone at a table surrounded by books, and possibly in a group with fellow students—and it happens over and over again.

Just as a viewer has to visually reconcile the numerous and possibly competing perspectives of *Les Demoiselles d'Avignon*, and may, in the process, see something he hadn't seen before that compels him to reconsider the entire work, so a researcher has to search and re-search her sources for connections and disjunctions, and perhaps catch new glimpses of the ever-changing scholarly conversation. Librarians can (and do) serve as indispensable guides to this entire enterprise, helping others see the myriad ways in which literary research can develop; grounding the research process in its contextual foundations; and teaching, in collaboration with English faculty, an academically interdisciplinary approach to research that accommodates the complexity of this wide-ranging, scholastic endeavor.

This is all well and good, one might ask, but precisely how does this work in the real world? At the risk of taking refuge in relativism and incurring general ire, it depends. It depends upon the faculty member and how much time s/he can allot to the librarian, it depends on the individual librarian, it depends upon the course and its assignments, and above all, it depends on the students. But I do believe that focusing library sessions on context as much as process, demonstrating (and reminding) students of the recursive nature of literary research, and getting them back into the library building are all key elements in promoting a Cubist vision of literary research. This approach, with persistence and a fair amount of luck, can lead to more complex questions from students and faculty, more meaningful collaborations among librarians and faculty, and possibly a greater understanding, among all parties, of the complex nature of literary research.

APPENDIX I: Sources for Bibliography and Methods of Research in English

Handout for the four-part library instruction session for a graduate-level English Research Methods class at the University of Southern Mississippi, taught during the fall semester, 2003

CATALOGS

British Museum Catalogue of Printed Books (Z 921.B86 Reference)
Entries include author, title, year, and a scant physical description. Based on the *Catalogue of the Printed Books in the Library of the British Museum*, this catalogue covers books published from about the sixteenth century to the early twentieth century.

National Union Catalogue of Pre-1956 Imprints (Z 881.A1 U3742 Index area)
This is a cumulative author list representing the Library of Congress printed cards and titles reported by other American libraries. Entries include author, title, edition, location and year.

National Union Catalog of Manuscript Collections (Z 881.A1 U3771 Index area)
Provides a list of manuscript collections, detailing their purchase history and location.

Pollard and Redgrave's Short Title Catalogue, 1475-1640 (Z 2002. P77 1976 Reference)
Also known as STC I, this catalogue traces variant editions and issues of works, and functions as a handy finding list, NOT (as Pollard once put it) a census of copies. Includes books written in English and printed both within and without the British Isles, as well as books in other languages printed in the British Isles. Entries include titles, authors, imprints, dates, publishers, format, head notes, and location.

Seventeenth-Century Imprints (Z 1015.W63 Stacks)
This print source contains compilations, descriptive listings, annotations and occasionally book biographies of 17th-century books at Wofford College Library, and possibly includes some titles not listed in the STC I and II.

Thomason Tracts (Z 2018.B852—Microfilm)

Covering the years 1640-1661, this source is a compilation of the books, pamphlets, newspapers, and manuscripts collected by George Thomason and housed in the British Library. Entries include author, title, tract number and reel number.

Donald Wing's Short Title Catalog, 1641-1700 (Z 2002.W52 Reference)

This catalogue, also known as STC II, picks up where Pollard and Redgrave's STC leaves off, providing an enumerative (not descriptive) bibliography of pre-18th-century books. Entries include author, title, imprint, date, format and location.

GUIDES

Literary research guide: an annotated listing of reference sources in English literary studies. (PR 83.H34 1998 Reference)

A thorough introduction to and evaluation of reference sources for British and American literatures. Written for graduate students as well as experienced scholars, James Harner's guide offers selective but rigorous coverage of books and journals. Highly recommended for all aspects of research.

A Reference Guide for English Studies (PR 56.M37 1990)

Michael Marcuse's annotated guide has a cutoff date of 1985, but provides informative entries about reference sources for British and American literatures, with a neatly subdivided table of contents and several helpful indexes. While it's less selective than Harner's guide, this source nevertheless offers helpful starting points for graduate students and full-fledged scholars.

DATABASES

Early English Books Online

Encompassing titles from both STC I and II, the Thomason Tracts, and the Early English Books Tract Supplement, this database contains citations, full page images and illustrations for books, pamphlets, and broadsides printed between 1475 and 1700. It also allows you to print, email and/or download citations, and download images. Definitely the place to start when researching early English texts.

Humanities Abstracts

This database indexes and abstracts articles about art, classical studies, communications, film, folklore, gender studies, history, journalism, linguistics, literary and social criticism, music, performing arts, philosophy, religion, and theology. Indexing and abstracting begins in 1984, and full-text coverage begins in 1995. Try using the index and search history features for more comprehensive research.

JSTOR

This full-text database provides articles about language, literature, history, philosophy and other areas within the humanities, as well as the sciences and social sciences. It only provides articles published as recently as 2000, given its agreement with various publishers, but draws on reputable, established journals. Choose the "Expand the journal list" to search within particular journals.

MLA International Bibliography

Has bibliographic records pertaining to literature, language, linguistics, and folklore, and coverage extends from 1963 to the present. The database provides access to scholarly research in nearly 4,000 journals and series, offering citations for books, working papers, proceedings, bibliographies, and other formats. As with Humanities Abstracts, use the index and search history features to ensure thorough research.

WorldCat

Containing millions (yes, millions) of citations, WorldCat provides indexing for books, journals, articles, websites, manuscripts, maps, sound recordings and just about anything else you can think of. Indispensable for research in any area. Use the "Advanced Search" to limit items by type, location, year and language.

WEBSITES

Research Centre in the History of the Book is a useful resource for book history buffs, and has a list of links—click on "Book History Links"—leading to other terrific sites. **http://www.sas.ac.uk/ies/RCHB/RCHB.htm**

Library of Congress's American Memory Project contains digitized texts and images (over 7 million!) from numerous historical collections on the culture and history of the United States. **http://memory.loc.gov**
Literary Resources on the Net—Bibliography and History of the Book is essentially an online bibliography of useful links about the history of

authorship, reading, publishing, and (of course) the books themselves. http://newark.rutgers.edu/~jlynch/Lit/biblio.html

Remote Access—or, doing research on your couch
You don't need a special login to search ANNA from the comfort of your own dorm, but you do need a PIN number which you can get from circulation. You have to get it in person, but once you do, you can renew books online, fill out online forms for Interlibrary Loan, and (best of all), do research in your pajamas. To search other databases, you need to be a current student at USM. When logging in from home, enter the 10-digit number that appears on your student ID card, and make sure cookies are enabled in your browser. That's it.

Web Services—or, getting what you need when the library doesn't have it
Web Services is a gateway to document delivery services, such as Infotrieve and Interlibrary Loan, both of which allow you to obtain books and journal articles that you can't find at USM's Libraries. First-time users should visit the following site: **http://www.lib.usm.edu/webservices/begin/index2.php**. Then you'll need the 10-digit number on your ID card, and can register by clicking on the "register" link. Once you've done this, you'll need to think up a password and log in. Now you're ready to register and log in to Infotrieve.

Infotrieve is an article-retrieval service for students, faculty and staff at USM. If you can't find an article you need at USM's Libraries, register (only once) with Infotrieve, typing in your name, address, phone number, and creating a user name and password. Then log in to Infotrieve with your user name and password, and put in a request for an article by entering the citation information (the author, the article title, the journal title, and the date). **Keep in mind that the more complete and correct your citation, the faster you'll get the article. You can choose to have the articles either mailed or faxed to you, and will get email updates on the status of your orders.

Interlibrary Loan is the department which borrows books and dissertations from other libraries that USM's libraries don't have. The forms are available through Anna, the USM catalog. A caveat: **expect delays when ordering from ILL.** A book can take up to 2 weeks—and sometimes longer—to arrive, so place your orders as soon as humanly possible. If you have any questions about or problems with this service, please call (601) 266-4249, and the folks at the Information desk at Cook can help.

NOTES

1.   Helene C. Williams, "User Education for Graduate Students: Never a Given, and Not Always Received," in *Teaching the New Library to Today's Users*, ed. Trudi Jacobson and Helene Williams, (New York : Neal-Schuman Publishers, 2000), 157-163.

2.   Anita Kay Lowry, "Beyond BI: Information Literacy in the Electronic Age," *Research Strategies* 8, no. 1 (Winter 1990): 24.

3.   Pamela S. Bradigan, Susan M. Kroll and Sally R. Sims, "Graduate Student Bibliographic Instruction at a Large University: A Workshop Approach," *Reference Quarterly* 26, no. 3 (Spring 1987): 336.

4.   Judy Reynolds, "The *MLA International Bibliography* and Library Instruction in Literature and the Humanities," in *Literature in English: A Guide for Librarians in the Digital Age*, ed. Betty Day and William Wortman, 237 (Chicago: Association of College and Research Libraries, 2000).

5.   Reynolds, 237.

6.   Reynolds, 238.

7.   Barbara Fister, "Teaching the Rhetorical Dimensions of Research," *Research Strategies* 11, no.4 (Fall 1993): 214.

8.   Fister, 217.

9.   C. Paul Vincent, "Bibliographic Instruction in the Humanities: the Need to Stress Imagination," *Research Strategies* 2, no. 4 (Fall 1984): 183.

10.   Harrison T. Meserole, "The Nature(s) of Literary Research," *Collection Management* 13, no. 1/2 (1990): 72. He derives these emphases from Joseph Garibaldi's *Introduction to Scholarship in Modern Languages and Literatures*.

11.   Meserole, 69.

Libraries, Librarians, and the Resources of Literary Study

William A. Wortman

"This Will Never Do," Richard Altick's acerbic review in 1979 of Margaret Patterson's *Literary Research Guide*, the *Guide* that now under James L. Harner's authorship has become arguably the single most important professional resource for literature librarians, brought upon me early in my career the realization that librarians should tread carefully in their relations with faculty.[1] What distressed Altick, however, was not the resources Patterson listed but her annotations about their content and uses. Disciplinary faculty's concern with the methods of research, scholarship, criticism, and teaching is deep, lively, and closely guarded. The librarian's primary role, as I conceive it, is to collect and maintain the resources for literary study and research: libraries have the resources, and what librarians know and understand is what these resources are and how they are categorized, organized, and accessed. For me, instruction has to be primarily in terms of resources, and this chapter is an argument for a particular kind of instruction that is in some respects quite traditional yet in its embrace of digital resources quite new. After a brief introduction to define terms and roles, I then discuss several categories of literary resources (with examples of assignments) and report on one model of new digital research. As digital resources become more prevalent and more important in literary study, we all—librarians, disciplinary faculty, students—find ourselves pioneers with new opportunities for meaningful collaboration among us in teaching about and actually practicing literary research. Altick's sharp, negative reaction helped me define my sense of librarians' expertise, but now some thirty years later librarians and disciplinary faculty find themselves in a newly positive and fruitful relationship as together we help students come to understand the resources of literary study.

RESOURCES, METHODS, AND INFORMATION LITERACY: DEFINITIONS

The term "resources" includes virtually everything libraries collect and provide for readers and covers print, digital, microform, manuscript, photographic, aural, and more. Each discipline has its own set of resources, and the disciplinary resources of and for the study of English language literatures include primary resources—the books of poetry, novels, and plays; the literary magazines; the scholarly editions of major works and writers' letters; the major statements of critical approach and theory—and the secondary resources such as critics' specialized monographs and journal articles, teachers' introductory overviews, and scholars' reference sources. Traditionally, resources are created by writers, scholars, and critics and produced by commercial publishers, scholarly associations, periodical editors, or website producers, but increasingly scholarly web-based resources are being built by scholars and librarians working collaboratively.[2] "Methods" refers to what is done with resources, and disciplinary faculty are committed to the methodologies of research and teaching. They publish explicitly methodological books and articles; the Methods of Literary Research division of the Modern Language Association (MLA) holds regular sessions at annual meetings; volumes in the MLA's *Approaches to Teaching* series continue to appear (over one hundred titles as of this writing); articles in *Profession*, the annual from the Association of Departments of English division of the MLA, regularly tackle issues of the curriculum.[3] Although the once-common research methods course in literature seems generally abandoned (or no longer required), faculty are far from abandoning concern for methods and, indeed, there may be a resurgence: in her introduction to *Teaching Bibliography, Textual Criticism, and Book History* (2006), Ann R. Hawkins notes, "Certainly, the teaching of bibliography declined in the years leading to the height of literary theory, but there appears to have been significant renewal of interest in such training."[4]

Librarians, too, are concerned about methods. We work daily with students struggling to make sense of our resources, and much of our liaison, instruction, and reference activities are designed to bring students and resources together effectively. In 2000 the Association of College and Research Libraries (ACRL) out of their concern about "the rapid technological change and proliferating information resources" issued guidelines to deal with the "escalating complexity of this environment." The guidelines emphasize process—"Information literacy is a set of abilities"—and set forth a long list of "performance indicators" and outcomes.[5] Somewhat abstract, these abilities needed to be redefined for different subjects and different kinds of libraries. The Instruction Section of ACRL proceeded in the next year to define "objectives for information literacy" that included a more specific understanding of publication formats, the publication cycle, and effect of different formats may affect usefulness.[6] Over the next few years another section of ACRL, the Literatures in English Section (LES), drafted its own research competency guidelines that made an even more explicit reference to resources: "Although based on [the] framework of the ACRL Information Literacy Competency Standards for Higher Education (2000), these guidelines address the need for a more specific and source-oriented approach within the discipline of English literatures, including a concrete list of research skills."[7] In the first section, titled "Understand the structure of information within the field of literary research," the LES librarians listed seven subheadings, all focused on resources, which I paraphrase:

1. Differentiate between primary and secondary sources.
2. Understand that literary scholarship is produced and disseminated in a variety of formats.
3. Learn the significant features of documents needed for correct citations.
4. Differentiate between reviews and criticism.
5. Understand the concept of peer review.
6. Understand that literary texts exist in a variety of editions.
7. Understand the process of literary production.

The LES statement on research competencies, it seems to me, shifts the emphasis from information literacy to resource literacy, and this emphasis underlies the model of instruction I describe here.

I am not arguing for an opposition between information and resources literacies but for the recognition that in the field of literary studies it is important to understand the nature of the discipline's resources. We as librarians are professionally responsible for resources and have developed a sophisticated knowledge of them. Students, however, are seldom able to distinguish clearly among the various kinds of resources, and certainly Google has only made it harder for them to understand that they are not fishing in a vast, undifferentiated sea of "information." Librarians, therefore, are well positioned to make a real contribution to the development of disciplinary knowledge.

THE RESOURCES OF LITERARY STUDY

The core book about resources is James L. Harner's *Literary Research Guide*, which emphasizes kinds of research sources and organizes them by nation, period, and genre.[8] We should recommend its use in most period and genre courses for undergraduate majors and urge graduate students and our faculty colleagues to buy their own copies, and librarians should use it to develop collections and design their own instruction programs. Harner's book, however, is a bibliography not a manual of methods, and in teaching from and with it we cannot simply go through item by item or section by section: we need a framework or model with which to build an effective instructional program.

Texts and Textuality

There is a fundamental distinction between a work and a text: libraries are full of texts, not works. The simplest search immediately brings up this fact: students ask for a copy of *Leaves of Grass*—or any other title—and the catalog provides them confusion untold, until we convince them that literary works are embodied in specific (usually material) texts, and it is these texts that we have in the library and that they must choose from. The nature of texts—their textuality—encompasses several related features. Texts of a work often vary; many literary works exist in more than one version, the different versions sometimes resulting from printer's error, publisher's house style, or editor's meddling, but often resulting from their authors' evolving intentions and artistic abilities. Texts are almost always physical; they exist as published items in periodicals and in a variety of book formats, and this physicality combined with the paratexts of dedications, introductions, annotations, design, and other features provided by author and/or publisher, may affect how they are read. There are different kinds of texts—original editions (periodicals, first book) followed by so-called cheap editions (such as paperbacks) and then by collected editions and finally by student and then scholarly editions—and these come typically in the sequence just described. Texts have a social as well as literary context; that is, they appear in the world of print at a particular time and place and inevitably gain or lose through comparison with other contemporaneously published books or earlier books that may be seen to have influenced or pre-figured them. Critical interest today seems to have shifted from the best text and scholarly edition to the material text and the cultural presence of literary texts, from text to textuality.

I have used three examples to help students recognize and understand these different aspects of textuality. The first is Robert Frost's "Stopping by Woods on a Snowy Evening," which exists in at least four meaningfully different versions starting with its first appearance in *The New Republic*, through his books *New Hampshire* and *Complete Poems*, to the posthumous, edited *Poetry*, and including a long presence in numerous anthologies.[9] We see in this example both textual variety and a typical sequence of publication for a now canonical work (and perhaps America's most famous poem). Students can spend a few minutes arguing about the interpretive effects of these different texts and be brought to understand both the value of close reading and the instability of texts. Then we can turn to our scholarly resources—to the catalog for a record of Frost's publications in our own and other libraries and of relevant bibliographies, handbooks, and textual studies; to indexes to periodicals and poetry anthologies; to critical books, articles, and other secondary resources that point back to primary resources.

Another example uses T. S. Eliot's *The Waste Land*, Virginia Woolf's *Mrs. Dalloway*, and Jean Toomer's *Cane*. This time, instead of examining the texts closely, students read standard reference resources about the history of composition, publication, and reception.[10] The various *Oxford Companions* and the *Cambridge Guide to Literature in English* provide good articles about these works.[11] That all—Eliot, Toomer, and Woolf, as well as Frost—published almost simultaneously in the high modernist period (1923-25) makes these examples also work well in examining authorship and contexts.

As a third example of textual history, we can hand out recent books of poetry to students and then examine the copyright and acknowledgement pages. Nearly every contemporary book of poems reveals the process and the system of literary publication. The poet's acknowledgements page thanks editors of magazines, anthologies, and prize contests for accepting and publishing most of the poems included in the volume in hand, and frequently mentions that some of them have been revised: so we see the process or sequence of publication and, often, of revision. Typically the poet is employed as a creative writing teacher, has received grants, residencies, or reduced loads, and had opportunities for readings and sharing with colleagues: so we see a system that supports writing and publishing poetry. Frequently the publisher too acknowledges grants and gifts that support publication, and the copyright page further reveals this process and system through its CIP, copyright notice, edition statement, and designer and printer credits.

The resources of textuality are primarily the texts in their many versions, formats, and editions. The library collection needs a representation of the textual history of a works and not only the latest or the earliest or the "best." The different genres and different eras of literary production each have their own characteristics, such as a text of a play that records performance information; a Victorian novel in its parts, its three-volume, and its cheap formats; a twentieth-century poem as it appeared in a little magazine and then in book volumes. Textual resources also include the standard bibliographical and indexing resources. The catalog, the consortial catalog, and WorldCat can yield a multitude of texts of a work, as might online bookstores and indexes to out-of-print titles such as Amazon.com or abebooks.com. Author bibliographies, trade and national bibliographies, literature bibliographies such as the *Bibliography of American Literature* and the *Cambridge Bibliography of English Literature*, more focused indexes such as *Play Index* or *Columbia Granger's Index to Poetry*, and also indexes to periodicals—current indexes such as *Academic Search Premier*, retrospective indexes such as Wilson's *Readers' Guide Retrospective* and the digitized editions of Poole's *Index to Nineteenth-Century Periodicals* (*19th Century Masterfile* and *19th Century Index*).[12]

Textuality is really the essence of literature, but, unfortunately, there are virtually no standard sources that compile textual information, in contrast to the many dictionaries of terms and author biographies and collections of plot summaries. Scholarly publication on textual analysis is spotty; the evidence in scholarly and variorum editions dense, intimidating, and very expensive. Nevertheless most students, undergraduate no less than graduate, can perform serious (and often original) scholarly work in identifying different texts of a work. Graduate students must engage textuality and not be allowed to accept a text of a work as the work itself. We see here the central appeal of literature—texts in their beauty and their variety and readers' elemental need to puzzle out, record, and examine, as well as read and re-read texts.

Authors, Publishing, and Authorship

Texts are written by authors and produced by publishers. Many authors create a body of work, and readers are as interested in the totality as in the individual texts—and, often, as interested in the person as the work. Lay readers find authors deeply interesting and important cultural figures and have made pilgrimages variously to Walden Pond, the Brontës' parsonage, the City Lights Book Store, but literature students—disciplinary readers—must examine the overall achievement and the specific moments of active composition. Literary study investigates four elements of authorship:

the author's life, achievement, reputation, and the process of creation and publication. The resources of authorship include both the primary materials such as letters and diaries that scholars use and the secondary biographies and biographical reference sources these scholars produce.

For students, a key resource is what I call the "critical introduction," that is, articles in the *Dictionary of Literary Biography* (DLB), the Scribner British and United States Writers sets, and the Wilson Author Series, and the longer treatments in the now-ceased Twayne series on American, British, and World writers.[13] A critical introduction provides details about the author's life, description of the author's central themes, style, and intentions, and an assessment of the author's achievement, current reputation, offers discussion of some individual works, and cites additional sources for further reading, all from the perspective of current critical thinking. One could ask students to read the DLB articles on, for example, contemporary playwrights Arthur Miller, Harold Pinter, and Caryl Churchill and be confident they now had in hand sound and fairly comprehensive critical as well as biographical information. Shorter articles such as in the *Merriam-Webster Encyclopedia of Literature* or *Wikipedia* are usually accurate and informative, but necessarily limited in usefulness.[14] If a student has merely to gain simple recognition of a writer, then these latter two are quite adequate, but if a student, say, has to make a twenty minute class presentation, the more ambitious critical introductions must be used, at the least.

Although some complain about the *Dictionary of Literary Biography's* practice of offering multiple articles in multiple volumes on many individual authors—for example, Virginia Woolf as novelist, short story writer, and essayist treated in as many different volumes—I think we can also acknowledge the value of multiple perspectives and multiple authoritative voices, especially with writers with multiple strengths. Virginia Woolf also provides an example of another well-known phenomena, that of changing reputations. The *Oxford Companion to English Literature* in its 3rd and 4th editions, 1946 and 1967, offered one short paragraph about Woolf, but twenty years later in the 5th edition, 1985, a new editor in a new era gave her a full, dense page. Changed reputation and status are not limited to the writer's work and achievement but also apply to biography. What the lay reader sees as a significant culture figure, literary students might see as an oppositional figure standing in political and ideological defiance, as a disruptive figure appealing to ludic readers and queer theorists, perhaps an outsider pushed by race, gender, or sexuality or driven by inner psychological forces to the culture's margins.

The nature of biographical scholarship itself is of interest, and when we see the full range of biographical studies on a significant author we realize how thin a term "biography" is. The many kinds of biographies serve various specific investigations and interests—the exhaustive account of a life, the critical analysis of the writing in terms of the life, the experience and influence of youth, the effects of education and reading, the family crucible, the many literary relationships, the various sociological and psychological explorations of race, class, gender, and identity. Melville, for example, has attracted biographers interested in his South Seas adventures, his youth and education, his experiences as a whaler, his psychology, his sexual identity, his relations with his wife and family, the creative dynamics of his writing, and the deep relationship between his life and his work, the daily log as well as the whole trajectory of his life.

Biographies are built on biographical resources that not only support the published biographies but also repay continuing examination and re-examination. Authors' letters, diaries and journals, memoirs and autobiographical writings, the memoirs and memorials of acquaintances, interviews, comment on other writers and works, occasional writing on topics of the day, the kind of public engagement common when the writer is actively reviewing rival books, interviewing, writing op-ed pieces or travel articles. Of these biographical resources, letters often provide the most valuable information because of their range of topics. They can reveal the full range of the writer's acquaintance, let the writer's unbuttoned voice speak, reveal insights into a writer's motivation or hopes or fears. Some let us virtually "hear" the writer live before us, Keats or Clemens or James or Dickinson. No biographer takes letters or public statements at face value, of course, but every biographer depends on the detailed information in them. Thus, a central scholarly project has long been the production of annotated editions of writers' correspondence; these resources can be analyzed for many different purposes and there is plenty of biographical sleuthing to be done in them that undergraduates as well as graduate students can handle.

Just as textuality inevitably involves the publishers of texts, so too the concept of authorship takes us beyond the individual writer to the process through which writers and others collaborate to bring their work to completion and publication. Its author developed it through rough notes, preliminary drafts, early versions in magazines or original anthologies, and initial book publication, while continuing to review and revise through subsequent publication, often with the advice of friends, teachers, and editors. Publishers take a manuscript and produce its physical presentation. Their choice of format, production values, packaging of the text, and marketing give us the material books and magazines we know, with their book jacket photos, blurbs, and design. Even before Roland Barthes' and Michel Foucault's postmodern conceptualization of the author-role as a construct in (or of) literary culture, it was acknowledged that authors worked collaboratively (if not always willingly) with multiple agents, among whom were actors in the theater, licensers in the court, editors at magazines, publishers and their sense (or fear) of buying public's sensibilities, in the process of embodying their work in a material text.[15] Like authors, publishers too can create a body of work. Jacob Tonson in eighteenth-century England, Ticknor and Fields in nineteenth-century United States, and City Lights in the latter half of the twentieth century were responsible for identifying, selecting, publishing, and maintaining in print a recognizably coherent set of writers and their texts. Authorship is a complex phenomenon.

Criticism and Theory

Ironically for my argument here, probably the most common request from faculty is to teach students the use of the *MLA International Bibliography* (*MLAIB*); this is certainly a methods- and skill-centered session and one in which several issues of information literacy can be addressed.[16] Nevertheless, I start by identifying the kinds of sources the *MLAIB* cites—books, chapters, articles, and dissertations. The next steps depend upon the time available, and they include locating these sources in the library or using library services that supply them, using the catalog (the library's and our consortium's) to find books and book chapters not always listed in the *MLAIB*, using the catalog to find specialized resources such as author bibliographies, encyclopedias, handbooks, and textual studies, and finding—and of course augmenting the *MLAIB* and the catalog with more specialized indexes to current periodicals or to, say, film studies or religion sources.

Simply listing and defining the kinds of resources is a sure soporific, so I ask students to all do a quick search in the *MLAIB* for citations about a literary work. First, we all do the same one and then go through identifying books, book chapters, articles in scholarly journals, and dissertations. Having done this search ahead myself, I will have brought in copies of the actual books and journals (if we have them in print) and can also talk (briefly at this point) about locations and access. Next, the students can do searches of their own and identify each of these four kinds of sources. Everyone is confused by the overlapping formats we provide now—print journals, electronic journals, online articles linked from indexing services, microfilm collections of back runs, not to mention the plethora of acronyms and products in JSTOR, ProjectMUSE, EBSCO, Ingenta, and local and consortial products. And since students (faculty too) are likely already to have used Google, we should push them along to Google Scholar and then have them compare results from that search with the sources mentioned here. Resource and access are linked. As students at their workstations move seamlessly from catalog to index to online article to their word-processed papers, the borders that used to define resources so clearly disappear. My emphasis, again, tries to be on the kinds of resources students will need and likely find more than on the tools used to find them.

Criticism and the *MLA International Bibliography* are not synonymous: working effectively with literary criticism must be distinguished (although not separated) from searching effectively with the *MLAIB*. There are alternatives and supplements to it. Students are at several different levels in age and experience and also in commitment to literary study. For lower-level undergraduates we might better use the resources that are part of the general arsenal of library resources we try to introduce early on, chiefly our online catalogs and general periodical indexes. As a student's first efforts with the *MLAIB* and the catalog are likely to turn up only the most special-ized and critically sophisticated kinds of courses, it is also important to try to help them find reasonably authoritative overview and introductory treat-ments, such as Cliffs Notes and Twayne-type books.[17] In many situations we might just a well start with literary databases, namely Gale's *Literature Resource Center*, EBSCO's *Literary Reference Center*, or ProQuest's *Litera-ture Online* (LION), that offer very selective sets of online critical articles along with basic and introductory articles from online reference sources.[18] At the upper end of the student spectrum (majors and graduate students) the *MLAIB* must be supplemented with more specialized genre, period, author, and subject serial bibliographies. Faculty often suggest their own personal techniques, the best one being to follow up the bibliographies in articles that have proved useful.

At a more advanced levels we can distinguish explication of textual details from theory that asserts the meaning or significance of a text, and we can expect that students be able to recognize the approaches and assumptions in critical writing. The resources of theory are quite extensive, and this makes all the more useful the various dictionaries, introductions, and synthesizing treatments. Theory is a constantly shifting scene as well, so we can point out the progression from basic dictionaries, such as the *Oxford Reference Online* database, through the encyclopedic Johns Hopkins Guide to Literary Theory and Criticism, to the annual survey and evaluation in *Year's Work in Critical and Cultural Theory*, and ultimately to the catalog of monographs and treatises.[19] At all levels, however, I emphasize the idea that there is a "critical conversation" in which participants are essentially provisional (no matter how dogmatically and confidently expressed) and in which "correct" is not a universally applicable term. The critical conversation assumes participation, assumes response and referral, demands citation, and forgoes simple assent or approval; it assumes students are participating in order to further their own understanding. We can talk about peer reviewing; suggest that reprinting and excerpting indicate acceptance and approval or that conference papers present the cutting edge of the field; and help students discover specialized journals for authors, genres, periods, or topics. If a big hurdle for younger students is to understand that scholarly writing about literature is not simply a matter of various persons' opinions, an equal challenge for advanced students is to understand theory as provisional and open to revision rather being a rigid template to apply to literary issues.

Contexts and Cognates

Literature is written, published, and read in specific contexts, and students of literature must "read" the contexts as carefully as the texts. Authors write within the traditions of literature, whether national or genre or group and movement, but they also write in the language of people, not just the language of literature. Every text embodies its author's style and themes but also is an example of literary genre and rhetoric. Authors also live in, and their works are set in, specific times and places. Publishers choose not only what to publish but how their choices are to be presented, and every published text inevitably becomes part of the commercial marketplace where its value is assessed relative to similar texts—and where publishers jockey to present their texts effectively, in commercial terms. We who read and who study writing likewise live and work in our own contexts and come at literature aware of cognate fields and their interests. Thorough study of any context would require thorough immersion in that subject, so my purpose in this unit is not to produce lexicographers, historians, or sociologists but rather to suggest a few ways serious students can explore the wider contexts of any writing and reading by making use of core resources in these fields.

One exercise I have used successfully with graduate students is to take in to class a cart of reference books—subject bibliographies, chronologies, dictionaries, directories, encyclopedias, handbooks, manuals, and year-books—and after a very brief explanation of each, work through a set of questions in class involving definitions, explanations, dates and locations, and citations. In half an hour we can cover a good deal of reference ground, and the exercise can then be followed up with independent work as above and also with some examples of online versions of these kinds of reference sources. A variation on this is to work with only with a small set of literary reference books and ask students to find brief definitions of, for example, Georgian poets, synecdoche, naturalism, aporia, *Bildungsroman*, or any of hundreds of other terms for genres, periods, movements, groups, and theoretical concerns that are defined in *Cambridge Guide to Literature in English*, the *Johns Hopkins Guide to Literary Theory and Criticism*, and *Oxford Reference Online*. Students gain familiarity with important disciplinary resources, some understanding of the structure of information resources, and the realization that readers are quickly taken beyond an author's words.

Literature obviously relies on language, and authors work with the language given them. The *Oxford English Dictionary* (*OED*) is important to literary study because it helps reveal the ways language has been used.[20] I ask students to read the entries for "stage," for example, and then consider the ways theater has entered our language, when it has done so, what sources are cited, and where the evidence has been published. Here we see language in its social context. To see more strictly lexicographic issues (if appropriate), I have students compare excerpts from introductions to different dictionaries on prescription, description, and authority, and then compare three or four contemporary dictionaries on their definition, pronunciation, and etymology of a word such as "battery" that has a long history, many definitions, a variety of literary and metaphorical uses in many different fields, and multiple pronunciations.

To help students understand that cognate fields have their own au-thorities, depth, and perspectives I use a series of short exercises. I have had them read the *Dictionary of the Middle Ages* to learn about the dance of death, the plague, the typical lives of women and children, and the social role of pilgrimages in medieval cultures. Similar in-depth resources exist for other places and time periods. Conversely, to see that different fields provide different perspectives, I ask students to read entries on blood or death in standard dictionaries and encyclopedias of folklore, religion, and philosophy. Finally, to reinforce the importance of disciplinary indexing databases, I have students look for articles discussing drama in education (*ERIC*), modernism as discussed by historians (*Historical Abstracts*), or copyright and publishing in law reviews and business magazines or journals.[21] These small assignments introduce students to both a set of resources and different ways of thinking about issues they encounter in literature.

Literature resides within the context of print culture, and book history is the broad discipline that studies publishing (not just literary publishing), copyright and intellectual property, popular culture, and the history of genres and formats. Interest and activity in this growing academic field has been stimulated by culture studies in general and studies of popular and material cultures specifically, along with a widespread sense of the "constructedness" of so many of our attitudes and values. The primary model in book history—the "communications circuit" (in Robert Darnton's well-known characterization) involving people and the process of authorship, printing, publishing, bookselling, and reading all within social and political conditions such as copyright, censorship, popular tastes, literacy and education, rival media, and more—has obviously influenced the model of instruction I am presenting here.[22] Our libraries contain the resources of book history, and it is fairly easy to gather those relevant to literary study. The *Cambridge History of English Literature* in its original and new second edition includes excellent chapters on publishing, authorship, and reading and reception. Studies listed in catalog author-subject subheadings "authorship" and "textual studies" are useful, as are the textual history sections of scholarly editions. The book history field itself now has basic textbooks and readers.[23] Although literature is identified with print, any study of contemporary literature and book history must include the digital and telecommunications cultures.

Web Resources

Although electronic resources are an integral part of these various categories, we should also treat them as a separate, new kind of resource. Doing so focuses students' attention on the fact that there are many different kinds of web resources, some of them replicating print resources such the

Oxford Online Reference collection of many of its valuable reference books; others offering improved versions of print, such as the *MLA International Bibliography* in its various online versions; some are teaching sites that faculty have created to support courses; others compare with scholarly monographs or standalone reference books such as James Harner's web supplement to his *Literary Research Guide*. Still others are entirely new, for example, gateway sites and thematic research collections.

Gateway sites are in one sense a catalog of sites, although they do not take on the responsibilities of a library catalog to offer authoritative classification and description nor full-fledged indexing. Instead, to quote from the *Voice of the Shuttle*'s introduction, they "... may be said to be about 'the ordering of things'—the ceaseless reconfiguration of humanities knowledge assisted by the new technologies of dynamic information." They list web resources in convenient but flexible categories, provide direct links to these listed sites, let users browse and also do advanced searches. Three well-known web gateways for literature are *Intute: Arts and Humanities* (formerly Humbul Humanities Hub), which covers the arts and humanities but includes only selected links; *Literary Resources on the Net*, which focuses on English and American literature; and *Voice of the Shuttle*, the most comprehensive of these three.[24]

Thematic research collections bring together a range of digital scholarly resources that, like a good library, provide resources and stimulate new thinking. As Carole Palmer describes them, thematic research collections such as *The Walt Whitman Archive, The William Blake Archive, and The Rossetti Archive* focus attention on an author or work, select carefully from among available websites, and primarily serve scholars.[25] Each contains primary resources, secondary books and articles, indexing and reference resources. Most combine texts and images, and in doing this emphasize physical objects (manuscripts, books and periodicals, buildings, sculptures, etc.) as well as intellectual content. Most are explicitly interdisciplinary and encourage scholars with interests in art, music, history and culture, as well as those more focused on literary matters. Although primarily created for scholars, they can be used effectively by undergraduates and graduate students and can be very useful in teaching. They are open to the addition of other related digital resources produced by scholars or perhaps drawn from collections of other libraries.

As an assignment, we could have students create a web resource of their own, such as a hypothetical site devoted to a single poem, Robert Frost's

"Stopping by Woods on a Snowy Evening." It could include text(s) of the poem and the history of their publication and the textual details requiring or deserving annotation; authorship, including manuscripts, Frost's comments about the poem's creation, and editors' actions in publishing it; reception, including how reception is defined and assessed. It consolidates what students learned in earlier segments, that every literary work has its textual and authorial history and is situated in a context of language, other literature, and social, political, and cultural events and currents. This digital project, then, asks them to think about textuality, authorship, criticism, and contexts and to gather and present resources that will make their web site an exemplary—and potentially public—literary resource.

Something similar is emerging at a number of institutions where students are launched into serious digital scholarship with major implications for expanding the teaching of literary research. One particularly successful example is the University of Nebraska-Lincoln's Center for Digital Research in the Humanities (CDRH, http://cdrh.unl.edu/), established in 1998, a primary site for *The Walt Whitman Archive* (http://www.whitmanarchive.org/) and *The Willa Cather Archive* (http://cather.unl.edu/), home to projects arising from nine departments, with over 100 students involved to date in digital scholarly projects, and, not incidentally, co-directed by two faculty, one from the University library and one from the English department.[26] Some of its work has been described in a series of interviews with those involved that emphasizes the Center's primary emphasis on research and teaching, the ways students are involved, the necessity and benefits of collaboration, and renewal and extension of literary and humanities scholarship.

An emphasis on research has been the impetus for engaging faculty as well as students in significant digital scholarship. Co-Director Katherine Walter (Chair of Digital Initiatives and Special Collections, University Libraries) distinguishes the CDRH from other humanities digital projects: "At many schools, E-Text centers were geared toward mass digitization of library collections without regard to a scholarly perspective … From the beginning, we focused on the scholar and the scholar's desire to work in a digital medium on their own humanities research."[27] Students are welcomed and they become involved. Andrew Jewell, Assistant Professor of Digital Projects, UNL Libraries, and Editor, *The Willa Cather Archive*, describes his own initiation into digital scholarship: "I got started working on the Whitman Archive, and right away … despite my student status, I was invited to debate with [CDRH Co-Director] Ken Price about project decisions."[28] Later as faculty, he noticed that "students get very invested in these projects, which is a phenomenon that seems distinctive to students doing digital work in the humanities ... This process invites real, active contributions by students. They get to see their work published online." This intellectual involvement comes from both collaboration and "the practical experience and skill-building that one obtains through work on an actual digital project." Students are pushed to understand why as well as how:

> Though sophisticated knowledge of the content area and the ability to be thoughtful about the theoretical implications of digital work [are], of course, crucial, if one does not have the practical skills to make the actual files, he or she is at a major disadvantage. Therefore, the teaching experiences I provide students always involve training on particular skills (text encoding, image scanning, etc.) combined with a discussion about the reasons why certain standards are adhered to, what motivates those standards, etc. In other words, rather than separate the theoretical and the practical, I try to unite them, to talk with students about the theory of text underlying the Text Encoding Initiative, for example, or about digital preservation in combination with high-resolution scanning.[29]

Collaboration between students and faculty and among faculty in digital humanities is central, as English professor Stephen Ramsay explains, echoing Jewell:

> The humanities fetishize the concept of the lone scholar in the attic ... But when you drop a computer in the room, how could you possibly know everything there is to know about what it takes to create the Whitman Archive, for example. We all need each other, so there is real mentoring going on, real collaboration. As professors, we would like to draw our students into our research, but historically it hasn't always been possible. There has always been something slightly strained about that relationship; tracking down journal articles is not collaborative. But now, with computing, it's different.[30]

Besides bringing students into dynamic relationship with faculty, collaboration also produces new kinds of questions as well, and new ways to present findings. Ramsay, a participant in the MONK [Metadata Offer New Knowledge] Project emphasizes that the time is right to analyze digitally the great online literary resources and that to do so requires specialized computer programs:

> Computer programs such as these don't just build themselves. The first generation of digital humanities work was about getting text online and was, ultimately, a data entry project ... Endeavors like the MONK Project demand computer programming skills in addition to knowledge of literature and the humanities. This new generation of research also utilizes high performance computing.[31]

CDRH Co-Director Ken Price (University Professor and Hillegass Chair of Nineteenth Century American Literature), speaking about a major project on Washington, D.C., in the Civil War era, observes that "We're just at this point pursuing where the questions lead ... We have broken down traditional ways of pursuing research, in that it's no longer solitary, no longer necessarily leading to an article or a book. It's pulling together a big team and exploring big research questions."[32]

CONCLUSION: LIBRARIES, LIBRARIANS, RESOURCES

Students and faculty engaged in digital humanities scholarship draw on all of the literary research skills involving texts and textuality, authors and authorship, criticism and theory, contexts and cognates, and book history, as well as learning new computer skills as they transform and expand literary research—and the methods for teaching it—into the digital future. Students of literature need more than ever to know about textuality, authorship, critical application of theory, and contexts; they gain immediate information from using the resources and they use resources they will inevitably return to. These resources are the literature of the field and we can help students learn of them, make effective use of them, and understand their place in the field they have chosen to study. Their professors are creating these resources, and this work of scholarship, no less than that of criticism, is at the heart of the literary discipline. We librarians are well positioned to teach these resources, to teach what we know best. This model allows us to integrate all aspects of our work in reference, liaison, instruction, and collection development; it pushes us to keep abreast of our collections and, complementarily, to keep faculty informed of new resources that they can use in their research and in their teaching. The library, librarians, and resources, then, remain at the heart of education in literature.

NOTES

1.   Richard D. Altick, "This Will Never Do," *Review* 1 (1979): 47-60; Margaret C. Patterson, *Literary Research Guide* (Detroit: Gale, 1976); and James L. Harner, *Literary Research Guide*, 5th ed. (New York: MLA, 2008). Prof. Altick, we remember, had published several significant volumes of research, most notably, *The English Common Reader: A Social History of the Mass Reading Public, 1800-1900*, 2nd ed. (Columbus: Ohio State Univ. Pr., 1998), and three widely used volumes on research resources and methods, *The Scholar Adventurers* (New York: Macmillan, 1950), *The Art of Literary Research*, with John J. Fenstermaker, 4th ed. (New York: Norton, 1993), and *Selective Bibliography for the Study of English and American Literature*, with Andrew H. Wright, 6th ed. (New York: Macmillan, 1979).

2.   Examples of such collaborative efforts include the Center for Digital Research in the Humanities at the University of Nebraska-Lincoln http://cdrh.unl.edu/ and Institute for Advanced Technologies in the Humanities at the University of Virginia http://www.iath.virginia.edu/.

3.   See for example *Approaches to Teaching English Renaissance Drama*, ed. Karen Bamford and Alexander Leggatt (New York: MLA, 2002); David Leon Higdon, "Ancient Madness or Contemporary Wisdom? A New Literary Research Methods Course," *Profession* (2002): 140-50.

4.   Ann R. Hawkins, "Introduction: Toward a Pedagogy of Bibliography," in *Teaching Bibliography, Textual Criticism, and Book History*, ed. Ann R. Hawkins, 8 (London: Pickering and Chatto, 2006).

5.   ACRL, Standards Committee, "Information Literacy Competency Standards for Higher Education," 2000, http://www.ala.org/ala/mgrps/divs/acrl/standards/informationliteracycompetency.cfm (accessed August 28, 2006).

6.   ACRL, Instruction Section, "Objectives for Information Literacy Instruction: A Model Statement for Academic Librarians," 2001, http://www.ala.org/ala/mgrps/divs/acrl/standards/objectivesinformation.cfm (accessed August 28, 2006).

7.   ACRL, Literatures in English Section, Ad hoc Committee on Literary Research Competencies, "Research Competency Guidelines for Literatures in English," June 2007, http://www.ala.org/ala/mgrps/divs/acrl/standards/researchcompetenciesles.cfm (accessed July 7, 2008).

8.   James L. Harner, *Literary Research Guide*, 5th ed. (New York: MLA, 2008).

9.   David Mesher, "Stopping by Woods," in *The Robert Frost Encyclopedia*, ed. Nancy Lewis Tuten and John Zubizarreta, 347-50 (Westport, Conn.: Greenwood, 2001); George Monteiro, "To Point or Not to Point: Frost's 'Stopping by Woods,'" *ANQ* 16, no.1 (2003): 38-40; and Donald Hall, "Robert Frost Corrupted," *Atlantic* (March 1982): 60-64.

10.   T. S. Eliot, *The Waste Land* (Richmond, Eng.: Hogarth, 1923); Virginia Woolf, *Mrs. Dalloway* (London: Hogarth, 1925); Jean Toomer, *Cane* (New York: Boni and Liveright, 1923).

11.   *Oxford Companion to English Literature*, 6th ed., ed. Margaret Drabble (New York: Oxford Univ. Pr., 2000); *Oxford Companion to African American Literature*, ed. William L.

Andrews, Frances Smith Foster, and Trudier Harris (New York: Oxford Univ. Pr., 1997); *Oxford Companion to Twentieth-Century Poetry in English*, ed. Ian Hamilton (Oxford: Oxford Univ. Pr., 1994); and *Cambridge Guide to Literature in English*, revised ed., ed. Ian Ousby (Cambridge: Cambridge Univ. Pr., 1993). The Oxford titles are available online in Oxford Reference Online Premium, http://www.oxfordreference.com.

12.   *Bibliography of American Literature*, comp. Jacob Blanck and Michael Winship (New Haven, Conn.: Yale Univ. Pr., 1955-91, available online, http://collections.chadwyck.com/bal); *Cambridge Bibliography of English Literature*, 3rd ed. (Cambridge: Cambridge Univ. Pr., 1999- ; 2nd ed. as *New Cambridge Bibliography of English Literature*, 1969-77); *19th Century Masterfile* (Reston, Va.: Paratext, available online, http://poolesplus.odyssi.com); *19th Century Index* (Ann Arbor, Mich.: Pro-Quest, available online, http:c19index.chadwyck.com); *Play Index* (New York: H. W. Wilson, 1949- , available online, http:www.hwwilson.com/play.htm); and *Columbia Granger's World of Poetry* (New York: Columbia Univ. Pr., available online, http:www.columbiagrangers.org/grangers).

13.   *Dictionary of Literary Biography* (Detroit: Gale, 1978-); *American Writers* and *British Writers* (New York: Scribners, 1974-); Twayne's United States Authors Series, Twayne's English Authors Series, and Twayne's World Authors Series (Boston or New York: Twayne, 1961-2002). All are available online as part of *Literature Resource Center* (Farmington Hills, Mich.: Thomson Gale, http://galenet.galegroup.com).

14.   *Merriam-Webster Encyclopedia of Literature* (Springfield, Mass.: Merriam-Webster, 1998, available online in *Literature Resource Center* and *Literary Reference Center*) and *Wikipedia* (St. Petersburg, Fla.: Wikimedia Foundation, http://en.wikipedia.org/).

15.   Roland Barthes, "The Death of the Author," in *Image Music Text*, trans. Stephen Heath, 142-48 (New York: Hill and Wang, 1977); Michel Foucault, "What Is an Author?" in *Language, Counter-Memory, Practice: Selected Essays and Interviews*, trans. Donald F. Bouchard, 113-38 (Ithaca, N.Y.: Cornell Univ. Pr., 1971); and Jack Stillinger, *Multiple Authorship and the Myth of Solitary Genius* (New York: Oxford Univ. Press, 1991).

16.   *MLA International Bibliography of Books and Articles on the Modern Languages and Literatures* (New York: MLA, 1922- ; available online from several vendors).

17.   From the 1960s through the 1990s Twayne published several series of introductory treatments of authors and individual works, including Twayne's English Authors, Masterworks, Studies in Short Fiction, United States Authors, and World Authors (New York and Boston: Twayne, 1961-2000). Cliffs Notes is one of several series of study guides that offer plot summaries and discussion, and study questions on literary works and other topics (New York: John Wiley, 1958- ; available online http:www.cliffsnotes.com). Currently Chelsea House publishes several similar series including Bloom's Modern Critical Interpretations (on works) and Bloom's Modern Critical Views (on writers) (New York: Chelsea House, 1996- , many available online in EBSCO's *Literary Reference Center*, see next citation).

18.   *Literature Resource Center*, http://galenet.galegroup.com/servlet/LitRC?;*Literary Reference Center*, http://web.ebscohost.com/lrc/; and *Literature Online*. http://lion.chadwyck.com/.

19.   *Johns Hopkins Guide to Literary Theory and Criticism*, 2nd ed. (Baltimore: Johns Hopkins Univ. Pr., 2005, available online, http://litguide.press.jhu.edu/) and *Year's Work in Critical and Cultural Theory* (Oxford: Oxford Univ. Pr., 1994- , available online, http://ywcct.oxfordjournals.org/).

20.   *Oxford English Dictionary*, 2nd ed. (Oxford: Oxford Univ. Pr., 1989; available online, http://dictionary.oed.com).

21.   *Dictionary of the Middle Ages*, 13 vols., ed. Joseph R. Strayer (New York: Scribner, 1982-89); *ERIC* (Washington, D.C.: ERIC, 1966- ; available online from several vendors); *Historical*

Abstracts (Santa Barbara, Calif.: ABC-CLIO, available online, http://www.abc-clio.com).

22.   Robert Darnton, "What Is the History of Books?" *Daedalus* 111, no. 3 (1982): 65-82, and frequently reprinted, as in Robert Darnton, *The Kiss of Lamourette: Reflections in Cultural History* (New York: Norton, 1990), 107-37.

23.   *Cambridge History of English Literature*, ed. A. W. Ward and A. R. Waller (Cambridge: Cambridge Univ. Pr., 1917-27; available online, http:www.bartleby.com/cambridge) and *New Cambridge History of English Literature* (Cambridge, Eng.: Cambridge Univ. Press, 2002-). See David Finkelstein, *Introduction to Book History* (London: Routledge, 2005); *The Book History Reader*, ed. David Finkelstein and Alistair McCleery (2nd ed., London: Routledge, 2006); *Teaching Bibliography, Textual Criticism, and Book History*, ed. Ann R. Hawkins (London: Pickering and Chatto, 2006); *The Press of Ideas: Readings for Writers on Print Culture and the Information Age*, ed. Julie Bates Dock (Boston: Bedford Books of St. Martin's, 1996); and S. H. Steinberg, *Five Hundred Years of Printing*, 4th ed., rev. John Trevitt (New Castle, Del.: Oak Knoll, 1996).

24.   Intute: Arts and Humanities, 2006, http://www.intute.ac.uk/artsandhumanities/ (accessed August 30, 2006); Literary Resources on the Net, ed. Jack Lynch, 2006, http://andromeda.rutgers.edu/%7Ejlynch/Lit/ (accessed August 30, 2006); and Voice of the Shuttle, ed. Alan Liu and others, http://vos.ucsb.edu/ (accessed August 30, 2006).

25.   Carole L Palmer, "Thematic Research Collections," in *A Companion to Digital Humanities*, ed. Susan Schreibman, Ray Siemans, and John Unsworth, 348-65 (Oxford: Blackwell, 2004). Representative thematic research collections are The Walt Whitman Archive, ed. Ed Folsom and Kenneth M. Price, 2003- , http://www.whitmanarchive.org (accessed August 30, 2006); Uncle Tom's Cabin and American Culture: A Multi-Media Archive, ed. Stephen Railton, 2004, http://www.iath.virginia.edu/utc (accessed August 30, 2006); The William Blake Archive, ed. Morris Eaves, Robert Essick, and Joseph Viscomi, 2005, http://www.blakearchive.org/blake/ (accessed August 28, 2006); and The Rossetti Archive: The Complete Writings and Pictures of Dante Gabriel Rossetti, ed., Jerome McGann, 2006, http://www.rossettiarchive.org/ (accessed August 28, 2006).

26.   Sara Gilliam, "Future Bright for Digital Humanities Projects," Digital Research in the Humanities | Final in a four part series, *Scarlet*, May 8, 2008, paragraphs 4 and 5. http://www.unl.edu/scarlet/ (accessed July 7, 2008).

27.   Ibid., paragraph 6 (accessed July 7, 2008).

28.   Sara Gilliam, "Cather Archive Takes Nebraska Author Global," Digital Research in the Humanities | First in a four part series, *Scarlet*, April 17, 2008 paragraphs 14 and 16 (accessed July 7, 2008).

29.   Andrew Jewell, Assistant Professor of Digital Scholarship, University Libraries, Center for Digital Research in the Humanities, University of Nebraska-Lincoln, from unpublished Annual Review documentation, February 2008.

30.   Sara Gilliam, "MONK Project Expands Text Analysis Online Literature Archives," Digital Research in the Humanities | Second in a four part series, *Scarlet*, April 24, 2008, paragraph 12. http://www.unl.edu/scarlet/ (accessed July 7, 2008).

31.   Ibid., paragraph 7 (accessed July 7, 2008).

32.   "Future Bright for Digital Humanities Projects," paragraph 17 (accessed July 7, 2008).

Librarians Influencing the Literature Core Curriculum

Sheril J. Hook and Verónica Reyes-Escudero

INTRODUCTION

This chapter describes our efforts to integrate information literacy (IL) into the curriculum for English majors at The University of Arizona. Incorporating information literacy into the curriculum in a scalable manner is a high priority for The University of Arizona Libraries. We illustrate here our approach to this priority and the challenges we continued to face in ensuring that all English majors were achieving the departmentally-stated student learning outcomes around IL.

It is no longer the sole responsibility of faculty to measure what and how students are learning. The American Association for Higher Education's *Principles of Good Practice for Assessing Student Learning* recognizes that "...assessment is not a task for a small group of experts but a collaborative activity; its aim is wider, better informed attention to student learning by all parties with a stake in its improvement."[1] As more entities on university campuses become responsible for some portion of student learning, each must collaborate with the others to determine relevant learning objectives and measurable learning outcomes for students during four years of undergraduate education. These outcomes and objectives should produce life-long learners, benefiting the students long after graduation. As Farber and others (e.g., Winner, Leckie,) have said, librarians must be active participants in the teaching and learning processes of students by helping students learn how to use the library and by helping faculty design research assignments.[2]

The authors of this paper, while English and American Literature liaison librarians at the University of Arizona, were working at the departmental level to integrate IL into the core curriculum for the undergraduate major. Through their majors, students could continue practicing the IL competencies developed in their general education courses (including freshman composition) and learn additional competencies specific to their discipline. Within this disciplinary context, librarians and faculty work together to evaluate whether or not students are achieving IL competencies appropriate to a discipline, and to measure students' success in meeting stated objectives for a departmental curriculum.

ENVIRONMENT

The University of Arizona (UA) Library seeks to integrate IL across the curriculum and to measure its success in doing so. To this end, the University of Arizona Main Library works with the university-wide General Education program, which includes foundation courses, such as freshman English composition. Librarians and composition coordinators have developed IL learning outcomes for freshman composition (Appendix A). Subject liaison librarians work with their departments to build on the IL competencies developed in freshman composition. Additionally, the University-Wide General Education Committee (UWGEC) adopted a set of guidelines for faculty regarding the inclusion of IL in all new course proposals. For example, general education courses are expected to "introduce students to important sources of information related to the content of the course."[3] A librarian and other members of the UWGEC evaluate all new course proposals to ensure that there are stated IL objectives that can be achieved without direct in-class instruction from a librarian. Given a lack of resources, changes in university focus, and a need to become more effective with the few resources available, UA librarians are currently moving away from in-class instruction for general education classes. Rather, librarians concentrate on integrating information literacy into the disciplines and offer in-class instruction for courses in their liaison departments. Our work with the English department helped establish a direction and focus for the library's information literacy program.

UNIVERSITY OF ARIZONA DEPARTMENT OF ENGLISH

There are four graduate programs: Creative Writing; English Language/Linguistics; Literature; and Rhetoric, Composition, & the Teaching of English. There are four undergraduate areas of concentration: British Literature; American Literature; Literature and Composition; and Language and Literature. Over 700 students are in the department. In 2003, the Undergraduate English Curriculum Committee (UGECC), with two liaison librarians (the authors of this paper) as members of this committee and as members of several course-specific subcommittees, completed a revision of the English undergraduate curriculum as part of a campus-wide assessment initiative. As liaison librarians, we were responsible for collection development, research consultations, reference, and instruction. We communicated with over seventy faculty plus numerous adjunct faculty, teaching assistants, and staff in the department.

OUTCOMES ASSESSMENT, A UNIVERSITY OF ARIZONA CAMPUS INITIATIVE

The University of Arizona Office of Assessment requires academic units to state goals for their majors, develop student learning outcomes, and describe the methods used to measure those outcomes. As a result of this initiative, the English Department revised its curriculum for the undergraduate major, identifying six goals for the major, stating student learning outcomes, listing measurement methods, and reporting the results of those methods.[4] The department later developed student learning outcomes for specific gateway and core courses. When we joined the UGECC, the department had already developed six goals (Appendix B) for the major and had been using student self-reflection portfolios as a method of assessment in the senior capstone course.

As part of their portfolios, students are required to reflect on their progress toward reaching one or more of the six goals of the English major. Many students' portfolios did not demonstrate the type of learning that faculty had expected at the senior level. Learning outcomes would need to be developed for specific core courses in order to achieve the departmental goals for the major. For example, many students, in assessing how well they had reached goal five—ability to conduct and use literary research—relayed that they did not feel adequately prepared to use the library and its resources for their literary studies. The faculty who taught the senior capstone courses shared this sentiment. Faculty were surprised that students were entering the senior capstone classes unaware of some of the most essential tertiary resources for literary studies, such as the *Oxford English Dictionary* (OED) and *Modern Language Association International Bibliography* (*MLAIB*). The faculty also acknowledged that senior students lacked an understanding of primary sources (including accepted editions of literary works), as well as how to access, locate, and select appropriate secondary sources for literary criticism. In gathering comments from both students and faculty on the current assessment process in the department, the UGECC realized that they would need to revise the curriculum "in order to better serve the needs of [their] students, and more fully use the talents of [their] faculty."[5]

Recognizing that "student learning is a campus-wide responsibility"[6] and wanting to make the most out of our instructional endeavors with the students and faculty in English, we began collaborating with the English Department in 2001 to integrate IL into core English courses and to help the department realize its fifth goal for the majors: ability to conduct and use literary research.

We started by working with the Director of the Undergraduate English Curriculum to explore options on how students might accomplish goal number five. We were invited to join the UGECC as well as one of three curricular subcommittees, a subcommittee for the gateway course English 380. The committee was charged with determining the learning outcomes for the course. As a gateway course to the major, English 380 required students to develop skills in close reading. We worked with the chair of the subcommittee, who was also one of the instructors, on an English 380 pilot course. Our aim was to develop the course so that IL was integrated into the curriculum to the extent that IL competencies were included in the course objectives and assignments would be created to help achieve these objectives.

PILOT PROJECT: ENGLISH 380, LITERARY ANALYSIS

English 380: *Literary Analysis* was a gateway course for all English majors, with students required to receive a grade of C or higher in order to continue in the major. As a gateway course, the UGECC thought it would be an appropriate venue for introducing students to key literary research resources that would enhance close-reading of a text. Although researching the secondary literature was not required, it was required that students would investigate allusions in the texts they were reading and explore words to understand their derivation and meanings to enhance their ability to interpret a text. Both of these requirements were intended to engage students in furthering their understanding of a text and to help them build interpretive skills. In the section of the class with which we were working, students also had to find and use biographical information about the author to inform their interpretations. Thus, we created assignments that introduced them to a variety of tertiary resources (indexes to mythological characters, art work, architecture, as well as biographical sources and a variety of encyclopedias and dictionaries) with the goal of developing their conceptual understanding of how and why such resources are created, as well as how understanding allusions and play of words could bear on their understanding of a text.

For the pilot section of the course, students read a variety of short stories and poems. In collaboration with the professor, we created two graded assignments for the students. The first assignment required students to identify the proper names in a poem and to use tertiary sources to find out more about them and then discuss how knowing more about such things as named places, mythological figures, an art work mentioned had influenced their interpretation of the poem. Additionally, the students had to learn more about the poet. Similar to the intention behind identifying the proper names, the students then discussed how knowing more about the poet's background had contributed to their understanding of the poem. During one class period, we met the students in the reference area of the library, briefly discussing the types of sources they could use and how the sources were compiled: *Proper Names Master Index*, *Dictionary of Literary Biography*, and *Contemporary Literary Criticism*. Students were grouped together and spent most of the class time using the sources, consulting us when necessary. Students were required to summarize their findings individually, describing how they had used the sources and how they had analyzed the poem in light of the sources they had used. They also made short presentations to the class about their group process in using the resources and what they had discovered about using them. We attended those presentations and provided feedback to the groups.

The second assignment asked students to investigate words that were unfamiliar to them in the texts they were reading. For this particular assignment, we wanted students to build skills in the use of the *Oxford English Dictionary* (OED), so it was more tool focused than the previous assignment. We met with the students in the library to explain how the OED was created; why one would use it; how to use it; and how to interpret each entry. Students then completed an assignment that asked them to respond to questions that would show their understanding of *how* to use the OED. Like the first assignment, they worked in groups and gave presentations about their understanding of how their literary analysis could benefit from using the OED.

While introducing the students to tertiary resources was necessary, as they are essential resources for the disciplinary community, we found that a beneficial part of the course occurred during the group presentations. During the presentations we were able to discuss the students' research process at a more conceptual level. The conversations led to discussions of the validity of information on web-sites, the changing meaning of words and allusions over time, and the creation of discipline-based information resources and their purposes to the academic community. Students were engaged during these discussions and would often relate their research experiences in this class to other courses they were taking. They seemed excited about the resources and concepts they had learned, and more importantly, they expressed confidence that they had improved their skills in close-reading.

GUIDELINES RATHER THAN MANDATES FOR DEPARTMENTS

Following the pilot class, we worked with two other sections. The two courses were distinctly different, which presented our first challenge: while the first section introduced students to an array of short stories and poetry throughout the course and required very little secondary material (thus making it similar to the goals of the pilot course), the second section introduced students to a single work, *Hamlet*, and required the students to do extensive research into the secondary material.

Although the two sections had similar outcomes, such as the expectation that students would develop appropriate interpretive strategies (see English 380 goals below), each faculty member had a different approach for how students would develop these skills. Despite the course having been deemed to have a close-reading approach, some professors were requiring extensive research. The differences in the methods faculty use to teach students interpretive strategies make it difficult for us to agree on objectives for research goals across all sections of a course. For example, it would not be helpful to expect all students enrolled in multiple sections to be familiar with the *MLAIB* and the complexity of using such a resource, including evaluating the results, if not all professors of the class were going to require students to locate, evaluate, and select the most appropriate types of materials. It made sense that when we designed assignments, we had to introduce resources and concepts that helped to achieve the objectives of the course, which were ultimately aligned with the methodology faculty used to interpret a text. By being flexible, and developing guidelines for the course learning objectives, rather than mandating specific learning outcomes across all sections, we were able to design IL student learning outcomes for each section in alignment with the course content and methodology.

Both the content of the class and the methodology students were to use in their interpretations of a text were different in the two sections described here. This flexibility allowed faculty to teach within their areas of expertise and to determine the level of research in which they wanted their students to engage. Thus, the outcomes created by the subcommittee were "general expectations to guide but not constrain individual instructors of the course."[7] The English 380 guidelines stated that students were

1.   To develop and sustain viable and appropriate interpretive strategies;

2.   To show a close working relationship with the language and form of texts being interpreted;

3.   To write a clean, clear, perhaps even graceful, critical prose;

4.   To know how to treat a text as if it were a literary text;

5.   To be able to distinguish between and among text-based, author-based, and reader-based criticism(s);

6.   To be familiar with the conventions of reading and writing (among other things) prose fiction and poetry;

7.   To know and use key terms and concepts associated with traditional text-based criticism, or close reading (e.g., narrator/speaker; theme; metaphor/trope; image/symbol/sign; irony; rhyme/meter; rhetorical situation);

8.   To argue logically and persuasively, especially in modes associated with text-based criticism(s);

9.   To successfully complete written assignments of varying lengths, kinds, and formats that demonstrate 1-8.

Because we wanted to work with faculty to develop the curriculum, it was necessary to remain flexible in creating assignments that stayed true to the content of each section of the course. We found that while some research resources and their uses in literary studies could be introduced in *all* sections (e.g., *OED*, *Proper Names Master Index*), the course was not a good candidate either for teaching the research process or for introducing major research resources (e.g., *MLAIB*, WorldCat), as the amount of research required for students was not the same for all sections of the class. By the end of the year, the English 380 curriculum subcommittee determined that although the course was a good place to introduce a few tertiary resources that would help students to develop interpretive strategies through the close reading of a text, it was not the place to teach comprehensive research methods. The UGECC needed a different course for this.

NEW LITERARY RESEARCH COURSE PROPOSED
While we were working with the department, it became clear that in order to achieve the goals of the English major there would need to be a course designed to teach research methods. Because such a course did not exist,

the UGECC proposed to the College of Humanities Curriculum Review Committee (COH CRC) a new course: a junior pro-seminar, English 396, which was approved. The course was "designed to introduce students, through the study of a specific and relatively narrow aspect of literary study, to the methods and materials of literary research. University librarians will work closely with the class, individually and as a group, to introduce students to the use of research materials necessary for literary study.[8]" It is worth noting that the voting membership of the English Department favored the new curriculum with a vote of 45 to 3. We developed seven learning objectives for students in English 396 (Appendix C).

The English 396 curriculum committee used the 2002 *Research Competency Guidelines for Literatures in English: DRAFT* to assist them in developing the goals for the course. These guidelines were developed by an ad hoc committee of the ACRL Literatures in English Section. (The final version of the *Research Competency Guidelines*, approved in 2007, is in the Appendix of this book.) The faculty found some of the competencies to be too general in some cases and felt that all students, regardless of their majors, ought to have some level of proficiency in some of the competencies listed, such as "identify and use librarians…in the research process"; use interlibrary loan for materials not available at one's own library; use Boolean operators appropriately; differentiate between resources provided free on the internet and fee-based resources. We agreed to strike non-discipline specific competencies and focus our efforts on the LES competencies specific to the major. After multiple lengthy discussions, we arrived at the objectives listed above for English 396, the research methods course.

Like the two sections of English 380, the first two sections of English 396, taught by different faculty members, covered different content and taught different approaches to conducting research. One section covered Shakespeare, while the other focused on Zora Neale Hurston's work. Because most faculty taught two sections of this course per year, we were usually able to work with the same faculty for one year. Additionally, at least one instructor would teach the course a second year so that there was continuity from one year to the next. At the beginning of each semester, we meet with the course instructors to discuss the goals of the course.

As librarians, we concentrated on teaching the use of resources appropriate to the discipline and we had multiple opportunities to attend class discussions of the research process so that we could also ensure that students had a conceptual understanding of how and why these resources were created, with particular emphasis on how the resources were designed to meet the needs of a particular scholarly community. We met with several of the classes after they had completed their research assignments. During these sessions, students reported on their research processes, elaborating on difficulties they encountered during the research process. We had the opportunity, then, to clarify and help them think about solutions to these difficulties.

STUDENT RETROSPECTIVE ASSESSMENT OF THE MAJOR
The Department of English assesses students by using both formative and summative assessment tools throughout the curricula. Some of those assessment activities are available from the University of Arizona Outcomes Assessment website.[9] As we mentioned earlier, one summative tool is The Retrospective Assessment of the Major, which is conducted as part of the senior capstone course (English 496). Students, with guidance from the faculty teaching the capstone course, are asked to assemble a self-reflective portfolio of their intellectual development in reaching the goals outlined for the major. The portfolio serves as a means to assess the overall effectiveness of the major. In their portfolios students may include a paper from their gateway course (English 380) and one from the Junior Pro-seminar (English 396); it must include a reflective essay responding to their achievement of at least one of the goals of the English major.

We had the opportunity to review the students' portfolios on several occasions since the implementation of the English 396 course and the changes in English 380. We found that the majority of students, when commenting on their "ability to conduct literary research," felt that although they had benefited from being exposed to resources, particularly in English 396, they would have liked being exposed to these resources much sooner in their programs. Overall, however, students claimed they felt much better prepared in their ability to conduct literary research as a result of their research experiences in English 396.

REFLECTION
In early discussions with the department, several faculty felt that if they could learn how to conduct research on their own, so too could their students. We have shared our concerns with them about allowing students to stumble through the research process and the highly complicated knowledge organization systems that exist. Through storytelling (e.g., stories of our encounters with students who spent hours researching only

to end up in tears at the reference desk or students who arrive at the desk not knowing how to look up a title in the library catalog) and discussion, we think they have begun to understand that we can work toward reducing barriers to student success by helping them understand and use the vast array of resources and materials available to them. Faculty have also begun to embrace the role they play in helping their students understand the disciplinary resources that are essential to their academic community, resources that they have helped to create and to which they contribute their own scholarly works.

Being part of the curriculum committee and various subcommittees, as well as being involved with instruction in two core courses, allowed us to test and explore various methods for integrating IL into different sections of the same courses. Participating on the committees and working with the students in these courses offered us a sort of bird's eye view into pedagogical differences among faculty and how these differences affected students' use (or lack thereof) of library resources. We shared these experiences with the committee members. In turn, they reflected on and suggested approaches to address the concerns we had about IL. We also determined what learning objectives belonged in which courses to ensure that all students could meet the goals of the department.

During this process, we have learned a great deal about the variety of methodologies used by faculty in a diverse department. Their methods of research vary and that variation is carried over into teaching. Some belong to a more theoretical school and employ various literary theories to their literary criticism, while others impose a more traditional approach to research, as was the case with the first course we piloted; and yet others employ a more experimental approach to research, where anything goes. In this last approach, a faculty member introduced several websites with a variety of domains (e.g., .com, .org, .net., .edu) that dealt with a particular literary work and theatrical productions of that work. He encouraged students to use these sites, rather than locate, evaluate, and use the enormous amount of scholarly material available through the disciplinary resources. He discussed how to evaluate the quality of the information they found on these sites and encourages them to think critically about the information.

As librarians, we were challenged to write objectives that could be met no matter the methodology being taught. There was agreement among the faculty in teaching students the use of specific resources (e.g., *OED*) in all sections of a single course, but where do the other resources fit into the core curriculum? The learning objectives for each core course needed to reflect when certain resources and concepts would be introduced. Of course, we were concerned with more than just the resources that students would use, but if students were never given the opportunity to learn about and use the basic resources for their discipline, then they could not be expected to achieve the fifth goal of being an English major. Although we made inroads in integrating IL into the curriculum, much will need to be considered as the faculty continues to develop course objectives for the department.

What we had hoped to gain was a partnership that would allow us the opportunity to voice our concerns and share our expertise as curriculum was planned and implemented. We achieved this. As Leckie states, a curriculum-integrated approach allows us "to concentrate on developing [our] working relationships with faculty, fostering an environment where the skills and knowledge of both groups can be harmonized to better benefit students and enhance the institution.[10]" The UGECC committee is now talking about making the goal number five of the English Major—ability to conduct and use literary research—more explicit. Although, we worked with two courses: both English 380 and English 396, our involvement with each section of each course varied. Some instructors worked closely with us for two years and felt confident that they could now teach what we originally taught, saving us time to work with them in another capacity, such as looking at students' final papers. Additionally, spending less time in one section, allowed us more time to work with faculty teaching these courses for the first time.

SUMMARY

There are countless examples of faculty/librarian partnerships that illustrate some aspect of curriculum-integrated instruction where the librarian is a true partner throughout the class. Librarians are partners in everything from co-teaching a class, writing syllabi, and developing assignments. It seems, however, that many of these partnerships are discontinued because librarians cannot continually commit substantial time to a single class. If we are to integrate IL into the curriculum, we need to share the responsibilities of integration with faculty. Understanding each other's goals and developing common objectives with measurable learning outcomes can help us achieve this integration. The faculty we have worked with thus far have become cognizant of their roles in IL, and are beginning to change their teaching practices. They have also revised assignments to make information literacy objectives clear, and alerted students to our services by including our names on syllabi or in class announcements.

A previous version of this chapter appeared as "Where It Counts: Departmental Curriculum Committees and Librarians" in *Learning to Make a Difference: Proceedings of the Eleventh National Conference of the Association of College and Research Libraries, April 10-13, 2003, Charlotte, North Carolina*, ed. Hugh A. Thompson (Chicago : Association of College and Research Libraries, 2003).

APPENDIX A: UA English Department, English 102 IL Learning Objectives

1. Explores a topic and formulates a focus. Through reading and reflecting, are able to narrow and broaden topics as needed. (Instructor should provide time for exploration – see Kuhlthau handout.)
2. Knows how to get to SABIO, the Library's Information Gateway
3. Knows that assistance is available from a variety of sources – library reference desk, writing center, etc.
4. Uses a variety of search systems, such as indexes, catalog, and web search engines when appropriate and understands the differences among them
   a. Searches the catalog (by selecting the Catalog icon) to identify and locate books & other items the library owns
   b. Uses indexes (by selecting the Indexes to Articles icon) to search for articles from journals, magazines and newspapers
5. Writes a research statement or question
6. Select keywords or phrases along with Boolean operators to create an effective search strategy
7. Identifies the parts of a citation and knows what to search in the catalog
8. Can physically locate a book or journal issue in the library from citation information
9. Distinguishes between scholarly articles from journals and popular articles from magazines or newspapers
10. Evaluates information for appropriateness to a topic and assignment and for its reliability, validity, accuracy, authority, timeliness, and point of view or bias
11. Recognizes prejudice, deception or manipulation
12. Demonstrates an understanding of what constitutes plagiarism

13. Creates citations for sources (bibliography) used in papers, according to a determined citation format
14. Synthesizes the information found to create his/her own argument

APPENDIX B: UA English Department, Goals for the Major

1. Knowledge of foundational texts of British and American literature
2. Understanding of the historical and cultural range of literature written in English
3. Understanding of the development of the English language as used in works of literature
4. Understanding of strategies of textual interpretation appropriate to different literary genres
5. Ability to conduct and use literary research
6. Ability to write clearly and effectively.

APPENDIX C: UA English Department, English 396 Learning Objectives

1. Make effective use of library resources at the University of Arizona and around the world, recognizing how information is organized and disseminated;
2. Show familiarity with the major databases, essential reference works (such as concordances, dictionaries, and bibliographies), and scholarly articles and books in language and literature as well as related disciplines;
3. Make correct, appropriate, and ethical presentation of research findings;
4. Make fair representation of an author's work, using paraphrase and quotation appropriately and documenting sources correctly;
5. Summarize, evaluate, and critique secondary sources;
6. Use primary and secondary sources to support original arguments in a variety of ways (e.g., as a point of departure, as theoretical grounding, as historical background, as evidence);
7. Follow MLA guidelines for documentation and conventions (e.g., punctuation, subtitles, endnotes, bibliography), while sustaining a coherent and original argument about one or more texts.

NOTES

1.   American Association for Higher Education (AAHE), *AAHE Assessment Forum: 9 Principles of Good Practice for Assessing Student Learning*, (1996), retrieved December 10, 2002, from http://www.aahe.org/principl.htm.

2.   Evan Farber, "College Libraries and the Teaching/Learning Process: A 25-Year Reflection," *The Journal of Academic Librarianship* 25, no. 3 (1999): 176; Gloria J. Leckie, "Desperately Seeking Citations: Uncovering Faculty Assumptions about the Undergraduate Research Process," *The Journal of Academic Librarianship* 22 (1996): 201-208; Marian C. Winner, "Librarians as Partners in the Classroom: An Increasing Imperative," *Reference Services Review* 26 (1998): 25-29.

3.   University of Arizona University-Wide General Education Committee, "Guidelines for Information Literacy Component of General Education Courses," http://web.arizona.edu/~uge/gened/submit.htm.

4.   University of Arizona, "Outcomes Assessment," http://outcomes.web.arizona.edu/

5.   Laura Berry, Director of English Undergraduate Studies, memorandum, 20 September 2002.

6.   AAHE.

7.   University of Arizona English Department, English 380: Close Reading Goals, May 2001.

8.   Berry, memorandum: Recommendation to Establish a New Course, 24 June 2002.

9.   University of Arizona Outcomes Assessment, "English Department Assessment Activities," http://outcomes.web.arizona.edu/data.php?uid=384#activities.

10.   Leckie, 207.

Training Librarians for Teaching Literary Research Methods

Helene C. Williams

Today's literature librarians are privileged in a way few others in our profession are: we have access to some of the most modern technology and
methods of accessing and manipulating information, yet we also remain
grounded in the traditional print-based world of the humanities. In some
disciplines, past research is more ignored than honored, but not so with
literature. For literary scholarship to move forward, it is necessary to bring
the past along with us. Thus ours is the pivotal generation between the
old and the new: herein lie the excitement and fulfillment, as well as the
challenges and frustrations, of our careers. In order to preserve as well as
continue to utilize past research and literary texts, it is vital that today's
researchers know how scholarship in literature is created, accessed, and
incorporated into current projects. How, then, can we best train ourselves
and our constituents? This chapter attempts to outline some strategies for
achieving this goal. Although the examples used are geared toward librarians, they can easily be adapted for use by instructors in English or other
humanities departments who wish to incorporate research methods into
their teaching repertoire.

BACKGROUND

The traditional research methods course used to be a staple offering in
English departments nationwide, but gradually faded as a graduate requirement when English faculty burned out from the repetitive nature of
the course, retired, or changed their areas of interest. The focus on critical
theory rather than on texts also hastened the demise of the course in many
English departments. Now, bemoans noted literary scholar Jerome Mc-
Gann, the "long-standing philological practices in language study, textual
scholarship, and bibliography" are "but a ghostly presence in most of our
Ph.D. programs."[1]

"Ghostly" is an apt word to describe some of what I felt while taking
the research methods course in my graduate English work, some twenty
years ago. The instructor gave us exercise after exercise requiring us to
look up texts on microfilm, for no discernible (at that time) reason. The

microforms room was usually deserted and nearly dark, with large metal machines that seemed to have been made out of surplus military tank parts casting eerie shadows across the floor. The handle to wind the film was overhead, and my arm would tire as I hunted for what was inevitably the last entry on the reel from the monstrous *Early English Books* or *Eighteenth Century* film sets. I would scribble descriptions of texts, fonts, and illustrations on innumerable note cards, dutifully paper-clipped together in the proper order, to turn in during class. My reward for completing this project would be another assignment requiring a trip to a printed short-title catalog, the massive microform cabinets, and then back to the dark scary corner of the machines.

What I learned in that research methods course has proven invaluable in my career as a literature librarian: it is essential to explain *why* one is using a short-title catalog, *why* a text is in a non-print format, and *how* the technology works to access that text, be it a behemoth microfilm reader or a computer workstation which can burn a CD of the text for the researcher to take away. Although technology has changed many of the "hows" in research, the "whys" still remain, and it comes back to what we spend our time explaining, both at the reference desk and in instruction sessions—the process of research.

EDUCATION FOR LITERATURE AND HUMANITIES SPECIALISTS

Although knowledge of literary research methods is inextricable from our other skills as literature specialists, including reference, collection development, and general instruction, a review of the library science literature reveals little in the way of instructional information for subject specialists in any discipline. In spite of wide agreement that the roles of subject specialists are changing, very little has been published on practical training or mentoring solutions in areas other than collection development. The goal of this chapter is to show how best to take advantage of training opportunities and best practices, in libraries as well as in library schools and within the humanities disciplines.

One of the first places to look for training opportunities is in the library school curriculum. Most programs offer discipline-based reference or collection development courses, allowing students to have hands-on experience with the resources in a specific field. Traditionally, students received source lists for specific areas within a discipline and a set of reference questions that can be answered with those sources. The better one knows the process of research, the more subject knowledge one can absorb from these lists: if a question asks about locating a critical article, one can then focus on the indexes on the list, looking at how they work, what they cover, and how they differ from one another, leaving the other sources on the list to be dealt with later.

Today, however, students in these disciplined-based courses may not be as familiar with the research process due to the increased aggregation of sources and the proliferation of access points. For example, a question about locating an article of criticism could be answered with the *Literature Online* database—which could also answer a biographical question as well as provide a primary text. The blurring lines between types of sources is exacerbated by many students' need for, and belief in, instant gratification and one-stop shopping for answers. In recent years I have found myself banning the use of aggregators and search engines such as Google in answering the assigned questions; these can indeed serve valuable purposes in reference and research, but subject specialists need to have a solid grounding in the standard sources in their discipline. In the case of literature, many of these resources are only in print, and are likely to remain so. Once the students have grasped the various kinds of information available in literary research, and which specific sources are likely to provide the needed information, they are much better prepared to make carefully-considered decisions in the use of the many available online resources.

Unfortunately, some library schools are moving away from the traditional discipline-based courses in favor of technology-centered ones. The changing nature of library work does indeed require reconsideration of the qualifications of librarians and their education. Richard Hopkins says there is plenty of room in the profession for the librarian-scholar, and is a proponent of library schools teaching the organization of the literature of a discipline along with some of the content, and outlines his own course objectives and methods.[2] Michael Ryan discusses the need for library science courses to reflect the interdisciplinarity in today's research and to have articulated goals and objectives for the curriculum in order to meet those needs.[3] Since most library school programs (and students) are driven by the current job market, though, they are obliged, as Brendan Loughridge says, "to concentrate their efforts on those areas deemed most likely to make their graduates employable and have tended to sacrifice the more traditional areas of historical bibliography, conservation and preservation."[4]

I recently conducted an unscientific survey of course catalogs from ten library and/or information science programs across the United States reveals that indeed, some of the traditional courses, including humanities reference, no longer exist or are taught on an irregular basis as "special topics" courses. Out of the ten programs investigated, the five cases in which humanities reference was found to still be in the course catalog, only one program offered it annually, two offered it once every two or more years, one had not offered it for at least three years, and one offered a version of it through the English Department. In all cases, none of the instructors were full-time faculty in the library or information science programs, but instead were adjunct lecturers "borrowed" from the main research library on campus, or as noted above, faculty from the English Department.

This anecdotal evidence corroborates this author's experience with teaching the humanities reference course, as several local library science faculty recommended several years ago that subject reference courses be dropped from the catalog; luckily, pressure from students and teaching librarians convinced them otherwise. Their reasoning was, in part, job-market driven, along with the concern that the traditional resource-based classes were irrelevant and served more as scavenger hunts than "real" reference work. Unfortunately, the subject reference courses have often been taught as scavenger hunts, rather than in a process-based research methods paradigm, and I would argue that this is to some degree due to the status of those who teach the classes: poorly-paid adjuncts, who already have full-time employment elsewhere, who have no time for curriculum development, and who are often working off of notes left by their predecessors. An investment in revamping these courses around the process of research, incorporating new formats and technologies, with specific resources as examples rather than ends in themselves, would go far toward training students wishing to become subject specialists, and toward convincing those in charge of the curriculum of the positive, ongoing, value of these courses.

Other research indicates frustration with the discipline-based library courses and looks toward advanced subject degrees to provide necessary training in the underlying principles of a discipline; John Budd notes that while an advanced degree is not always required for a subject specialist position, it helps to "not just mediate between users and information structure but also between users and information content."[5] John Haar discusses recruiting difficulties and says libraries look in the wrong places for people with the skills necessary for the job, and echoes Budd in saying that there is no "substitute for subject-based graduate programs in developing an appreciation of how scholars create and use information."[6] Not every literature librarian needs a Ph.D. in English to be effective, but having graduate coursework and research experience will lend credibility to one's efforts to promote literary research methods instruction.

ON THE JOB/PROFESSIONAL DEVELOPMENT TRAINING

As literature librarians, we all teach research methods to some extent, most often in one-on-one interactions at a reference desk or in individual consultations. We may do one-shot instruction sessions on literary research, provide several presentations in a resurrected research methods course, or we may be fully responsible for the term-length methods course for an English department. Neither library school nor graduate coursework nor an advanced degree in English is enough in and of themselves to prepare you for your specific situation, however. Much of what is needed is local, contextual information, and the following must be considered:

- how collections, services, and programs work at your institution
- the specialties within the English department
- the varying needs within the English department and hearing how they are voiced; for example, the medievalists may be quite vocal, drowning out the quieter eighteenth-century specialists
- the focus of the English department, which may well be on critical theory, with little reliance on standard texts or non-digital secondary sources

An important part of learning to teach literary research methods is knowing the situation at hand, and responding appropriately.

When I landed my first library position that had substantial collections and liaison duties, my knees trembled and I feared that I was not capable of succeeding in the job. Did I have what it takes to be a subject specialist, and was there anything I could teach these people that they didn't already know? I turned to one of my mentors, an eminent English bibliographer from the old school of literary research. His advice: spend your days doing what your boss tells you to do, and your nights and weekends working like the dickens to learn the collection, to meet the English department faculty and students, and to read in the areas you avoided in graduate school. Though I did not follow this advice to the letter, it was sound and very effective. For the librarian new either to the profession, to the subject of literature, or to the concept of teaching literary research methods, the following suggestions may provide a manageable guide to achieving the level of training necessary to do your job, and ultimately, to teaching a literary research methods course. These strategies are not meant to be prescriptive; rather, the activities are ones which have proven effective for librarians currently in the field, and which can be adapted to meet the needs of new and different situations.

The skills necessary to be effective in specialized collection development and reference also apply to being prepared to teach a methods course. A structured way to gain these skills is to develop goals and expectations, identify activities, and assess progress: in other words, create a training program. These are several of the steps discussed by George Soete in terms of training new bibliographers. In the case of both bibliographer and methods instructor, success of the training program depends on "the readiness of (1) the organization, (2) the trainee, and (3) the training program."[7] In her article on the changing roles of librarian-bibliographers, Deborah Jakubs outlines the desired skills of collection development librarians[8]; the following list is a modification of Jakubs', and attempts to provide some manageable goals:

+ Knowledge of subject background and flow of information within the discipline (e.g. scholarly communication)
+ Understanding of processes at one's own library and larger institution (e.g. how budgets get allocated, and what communication mechanisms exist between the library and the English department)
+ Strong interpersonal skills, for networking within the library and with the departments, as well as to aid in establishing a network among counterparts at other institutions
+ Teaching skills, for reaching various levels of scholars, from first-time researchers to established scholars, and for using the many formats now available. Being able to think on one's feet to provide a research process aimed at a specific user is invaluable.

Each of these skills can be dissected further, to help in creating and evaluating specific activities. For example: focus on one time period, such as Victorian, and immerse yourself in the finding aids and literature. Then look at the primary and secondary sources available, in all formats, from microfilm to full-text web documents, to see the strengths and weaknesses of each. This will do much to increase your confidence in teaching users and recommending specific research paths. Other tools are available to assist with self-training in the area of literary research. For example, Candace Benefiel et al. provide checklists in baseline subject competencies; Maureen Pastine's conceptual framework for teaching literary research is also valuable.[9]

Reference works and professional literature update and supplement classroom and on-the-job experience. The following titles can form the core of a personal ready-reference collection for literature specialists, for use especially in teaching literary research methods, but also for consultation and collection development purposes:

- Altick's *The Art of Literary Research*
- Blazek's *The Humanities: A Selective Guide to Information Sources*
- Bracken's *Reference Works in British and American Literature*
- Gibaldi's *MLA Handbook*
- Harner's *Literary Research Guide*
- Keift's "Lit Crit, Snip Crit, the Nitty Grit, and the Work of Learning Literature"[10]

Reading, or at least skimming, the major disciplinary journals for emerging topics and new names in the field, is one way to keep up with developments in literary research. This can lead to ideas for incorporating newer resources, such as the *Early English Books Online* or *Eighteenth Century Collections Online* databases, into the classroom. Attending literary conferences, such as those sponsored by the Modern Language Association, or smaller, regional conferences provides first-hand experience with the hot topics in literary research, and is also a forum for discussions with literary scholars. Announcements for these meetings are advertised in the major literature journals such as *PMLA (Publications of the Modern Language Association of America)* as well as in the time- and genre-specific titles such as *Victorian Studies* or *Modern Fiction Studies*. On-campus activities such as faculty readings or graduate discussion groups provide valuable perspective on local research.

Taking classes in the English department at your institution is also an effective training tool. Many faculty are pleased to have librarians sit in on their courses, or, depending on the benefits at your institution, officially enroll. Even those librarians with advanced degrees in English can benefit by sitting in on classes; the content may be familiar, but the delivery, discussion, and student assignments are apt to provide a wealth of information to improve your own teaching, consultations, and even collections. If a research methods course currently exists in the department, attending it may well be the first step towards integrating yourself into it as an instructor.

Networking with colleagues can be one of the most useful development activities. Opportunities range from the ALA annual and midwinter conferences to activities offered by sections within the American Library Association , such as the Association of College and Research Libraries' Literatures in English Section (LES). The discussion groups within LES provide a forum to talk about literary reference, collections, instruction, and training issues, for literature librarians at any stage of their career. The section has also established a mentoring program and is making plans for training workshops.[11]

Mentors for literature librarians can range from English faculty to established librarians in the field, or mentorship can be provided through support networks of your local peers at any level. Mentors serve as a sounding board for local issues as well as unique perspective-enhancers. Some institutions assign formal mentors to new librarians, to help them through the institutional bureaucracy or promotional hurdles, but often a mentoring relationship is more organic. Meeting people in the field of literature librarianship, joining appropriate e-mail lists in both the library and literature realms, and making yourself known on campus are all ways to connect with people who you may view at one time or another as a mentor.

POLITICAL REALITIES

Immersing oneself in literature, selecting materials for a literature collection, and providing basic instruction in literary resources are all good preparation for teaching a methods course. Implementing such a course, however, can be fraught with political, financial, and logistical difficulties. My personal crusade for reinstating research methods at an ARL institution began when I met with an English graduate student who was at the point of defending her dissertation on second language acquisition, and one of her committee members had asked a question about some of the statistics she presented. In doing the usual reference interview, I asked what sources she had looked in to get the information she already had, assuming she would have a lengthy, coherent list of resources she had used. "I checked everything," she said. "Everything" turned out to be *InfoTrac*. Not the *Modern Language Association International Bibliography (MLAIB)*, not the *Educational Resources Information Clearinghouse (ERIC)*, not *Linguistics and Language Behavior Abstracts (LLBA)*, not even the library catalog. We have all had encounters like this, when patrons are unaware of basic resources, or when they say "I used the computer to find this," not understanding that a library workstation can offer access to hundreds upon hundreds of databases, as well as that chaotic world of the Internet. However, this consultation, which revealed the lack of understanding of the research process, not only on the part of the student but also on the part of her dissertation committee members, spurred me to action.

There has always been, and probably will always be, tension between libraries and English departments as to boundaries: who does what? Who teaches MLA citation style? Who teaches the research methods course, if there is one? This varies from institution to institution, and an understanding of the local situation is invaluable. In my case, it took three years of meetings with the English department chair, various faculty committees, and individual students and faculty to resurrect and update the research methods course. Topics such as descriptive and analytic bibliography were ceded to English, even though none of the faculty was teaching it at that point. Database searching, scholarly communication and copyright issues, and indeed, pretty much anything to do with technology, was integrated into the course. Thanks to strong support from the younger faculty, the class ended up being taught in a hands-on classroom, with a separate space for discussion sessions. The course could easily become team-taught, with the dropped segments added back in by a faculty member or special collections librarian; it could also revert to English Department control, with the librarian providing select portions of the instruction. In other words, there is no one "right" way to design or teach a literary research methods course. Much is dictated by the strengths of the institutional environment.

We must also keep in mind that the entire literary and scholarly community is going through some of the same disciplinary and professional angst as the library community; issues of territoriality, of the need to be seen as central to the university, or at least be seen as worth continued funding, are rampant on campuses. The future of literary studies, of the definition of literature itself, and of the humanities job market, are hot topics discussed by Modern Language Association members, and their counterparts around the world. Hans Gumbrecht describes the "dysphoria" felt by many literature scholars, as focus and connection decrease and the discontinuity in the discipline increases.[12] Does this sound familiar to those of us in the library world?

It would seem that the key for both literary scholars and literature librarians is to be able to continue to learn and change throughout our lives; this is, after all what we try to tell our students about lifelong learning, if not in those specific terms. Working collaboratively, learning from each other, will make for professional growth and a successful methods course. We need to train ourselves as well as our students and faculty, in order to overcome the cultural divide between librarians and scholars. As noted by Burnette et al., this takes time, and in many cases, space, where one can meet faculty and researchers on their own ground and not in the library[13]; in addition, these networking activities must be supported by library administration.

CONCLUSION

Being well-trained and keeping up-to-date on changes in our fields of both librarianship and literature means we need to be active on a number of fronts, which can be challenging. Creating manageable goals that can be assessed and revised is key to staying afloat. An excellent discussion of the responsibilities in the profession, of individuals, library science curricula, individual libraries, and library associations, is available online as part of the Association for Library Collections and Technical Services' Educational Policy Statement.[14] The appendix of the policy statement provides checklists of knowledge and skills in key areas; we can create similar checklists for our subject competencies as well.

Part of what makes librarianship so rewarding is that it is a profession that allows us to improve over time; the more we know, the more experience we have, the better we get at what we do. We can learn from our entire community of users, from novice researchers and experienced scholars, and that knowledge goes back into the system, in the form of materials selection, resource use, better instruction sessions, and perhaps a literary research methods course. There are many paths we can take to reach our common goal, of well-trained humanists with skills both critical and technical; including stakeholders from across those many paths, from those in library education to practicing librarians to research faculty across the disciplines, is vital to meeting these specific professional challenges.

NOTES

1. Jerome McGann, "Literary Scholarship in the Digital Future," *Chronicle of Higher Education* 49, no.16 (2002): B7.

2. Richard L. Hopkins, "Perspectives on Teaching Social Sciences and Humanities Literatures," *Journal of Education for Library and Information Science* 28 (1987): 136-51.

3. Michael T. Ryan, "Among the Disciplines: The Bibliographer in the "I" World," in *Recruiting, Training, and Educating Librarians for Collection Development*, ed. Peggy Johnson

and Sheila S. Intner, 99-112 (Westport, CT: Greenwood Press, 1994).

4.   Brendan Loughridge, "Information Technology, the Humanities and the Library," *Journal of Information Science* 15 (1989): 283.

5.   John M. Budd, "The Academic Librarian," in *The Academic Library: Its Context, Its Purpose, and Its Operation* (Littleton, CO: Libraries Unlimited, 1998), 302.

6.   John Haar, "Scholar or Librarian? How Academic Libraries' Dualistic Concept of the Bibliographer Affects Recruitment," *Collection Building* 12:1-2 (1993): 22.

7.   George J. Soete, "Training for Success: Integrating the New Bibliographer into the Library," in *Recruiting, Training, and Educating Librarians for Collection Development*, ed. Peggy Johnson and Sheila S. Intner, 160 (Westport, CT: Greenwood Press, 1994).

8.   Deborah Jakubs, "Staffing for Collection Development in the Electronic Environment: Toward a New Definition of Roles and Responsibilities," *Journal of Library Administration* 28:4 (1999): 71-83.

9.   Candace R. Benefiel, Jeannie P. Miller, and Diana Ramirez, "Baseline Subject Competencies for the Academic Reference Desk," *Reference Services Review* 25:1 (1997): 83-93; Maureen Pastine, "Teaching the Art of Literary Research," in *Conceptual Frameworks for Bibliographic Education: Theory into Practice*, ed. Mary Reichel and Mary Ann Ramey, 134-44 (Littleton, CO: Libraries Unlimited, 1987).

10.   Richard D. Altick and John J. Fenstermaker, *The Art of Literary Research*, 4th ed. (New York, Norton: 1993); Ron Blazek and Elizabeth Averso, *The Humanities: A Selective Guide to Information Sources*, 5th ed. (Englewood, CO: Libraries Unlimited, 2000); James Bracken, *Reference Works in British and American Literature*, 2nd ed. (Englewood, CO: Libraries Unlimited, 1998); Joseph Gibaldi, *MLA Handbook for Writers of Research Papers*, 6th ed. (New York: Modern Language Association, 2003); James Harner, *Literary Research Guide: An Annotated Listing of Reference Sources in English Studies*, 4th ed. (New York: Modern Language Association, 2002).; Robert Kieft, "Lit Crit, Snip Crit, the Nitty Grit, and the Work of Learning Literature," *CHOICE* 38:3 (2000): 457-72.

11.   Literatures in English Section, http://www.ala.org/ala/mgrps/divs/acrl/about/sections/les/leshomepage.cfm (31 March 2005).

12.   Hans Ulrich Gumbrecht and Walter Moser, ed., *The Future of Literary Studies/L'avenir des études littéraires*, Library of the Canadian Review of Comparative Literature, 9 (Edmonton, 2001), 12-22.

13.   Michaelyn Burnette, Christina M. Gillis, and Myrtis Cochran, "The Humanist and the Library: Promoting New Scholarship Through Collaborative Interaction Between Humanists and Librarians," *The Reference Librarian* 47 (1994): 181-91.

14.   Association for Library Collections and Technical Services, *Educational Policy Statement.* http://www.ala.org/ala/alcts/alctsmanual/conted/cepolicy.htm (31 March 2005).

Work in Progress: A Review of the Literature of Literary Research Instruction 1978-2003

Daniel Coffey

INTRODUCTION

The teaching of research is a constant among academic disciplines, and most undergraduates are exposed to some form of research instruction even before they declare a major. Yet, the field of literary research is somewhat distinctive on several counts, one being that the same repository that holds the research tools (or provides access to them) also houses the physical manifestation of the ideas that are being researched. Undergraduate literature students go to the library to obtain a copy of *Leaves of Grass*; they also enter into the scholarly research conversation by reading articles in the *Walt Whitman Quarterly Review*—at the library. Further, it can reasonably be assumed that they found the citations of those articles by using the *Modern Language Association International Bibliography* (*MLAIB*) database, either in the library or, at some institutions, from their dorm or off-campus apartment. Even in the latter case, the library is still omnipresent, as the student will realize by going through their library's web site to access the database.

The fact that the work of many literature students begins and ends in the library does not mean it is going to be easier for them to learn how to research their subjects effectively. On the contrary, whereas students in elementary education and agronomy come into the library to do their searches and get their journal articles before going to their labs or internships, literature students do not have the sense of separation between research tools and subjects. An advantage they do have is the close proximity of librarians, to help guide them through the research process.

Close proximity is not enough, though. Literature students, even at the graduate level, still demonstrate, to their instructors' chagrin or amazement, an inability to evaluate and effectively use literary reference and research tools. Literature librarians have an excellent opportunity to instruct these students on how to do research, since they are from time to time essentially captive audiences, but careful planning, thought, and reflection still need to take place—on both the part of the librarian and the course instructor.

In this chapter I intend to give a sense of some of the most original, engaging, and informative contributions to the literature on teaching literary research that were published in the last thirty years by librarians and teaching faculty. While the reader could, on her own, identify the articles and chapters included in this review, this review discusses approaches taken, ideas, exhortations, and reflections, and deals with wide and narrow foci in undergraduate literary studies as well as in graduate studies in enough detail to highlight the main points and to assist the reader in deciding whether to read the entire article or chapter.

The discussions place literary research in the contexts of professional preparation, pedagogy, theory, and technology. Although technology has changed radically since most of these articles and chapters were published, many of the core issues addressed in these writings remain relevant and challenging to those teaching literary research today. There are themes that link the writings on undergraduate and graduate research, but in order to make this chapter as useful as possible, the two areas are treated separately.

It should be said that this chapter is only concerned with surveying the literature of teaching research of a *literary* nature, a very small subset of the available literature that addresses concerns of teaching research in general. Examples of such non-specific articles may be found in the bibliographies of the other chapters in *Teaching Literary Research*. To locate the publications that are reviewed in this chapter, several indexes in particular were used: *Library Literature, ERIC, Educational Abstracts*, and *MLAIB*.

TEACHING LITERARY RESEARCH AT THE UNDERGRADUATE LEVEL

Lori E. Buchanan and Anne May Berwind intend in their excellent *Research Strategies* article to "show students how criticism fits into the literature of literature."[1] The authors discuss a methodology for introducing undergraduates to the process of using the card catalog to locate and identify literary criticism. Published in 1989, their article is interestingly placed in library history around the time of the advent of the OPAC (Online Public Access Catalog). Buchanan and Berwind are at their most helpful when they transcend the mere functionality of the card catalog, and examine the underlying purpose and mechanics of such an introductory exercise. This article is also useful as a reminder of how such a process might have been taught before the access points to library catalog records exploded in number.

Buchanan and Berwind mention the importance of ensuring that students realize that secondary sources—sources that deal critically with a given literary work (primary source)—come under the subject heading of the work's author; thus, beginning a search by looking up the author as subject is often the best approach. In this day of "subject keyword" searching, criticism of certain well-known texts will be accessible via the work's title, but the authors' admonition still stands: students should be aware of the subject heading hierarchy in order to make full and efficient use of the library catalog.

The authors also strive to teach their students about the roles that genre, nationality, temporality, and even gender play in subject headings, and how they can each lead to critical and interpretive works. The concept of "subject tracings" is also introduced for the stated purpose of helping students to find other resources when the ones to which their catalog search has led them have already been checked out by eager peers doing the same assignment. The authors could not have spoken to this in 1989, but being able to manipulate subject tracings will also help students to find materials not owned by their library, through the Online Computer Library Center's (OCLC) WorldCat, and similar strategies can be used in the *MLAIB* and other relevant online databases.

In addition to denoting important Library of Congress subject heading terms like "Criticism and interpretation," or "History and criticism," the authors discuss relevant subject terms for tertiary resources. The sub-heading "Indexes," or "Bibliography," when found under one of the headings listed in the previous sentence, will lead students to tertiary resources–publications that, in turn, will point students in the direction of useful primary *and* secondary sources.

Although flexibility is desirable when doing research, and the authors encourage it, one should be cautious about passing on the following suggestion to beginning researchers. Buchanan and Berwind posit the example of a student who finds nothing when looking for criticism of a Louis L'Amour story by searching in the subject catalog under the author's name, followed by "Criticism and Interpretation." They would tell the student to change her tactic by looking under "Western Stories— " with the same subheading. If it is still to no avail, she should demonstrate flexibility by further broadening her search in increments of "Short Stories, American—," "American Fiction—," and further still to "American Literature—," or "Literature—". This "flexibility" will prove discouraging for the student, as anything directly relating to L'Amour would, in fact, have shown up under the first few headings. Better to encourage the student to display flexibility by encouraging her to locate a tertiary resource or simply consult with a reference librarian. This criticism aside, Buchanan's and Berwind's article remains an excellent guide for new librarians who will be teaching literary research techniques to undergraduates. It is not outdated, despite its references to the physical card catalog.

Judy Reynolds, writing in 2000, focuses on literary research instruction, and indeed library research instruction in general, by way of discussing the nature of the *MLAIB*, and its relevance and teachability.[2] In order to give context to the main point of her essay—the *MLAIB* as a teachable resource—Reynolds gives a considerable amount of space to discussing in very broad terms such issues as faculty attitudes toward library instruction.

Reynolds avers that instruction librarians first need to understand the researching styles of humanities scholars before beginning to "design our instruction in concert with them to suit student learning needs."[3] Thus, she provides a thorough overview of the characteristics unique to their research methods, and how these methods have been aided and stymied by the advent of online indexes and other electronic resources. These issues will have to be addressed before humanities faculty will feel completely comfortable with their students receiving library instruction on the use of electronic reference tools such as the *MLAIB*.

Reynolds examines the specific ways that efficient use of the *MLAIB* can best be taught to students at varying levels of sophistication. She notes that most beginning students neither have a grasp of the "breadth of the field," nor "know the field well enough to focus on a specific question."[4] The full depth of the *MLAIB*, coupled with its many non-intuitive idiosyncrasies, may make it less than an ideal tool for beginning students who are not yet familiar enough with the field of knowledge covered by that database. Goals that Reynolds puts forth in teaching the *MLAIB* to beginning students tend to focus more on the author/title/keyword aspects of the database and less on the subject/descriptor aspects. Some examples of these goals include: being able to correctly read an *MLAIB* citation; engaging in free-form brainstorming to come up with useful search topics; successfully executing a simple author/title/literary character search; locating the cited item(s) in the library and being aware as well of alternate options, should citations lead to items not available in the library.

One way to approach this task at the beginning student level may be to *not* teach the *MLAIB*; that is, to start with resources such as *Contemporary Literary Criticism*. When instructors of freshman-level courses insist on using the *MLAIB* in their courses, librarians can "work with the teaching faculty member to make the assignment more specific, including more appropriate materials, so that the students will have a more interesting and fruitful experience."[5]

Intermediate level students will benefit from knowing the actual scope of the *MLAIB*, including its cross-disciplinary focus. They will have a better grasp of the subject matter and will be better positioned to use the database on a deeper level. These students need to be aware of the vagaries of the subject indexing in the *MLAIB* and be prepared to use "fuzzy" keyword searches as well as well as subject heading searches. Reynolds states that it is advisable here, as in many other instances, to instruct students to initiate their searches with keywords, and then follow up with searches on the subject headings culled from the resulting citations.

A very different use of computers for literary research is described by Dene Grigar. Much of Grigar's 1998 article on using hypertext to teach the work of Gertrude Stein focuses on the difficulty of teaching Stein at the undergraduate level, the technology itself, and how her students benefited from having *Tender Buttons* presented to them in hypertext.[6] In the context of this review, Grigar's requirement that students work their Stein research into hypertext format, linking critical writings on Stein's writing directly to the text itself, is the most interesting feature. Grigar is not concerned with the methodology of *doing* research, as such, but rather how the fruits of the students' research can be best used to increase their understanding of the process of literary creation. As well as being used as a means of textual representation in teaching works of literature, those of us teaching literary research can use the hypertext model to make the connections between literary criticism (once it is located) and the text more explicit and holistic, in order to help students to better understand the complexity of the relationship between the two.

Beyond using computerized resources such as *MLAIB* or creating hypertext to understand a literary work, the well-rounded literary researcher should also engage with archives. Bianca Falbo, an archivist writing in 2000, looks at teaching literary research from an archival point of view.[7] Leaving aside the issue of "how to do research," Falbo talks about the pedagogical usefulness of letting students conduct their literary research in a library's special collections department. Looking at primary source material (manuscripts or first publications) in an archival setting gives the students, Falbo argues, the opportunity to challenge their own notions, and form new notions, of what constitutes the "text" and the "reader." From a pedagogical standpoint, Falbo notes that, in having students go straight to the archives rather than working with texts that she has selected in advance, the role of "ultimate authority" is lifted from her, and she is able to engage in real discussions with the students about what they found rather than simply imparting her knowledge of her chosen texts.

What she has to say about the transfer of archival texts to online repositories is also insightful. While the accessibility of a text may increase in an electronic format, the text nevertheless is almost always robbed of its historical context. Students stand to learn a great deal if they can discuss the issue of the "electronic transformation" of a text, but only if they are able to see the text as it was originally presented. Wider use of Falbo's pedagogical strategy would make future graduate work in textual bibliography all the more meaningful and add to understanding of theoretical discussions of readership and cultural context.

Anita Lowry also discusses how electronic texts can be used in the process of teaching literary research.[8] Making a point similar to Falbo's, she argues that electronic texts make primary sources at once more and less accessible to students; while on the one hand, putting primary sources in electronic format allows for a wider distribution of the text, on the other hand, students are not able to see it in its original format and thus miss out on the sense of historical context. Here, research enters the frame: Lowry claims that electronic texts are not as easily browsed, and that students have to consider them in terms of text analysis and query formation. Before approaching the electronic text, they will need to have an idea of what information they want to retrieve, and their professor can use this as a means to instruct them on the "interrogation and interpretation"[9] of these texts, in using the retrieval and analysis apparatuses that exist alongside the electronic documents.

Lowry also cautions literature professors and librarians not to forget that there are other electronic resources at hand to facilitate literary research besides the MLAIB. While this tool has been a "godsend" for students who need to locate criticism, there are also software programs and packages (she mentions a CD-ROM that contains the full-text of the Riverside Shakespeare) that allow for direct interrogation and manipulation of the text for research purposes. Lowry's article was published in 1994, and since then the number of commercial CD-ROMs containing literary texts multiplied, and more recently has been overshadowed by the number of e-texts available in various standardized formats on the Web. They have simultaneously become more accessible in terms of being able to be read more like a traditional literary text and to be more easily interrogated. Lowry's point still holds, though, that instructors of literary research can use electronic texts to illustrate the nature and process of textual research as well as to illustrate the very nature of a primary resource.

Like Dene Grigar, Lowry cites hypermedia as a way for students to see how criticism, as well as other source documents, relates to the text in question. Using hypermedia, professors can show students vital correlations between these various documents in a way that can further illuminate the research process.

Talking primarily in terms of undergraduate research, Lowry makes the salient point that there must be cooperation between college/university administration, library administration, and computing services to make sure that there is enough financial, technical, and pedagogical support to make these electronic resources available to and useable by undergraduates. As she puts it: "In order to integrate electronic primary source materials successfully into the undergraduate academic experience, access to these materials must be as transparent and hassle-free as possible, and point-of-use assistance must be readily available."[10]

Barbara Guenther, while not limiting herself to strictly literary research, talks in the mid-1990s about the possibilities for creativity in the form of a research paper.[11] Guenther's background is in teaching composition to English as a Second Language (ESL) students, but what she says in this paper can hold true for all humanities students learning to write quality research papers. Guenther reports that many of her advanced ESL students exhibited an extreme level of unease with the research paper assignment. Her ideas for circumventing this discomfort were to encourage a creative approach to not only the research paper, but also to the methods used to undertake the research. While not eschewing academic rigor, students were able to present their findings in a form that made it more personal and meaningful to them, which made the writing more vital and engaging to the reader/instructor. Leaving aside the ESL angle, such an approach to the research paper assignment might be of particular interest to those in the profession who find themselves combining the teaching of composition, research, and literature to varying degrees. One of Guenther's students wrote a research paper on the subject of Man Ray's photography in the form of an open letter to Man Ray; another wrote a research paper in the guise of an informative monologue: the student presented what was learned through doing research as a written guide for a walking tour of a specific art gallery, all the while citing references and including a list of works cited. As Guenther puts it, "Jin's persona in this research paper is informative but not pedestrian, animated but not distracting."[12] Students doing literary research who are still, for whatever reason, not comfortable or proficient at producing a literary research paper might do well with such creative leeway.

Guenther mentions that it is important to explode the myth, if such a liberal approach to the research paper is used, that research can only take place in the library. She rightly notes that there are applicable and highly useful sources—such as interviews—that do not involve the academic library. Nevertheless, Guenther's view of the role that the contemporary academic library can and should play in the process of teaching research is distressingly reductive. "Because computers have made libraries so accessible to students," she writes, "activities that will enable [the students] to make full use of traditional academic resources ... need not consume a great amount of instructional time." Guenther goes on to say that "we need to spend time making students aware that a writer has a wealth of other sources as well: public records, surveys, polls, [and] videos."[13] College and university libraries have more to offer than what are referred to here as "traditional academic resources": most notably, the professional knowledge of the academic library reference staff that can show the student how to access non-traditional as well as traditional means of finding information. A more reasonable view of the academic library than the one Guenther espouses, coupled with a willingness to allow for responsible experimentation in the presentation of a research paper, would be truly helpful when dealing with ambivalent students.

Jeanne Gunner's short article, published in 2002—really a class assignment preceded by a short explanation of its nature—is a good indicator of how literary research can be folded into a composition/rhetoric program, and as such usefully complements Guenther's essay.[14] Gunner claims in her prefatory note that she aims to break down "calcified notions of research-based writing"[15] with this assignment, which asks students to read and respond to Chinua Achebe's *Things Fall Apart*. She instructs her students to do library research *not* to uncover criticism pertaining to Achebe's work, but rather to do their own evaluative research on the legitimacy of the text as a valid source of information on a certain aspect of African culture at the close of the nineteenth century. The payoff for the students in using the appropriate resources in their library's collection is that they will see that literary research can be done using other resources (relevant subject encyclopedias, historical studies) besides the standard literary criticism reference tools, and also be able to think about literature in ways, and using methods, usually reserved for graduate students.

In a fairly unlikely place (a composition textbook) Wendy Weston McLallen, writing in 2001, skillfully synthesizes the teaching of the literary research process with the teaching of the writing process.[16] Her audience consists of first-year writing students, but the alert and open-minded instructor would likely find this a useful refresher or source of new ideas. McLallen treats literary research as a part of the process of writing a research paper, and indeed her focus is on writing, and how research can be used to support that initiative.

We are reminded by McLallen that the literary research process begins with the first reading of the primary source. She encourages students to keep a reading notebook, using that written reflection on the text as a way to choose an appropriate and meaningful topic, and then to reread the text with an eye for generating research questions. The reading notebook can also be used in conjunction with the rereading of the text, to determine which portions of a longer work would be most useful to revisit.

McLallen stresses to her student readers that "anyone can go to the library, look up sources, and then report on that information,"[17] and that their instructor is more interested in how the acquired information is synthesized into the paper. She advocates a process of simultaneous writing and researching, which will help to prevent the student from forgetting any insights that occurred during her research, and also to ensure that each student's own thoughts and reactions do not drown in the multitude of other, more conventionally authoritative voices that she will encounter in the secondary sources. She also encourages students to temporarily suspend their research activities after a few weeks and go back to the primary source. Reading the text once again, the students use their notebooks to record the ways in which exposure to the secondary literature may have altered their reactions to—and understanding of—the text.

Maureen Pastine (1987) has written a very simple, but not simplistic, and certainly comprehensive, overview of the concepts and resources that librarians unfamiliar with English literature-focused bibliographic instruction need to know.[18] She stresses the importance of introducing, conceptually, the idea of publication sequence in terms of primary and secondary sources. Briefly touching on examples of important guides to primary sources, she quickly switches focus in a section entitled "Secondary and Tertiary Sources" (where she never really clearly defines what constitutes the latter). Here, Pastine explains the importance of book reviews, biographical sources, bibliographies, literary periodicals, indexes, dictionaries and glossaries, and literary surveys to the research process. She notes that the body of published criticism of poetry and short stories pales in comparison to criticism of longer works. Pastine also addresses the lopsided nature of bibliographic control of different aspects of literature: finding poems and short stories is often difficult unless they are anthologized, as they often are not indexed.

One of the most prestigious and respected organizations in the field of literary study in the United States is the Modern Language Association. As such, no review of the literature of teaching literary research would be complete without an examination of one of its major publications, the *MLA Handbook for Writers of Research Papers*, geared primarily toward undergraduate students.[19] The majority of the book is comprised of mechanical matters relating to the construction of a research paper: punctuation, margins and spacing, abbreviations, and proper methods of source documentation, including lists of works cited as well as citing sources within the text. While these features are useful to the student in the midst of composing or polishing their research paper, perhaps more interesting in the context of this review is the meditation on the need for such citation mechanics, offered in the second chapter, "Plagiarism."[20]

In this chapter, Gibaldi defines plagiarism, discusses the consequences of it, and distinguishes between its different forms. He links a profound understanding of plagiarism to being information literate, but also ties it into the research process. Despite the influx of new technologies that facilitate access to increasing amounts of information, Gibaldi maintains that "the essential intellectual tasks of a research project have not changed," and that students who desire to get beyond the information-seeking process and synthesize the information with their own thoughts "must rigorously distinguish between what they borrow and what they create."[21]

Gibaldi also prefaces the more technical aspects of this volume with an opening chapter on what a research paper can and should be. Without putting a great deal of emphasis on literary, or even humanist, research, Gibaldi attempts to counterbalance some of the mechanical leanings of the rest of the book, reminding the reader that doing research can and should be inspiring, and not merely "a mechanical exercise."[22]

A large part of the first chapter, subtitled "Conducting Research," deals with the role the library plays in the research process. Using the method familiar to anyone who has used the MLA or APA style guide, or the *Chicago Manual of Style*, Gibaldi presents, in a hierarchical outline, the various resources that the modern academic library has to offer, starting with the triumvirate he deems the "central information system,"—the library catalog, "bibliographic databases" (he uses *MLAIB* as an example), and "other electronic resources"—before narrowing his focus to enumerate and describe all types of resources, from "collections of abstracts" to "biographical sources." Perhaps strangely, given the humanistic focus of the MLA and its view of books as containers of important intellectual information as well as physical objects worthy of study, Gibaldi offers his readers a list of reasons why "online and CD-ROM databases have a number of advantages over print versions of reference works,"[23] but offers no comparable list of advantages for print resources.

The final section of this chapter is Gibaldi's attempt to introduce his readers to information literacy, in a section of the chapter titled "Evaluating Sources." Here, he couples the advice given in commonly found guides to assessing the scholarly usefulness of a web site's contents with pointers on evaluating the worth of a printed scholarly document. The peer review process is noted as a means of determining scholarly work, as is checking for "accuracy and verifiability" by examining the works cited in the publication. Gibaldi informs the reader that the list of works cited can verify the accuracy of the information presented in the text, as well as "tell you something about the breadth of the author's knowledge of the subject and about any possible bias."[24]

Because this information is presented in one of the most widely used publications of one of the most prestigious literary studies organization in the United States, it would seem to be an excellent place for students to begin to learn about literary research. However, Gibaldi consciously makes the information broad enough to apply to any student learning how to begin the research process, and thus a student would need to supplement this text with other information on doing research that is strictly literary in nature.

TEACHING LITERARY RESEARCH AT THE GRADUATE LEVEL

The Art of Literary Research by Richard Altick and John Fenstermaker must head any list of resources for teaching literary research at the graduate level. First published in 1963, the fourth edition (1993) was extensively revised to take into account the effects of computerization on literary research. The focus of the book, however, is not on technology, but rather on those habits of mind that a scholar must develop. In the first chapter, "Vocation," the authors position literary research as a crucial tool, but not as the end in itself. "Research is the means, scholarship the end; research is an occupation, scholarship is a habit of mind and a way of life. Scholars are more than researchers, for while they may be gifted in the discovery and assessment of facts, they are, besides, persons of broad and luminous learning."[25]

Chapter Two, "The Spirit of Scholarship," encompasses "Error: Its Prevalence, Progress, and Persistence; Examining the Evidence; Two Applications of the Critical Spirit: Fixing Dates and Testing Authenticity." The third chapter reviews "Some Scholarly Occupations," including "Textual Study, Problems of Authorship, The Search for Origins, Tracing Reputation and Influence, [and] Cultivating a Sense of the Past." Succeeding chapters deal with "Finding Materials," "Libraries," "Making Notes," "The Philosophy of Composition," and "The Scholar's Life." Although generations of technology have come and gone since this edition was published and some of the techniques and resources have changed radically, the sage advice proffered and scholarly values advocated by the authors continue to form the critical core of what a graduate student should aspire to accomplish.

Others have also addressed some of the challenges facing graduate students as they become scholarly literary researchers. Craig Abbott, a Northern Illinois University professor who taught Bibliography and Methods of Research, writes in *Literary Research* in 1987[26] about the changes that have arisen in the teaching of literary bibliography and research—the "pervasiveness of literary theory"—but perhaps more important to this discussion is his acknowledgment of "the proliferation (and uneven quality) of reference materials, and the greater availability of primary materials— books and manuscripts—in microform."[27] This problem, if one insists upon seeing it as such, has only been exacerbated, in the intervening years since Abbott's writing, by the onslaught of electronic reference resources and online storehouses of electronically rendered primary materials.

Abbott relates that, in his fifteen-year tenure as instructor of this course, adjustments have had to be made to allow for the recognition of the aforementioned changes, but that the essence of the course—the reason for teaching it as well as the outcome—is still the same.

Abbott knew something in 1987 that has not caught on as well as it should have by now in the field of bibliographic instruction: library and research skills—whether general or discipline-specific—cannot be learned in a vacuum, at least not as well as when taught in the context of a meaningful assignment. As he says, "the adequacy of the answer and of the strategy to find it depend on the context and without a context students lose sight of the relation of their search to the process of scholarship."[28] He stresses that his students needed to know the types of reference materials available more than they needed to know them each individually, and that it was still more important to know why these resources would be used. In Abbott's view, it was imperative for the students to understand the ends for which each resource could be used as a means.

Abbott also states in this article that the quality of reflection on the research process is at least as important as learning how to effectively perform literary research. "What is the object being studied? What is the relation of the study to other studies—that is, to the continuing scholarly 'conversation'?"[29] The changes in reference resources, availability of primary resources, and the advent of critical theory and intertextuality to the forefront of graduate studies in literatures in English has, ultimately, for Abbott, reinforced the desired end result of the course: for students "to gain a further understanding of the scholarly enterprise and to see the histories of texts as integral, if not central, to humanistic study."[30] It need hardly be noted that in the years since this article was published, not only has the number of reference resources increased, but also the number of ways to access these resources. Abbott's call for an understanding of why, and when, the resources should be used, as well as the necessity of reflection on their importance as part of the scholarly conversation is even more relevant now than it was in 1987.

Interestingly, David L. Anderson, writing in the *Literary Research Newsletter*, in 1978, makes a call for the inclusion of foreign language graduate students.[31] As a professor of foreign languages, rather than of English, he brings that perspective to this contribution. He claims that training in research methods is the highest priority in the teaching of graduate English, with training in literary analysis being a close second.

Emphasized the least, according to Anderson, is the reading knowledge of a foreign language. He argues that the reverse is necessarily true in foreign language graduate departments, where, obviously, fluency in a targeted foreign language is considered to be of the utmost importance, followed by historical linguistics or philological training, and ending with training in research methods as having the least emphasis.

Anderson makes the important point that instructors of English literature (and departmental administrators) would do well to remember that English is studied in the context of other languages—not as an island unto itself. Students can only benefit in their studies from a fluency in other languages. Conversely, students of foreign languages would benefit greatly from being taught research methods, instead of being more or less left to fend for themselves. This can be accomplished by accepting foreign language students into English research methods courses, while subtly changing the scope of these courses to include topics germane to worldwide literary issues, rather than solely those normally considered under the rubric of literatures in English. Anderson also suggests that English graduate students be allowed to benefit from the new foreign language pedagogical advances based on the Dartmouth/Rassias Method (see Horner and Stansfield's bibliography for further information[32]) that supposedly will allow a student to become fluent in a foreign language in the space of an academic year. Basically, in allowing foreign language students to take part in the research methods courses, English graduate students' education will be enriched as well, as they learn more about bibliographic and literary research issues in other languages and cultures.

Susan Handelman (1987) sees the disparate and opposed fields within English studies as something that is often kept from graduate students who are entering the profession, leaving them without a sense of their profession's intellectual history.[33] While they may be aware of the existence of different approaches to literary study (New Criticism, reader-response, feminist criticism), they are not given the knowledge of how these different schools of thought interacted with each other in the medium of scholarly debate. Handelman argues that while English professors are often loathe to discuss their own profession's fractiousness, students still need to have a sense, both historical and current, of the interplay between the different approaches. Without this, they will be much less employable.

The ubiquitous "Methods" course, Handelman argues, is an excellent place to insert discussion on the intellectual debates inherent in English studies. She asserts that the course mostly exists in English departments as yet another closed-off portion of the total playing field, without any direct intellectual or philosophical connection to other literary theories being taught. Since so many English scholars of all different theoretical stripes have a keen interest in textuality, it would make sense to incorporate their concerns into a course that is centered on "traditional" textual and bibliographic research.

Literary research, then, can be taught in the Methods course as it would apply to the different approaches. Handelman offers as an example the suggestion of "helping the student interested in reader-response criticism and reception theory learn how to find and analyze contemporary reviews of a work."[34] The Methods course, in this way, would not only serve to familiarize students with the different theoretical approaches to the study of English literature (Handelman here acknowledges the critics who claim that such knowledge would be better imparted in elective courses), but, in keeping with the established goal of the course, show them the different ways that research can be performed in each context. Student comments recorded in her article suggest that introduction to these various approaches to literary research could actually *supplant* the more traditional bibliographic and textual editing research, which will be more useful to students when they are closer to the end of their graduate career, and have become more specialized.

David Leon Higdon, writing in 2002, fifteen years after Handelman, and explaining the reasons why he has decided to revamp his own literary research methods course, echoes her sentiments regarding the inclusion of critical theories into such a course.[35] Where Handelman seems to be leaning towards minimizing the role of skills and areas of knowledge such as enumerative bibliography and documentation protocols, Higdon strives to link them to the various critical methods. He introduces the latter only as extensions of the former: introducing "deconstructionism when working with annotative supplements and word meanings, [and] new historicism when working with sources and intertextuality."[36]

R. H. Miller (1987), in looking at the "new directions" that the graduate research course in literature has been taking, singles out library skills: "A treatment of library resources that is bounded by an older tradition of literary-historical concerns does not serve graduate students or colleagues well at all."[37] He agrees with Handelman that students need to learn how to access information in other disciplines like psychology, sociology, and economics, to be able to meet the needs of more recent critical approaches. In naming these disciplines, Miller contributes to a necessary dialogue concerning practical issues that augments Handelman's discussion of theory.

Miller also is in agreement with other authors covered here in his call to demystify computers and the role(s) they can play in graduate literary research. He mentions the need to teach "strategy-based systems of research,"[38] by which he means learning how different library resources are supplemental and complementary to each other, and using that understanding to be able to plan a course of action before going to a certain resource. Miller claims that, among other things, this would help ease the transition from searching in print materials to using computerized reference sources. This was true in 1987, and is even more apt now, with the countless shades of grey that exist between print and electronic resources available in, or through, the academic library.

T. H. Howard-Hill (1978) writes that he decided to change the title of his course from "Bibliography and Methods in Research" to "Introduction to Graduate Study of English," taking into account the decrease of doctoral candidates as well as the tendency of the job market to place them in positions where they would most likely be more involved with teaching freshman composition than with textual editing.[39] More to the point, he notes that he calls what he does in this course "teaching bibliographical reference" rather than teaching "research."[40] Howard-Hill claims that most of the literary enquiries students have can be answered by literary reference works held in the library, and their use constitutes reference and not "research," which should be saved for doctoral students once they are specialized and have more experience.

In a similar vein, Harrison T. Meserole (1976) makes an important distinction between graduate and undergraduate literary research.[41] Before outlining the different units that make up the introduction to his graduate studies course, he notes that the literary research that undergraduates do largely consists of using their library's reference resources to obtain facts, and that the skills needed to accomplish this sort of research are those with which the beginning graduate student in English literature should be armed. Although Meserole has his students go on a "fact-finding" mission at the outset of his class, the purpose is to show them that the research they are now expected to do is of a higher caliber, and the questions that will arise in their work will not be answerable by the reference resources they were familiar with as undergraduates. Indeed, the exercise is designed to show the students that a mastery of the resources at their disposal combined with the necessary judgment to know which ones are appropriate is not enough; "graduate English requires perception, imagination, resourcefulness."[42] Meserole's students will learn that, although they have innumerable library resources at their disposal, they require an "appropriate skepticism,"[43] and they will hopefully learn to turn this skepticism not only towards the sources, but also towards the conclusions that they will eventually make.

Nancy Ide (1987) had the thankless task of writing about the problem of computer integration into literary research at a time just prior to the sudden leap in research-friendly computer technology.[44] She asserts that research methods courses should focus equally on teaching proper use of the tools and appropriate methodology, and that it is not enough to simply give the students a list of available databases. As is true with other authors covered in this chapter that write on the topic of new technologies in literary research, this assertion not only stands the test of time, but increases in validity as the academic community becomes exposed to ever more computational aids. Ide also reminds us that possibilities for computer-related research exist beyond using the *MLAIB* to locate criticism; students should be given the opportunity to learn how computers can be used to analyze style and content. This "quantitative methodology," she argues, should be represented in the "literary critical context," (echoing Handelman) since it can raise and answer questions about all manner of issues that are essential to literary study: "sources of meaning and reference, the autonomy of text, and the relevance of context."[45] Indeed, it is crucial for the use of computers in literary research to be folded into the methods and approaches that are taught in the introductory course. Finally, Ide calls for a follow-up course in the form of an elective that would treat in greater depth the ways in which computational methodology can enhance literary research endeavors.

A review of the published literature on teaching literary research at the graduate level would be remiss if it did not make note of one of its central organs, the *Literary Research Newsletter*, re-christened *Literary Research*, or *LR*, for the last five years of its existence. The periodical was published from 1976–1990, and during its run provided a forum for the professional discussion, mostly among professors of English, of matters relating to literary research. There is a great deal of literature contained in those pages that addresses pedagogical issues relating to literary research, and most of it concerns itself with the graduate level of study. Abbott, Anderson, Handelman, Ide, Meserole, and R. H. Miller, all of whose writings are discussed here, contributed to *Literary Research Newsletter*. In addition, there are several articles which deal with the same topics that deserve mention.[46] These, and indeed the whole run, should be perused by the professional who wants to get a more complete sense of the professional dialogue on literary research, including but not limited to pedagogical concerns.

Another relevant resource that includes, but is not limited to, pedagogical concerns is the online bibliography "Studies for Literatures in English Librarians," initiated by Scott Stebelman and currently maintained by Aparna Zambare and Michaelyn Burnette for the Association of College and Research Libraries' Literatures in English section.[47] Two sections of the bibliography, "English in Higher Education," and "Reference, Research, and Instruction," may prove especially useful to those seeking further literature on the topic of teaching literary research. Recommendations from users of the Bibliography are welcomed. The bibliography web site is currently updated on an irregular basis.

CONCLUSION

Perhaps it is fitting that, in the thirty-year span of professional and scholarly discourse on teaching literary research covered in this chapter, many of the same themes and discussion points arise. It is heartening, as a still recent addition to the ranks of librarians interested in teaching literary research, for me to know that the core values of this aspect of our profession remain the same. Methods and approaches to the study of literature are constantly changing, with the latest "new thing" inevitably heading for a fall out of favor, new pedagogical approaches to teaching composition *vis à vis* the research paper have been and will continue to flow from our English departments, and of course, technology certainly cannot be accused of standing still. For all that change, though, one fact, which was alluded to time and again in the literature, is that the past is the past, and the primary source material does not change. Neither does the role of the librarian in assisting students (and instructors) in learning how to navigate the "literature of literature."[48]

NOTES
1. Lori E. Buchanan and Anne May Berwind, "Using the Card Catalog to Identify Literary Criticism," *Research Strategies* 7, no. 4 (1989): 180-86, quote from 180.
2. Judy Reynolds, "The *MLA International Bibliography* and Library Instruction in Literature and the Humanities," in *Literature in English: A Guide for Librarians in the Digital Age*, ed. Betty H. Day and William A. Wortman, 213-47 (Chicago: American Library Association. Association of College and Research Libraries, 2000).

3.   Ibid., 223.
4.   Ibid., 229.
5.   Ibid., 230.
6.   Dene Grigar, "What is Seen Depends on How Everybody is Doing Everything: Using Hypertext to Teach Gertrude Stein's *Tender Buttons*," in *Dialogic Classroom: Teachers Integrating Computer Technology, Pedagogy, and Research*, ed. Joan Latchaw and Jeffrey R. Galin, 27-42 (Urbana, Ill.: National Council of Teachers of English, 1998).
7.   Bianca Falbo, "Teaching from the Archives," *RBM* 1, no. 1 (2000): 33-35.
8.   Anita K. Lowry, "Electronic Texts and Multimedia in the Academic Library: A View from the Front Line," in *Literary Texts in an Electronic Age: Scholarly Implications and Library Services*, ed. Brett Sutton, 57-66. (Urbana, Ill.: Graduate School of Library and Information Science. University of Illinois at Urbana-Champaign, 1994).
9.   Ibid., 59.
10.   Ibid., 60.
11.   Barbara Guenther, "De-Mythicizing the Research Paper," *Journal of the Imagination in Language Learning* 3 (1995-6): 54-8.
12.   Ibid., 56.
13.   Ibid, 54.
14.   Jeanne Gunner, "An Assignment for Encouraging Research," in *Strategies for Teaching First-Year Composition*, ed. Duane Roen, Veronica Pantoja, Lauren Yena, Susan K. Miller, and Eric Waggoner, 609-10 (Urbana, Ill.: National Council of Teachers of English, 2002).
15.   Ibid., 609.
16.   Wendy Weston McLallen, "Why Write Literary Research Papers?" in *The Subject is Research: Processes and Practices*, ed. Pavel Zemliansky and Wendy Bishop, 165-77 (Portsmouth, NH: Boynton/Cook, 2001).
17.   Ibid., 170-1.
18.   Maureen Pastine, "Teaching the Art of Literary Research," in *Conceptual Frameworks for Bibliographic Education: Theory into Practice*, ed. Mary Reichel and Mary Ann Ramsey, 134-44 (Littleton, Colo.: Libraries Unlimited, 1987).
19.   Joseph Gibaldi, *MLA Handbook for Writers of Research Papers*, 6th ed. (New York: Modern Language Association of America, 2003). Contrast this with Joseph Gibaldi's *MLA Style Manual and Guide to Scholarly Publishing*, 2nd ed. (New York: Modern Language Association of America, 1998), which is geared towards graduate students and professional scholars.
20.   Gibaldi, *MLA Handbook*, 65-75.
21.   Ibid., 69.
22.   Ibid., 4-5.
23.   Ibid., 15.
24.   Ibid., 44.
25.   Richard D. Altick and John J. Fenstermaker, *The Art of Literary Research*, 4th ed. (New York, London: W. W. Norton & Company, 1993), 20.
26.   Abbott, Craig S., "Goals and Methods in a Traditional Approach to Bibliography and Research," *Literary Research* 12, nos. 2 & 3 (1987): 95-8.
27.   Ibid., 95.
28.   Ibid., 97.
29.   Ibid., 96.
30.   Ibid., 98.
31.   David L. Anderson, "Graduate Research in English: A Foreign Point of View," *Literary Research Newsletter* 3, no. 1 (1978): 15–21.

32.   Jeanne Horner and Charles Stansfield, *The Dartmouth/Rassias Method: An Annotated Bibliography* (Educational Resources Information Center, 1980). ED181716.

33.   Susan Handelman, "Ending the Cold War: Literary Theory and the Bibliography and Methods Course," *Literary Research* 12, nos. 2 & 3 (1987): 115-35.

34.   Ibid., 120.

35.   David Leon Higdon, "Ancient Madness or Contemporary Wisdom? A New Literary Research Methods Course," *Profession* (2002): 140-50.

36.   Ibid., 141.

37.   R. H. Miller, "New Directions in the Graduate Research Course," *Literary Research* 12, nos. 2 & 3 (1987): 111-14.

38.   Ibid., 113.

39.   T. H. Howard-Hill, "Introduction to Graduate Research in English at the University of South Carolina," *Literary Research Newsletter* 3, no. 4 (1978): 151-62.

40.   Ibid., 161.

41.   Harrison T. Meserole, "The Design and Function of the 'Introduction to Research and Bibliography' Course in Graduate English Study," *Literary Research Newsletter* 1, no. 2 (1976): 53-68.

42.   Ibid., 56.

43.   Ibid., 57.

44.   Nancy M. Ide, "The Course in Methods of Literary Research: Integrating Computational Tools and Methodology," *Literary Research* 12, nos. 2 & 3 (1987): 107-110.

45.   Ibid., 109.

46.   The other *Literary Research* newsletter articles mentioned above include: John J. Fenstermaker, "The Introductory Course in Research Methods: A Fuller Context for the Eighties." *Literary Research Newsletter* 7, no. 1 (1982): 3-11.; Bradford Y. Fletcher, "'Unknowns' in the Teaching of Literary Research," *Literary Research* 11, no. 1 (1986): 11-18; Mary W. George and Mary Ann O'Donnell, "The Bibliography and Research Methods Course in American Departments of English," *Literary Research Newsletter* 4, no. 1 (1979): 9-23; Margaret Loftus Ranald, "And Welcome to the Club: The Mission of the Graduate Methodology Course in English," *Literary Research* 11, no. 4 (1986): 253-68; Susan Staves, "Revising the Pedagogy of the Traditional Scholarly Methods Course: The Brandeis Elizabeth Griffith Collective," *Literary Research* 12, nos. 2/3 (1987): 137-50; Scott Stebelman, "Teaching Manuscript and Archival Resources," *Literary Research* 12, no. 1 (1987): 23-34; and William A. Wortman and David D. Mann, "The Introduction to Research and Bibliography Course." *Literary Research Newsletter* 10, nos. 1/2 (1985): 5-16.

47.   http://www.lib.cmich.edu/bibliographers/aparnazambare/LESBibliography.htm

48.   Buchanan and Berwind, 180.

Work in Progress: A Review of the Literature of Literary Research Instruction 2002-2008

Kathleen A. Johnson

Over the past half a dozen years, a number of interesting articles and essays on teaching literary research have been published. In them, many of the themes and issues Dan Coffey identified in his literature review continue to be explored and discussed, albeit with new emphases, given the changing research environment. Searches in WorldCat; *Library, Information Science & Technology Abstracts; Library Literature; ERIC; Educational Abstracts;* and *MLAIB* produced the resources included in this update, covering the period 2002-2008.

ON THE NATURE OF LITERARY RESEARCH AND ITS RELATION TO INFORMATION LITERACY

Although not specifically addressing the teaching of literary research in English language literatures, in "Researching 'Undergraduate Research' in the Humanities,"[1] Reed Wilson clearly states the core issue of teaching and engaging undergraduate students in research in the humanities.

> At the very least, what we mean by "research" in the humanities should be the first "subject" of every course we teach.... We need to point out that in all disciplines, research is not just finding something that already exists, but an endless (in both senses of the word—lacking terminus and *telos*) process of discovery that creates knowledge, on in which subject and object interact to create new structures of reality.... To research is not to *retrieve*.[2]

In the works discussed below, "research" at times encompasses retrieval, but the distinction between the concepts is valuable and should inform all who teach literary research skills. This concept is worth reinforcing for each generation of librarians and literature professors; as long ago as 1978, as noted in Coffey's literature review, Howard-Hill distinguishes between bibliographical reference and research.[3] This clearly relates to Wilson's distinction, published in 2003, between retrieval and research. While not directly addressing the *teaching* of literary research, Rosemary Ross Johnston[4] argues for the value of literary research as "transformative and states that researchers are 'transformers': educators and teacher-scholars who sometimes shape new awareness of *what is*, by describing it, and sometimes 'draw out' and 'raise up' (*educo*) awareness of *what is not* but *could be*, perhaps suggesting reasons and resources for change."[5] Although the *ACRL Information Literacy Competency Standards for Higher Education*[6] includes statements about outcomes and competencies and needs and the Literatures in English Sections 2007 *Research Competency Guidelines for Literatures in English*[7] features words such as "understand," "learn," "differentiate," and "identify," neither document addresses Johnson's emphasis on the transformational aspects of literary research; her observation serves as a reminder to all that mastering the skills of literary research is not the ultimate goal, but rather a means to an end. This echoes the statement from *The Art of Literary Research* quoted in the previous chapter on how "[r]esearch is the means, scholarship the end...".[8]

What mastery of literary research skills means and what it requires are open to ongoing discussion. Stuart Boon and Bill Johnston report on their study of the "conceptions of information literacy" of twenty English faculty members from the United Kingdom; among their findings, they observed both congruence with and significant differences from information literacy research and standards created by librarians. For those engaged in teaching literary research, this article should raise questions of how information literacy relates to literary research and raise awareness of the related but sometimes different emphases and values held by English faculty and by librarians.[9] Coffey discussed a related issue in his coverage of Judy Reynolds' observations on the necessity of librarians understanding the research styles of humanities scholars.[10] Several chapters in *Teaching Literary Research* address this topic as well.

In her thoughtful article, "A Discipline-Based Approach to Information Literacy," Ann Grafstein argues that both librarians and disciplinary faculty are needed to teach students information literacy skills.[11] Drawing on the work of Gavriel Salomon, she distinguishes between *information* and *knowledge*: "Information is discrete, whereas knowledge consists of a network of connections." She maintains that "information—not knowledge—is constantly changing....This core knowledge–base of a discipline, moreover, is not in a constant state of flux. Rather, the core knowledge of a discipline is expanded and perpetuated in relation to a current theoretical or research paradigm."[12] She expresses concern that, in the rush to teach students to think analytically and critically and to become lifelong learners, one not discount the importance of the discipline's insights and values, because these can help the students to achieve these ends.

She delineates the areas in which, in her view, librarians and disciplinary faculty can work most productively toward creating information literate students: librarians should teach students search strategies, including how to use Boolean logic and controlled vocabulary, and how to narrow or broaden a search. Librarians also can teach "generic critical thinking skills" for students to use in assessing information, such as "timeliness," "authority," "bias," "verifiability," and "logical consistency."[13] Disciplinary faculty should teach "evaluating the content of arguments" and "assessing the validity of the evidence." Her concluding sentence summarizes her argument: "Librarians are responsible for imparting the enabling skills that are prerequisite to information seeking and knowledge acquisition across the curriculum, while classroom faculty have the responsibility of teaching those skills that are required for subject-specific inquiry and research."[14]

Generally speaking, Grafstein's division of labor between the librarian and the faculty member is reasonable, but this article does not address the role of a librarian who may also have an advanced degree in the subject. The division of labor may be in part a function of the small amount of contact time that a librarian generally has with students in a class, compared to a faculty member over the period of a semester or quarter. She also does not directly address types of more extensive collaborations that some librarians and disciplinary faculty have created.

Grafstein's declaration that "disciplines have different epistemological structures, and, for this reason, the research process is not identical across disciplines"[15] bolsters the argument for a book dedicated to teaching *literary* research as opposed to other kinds of research.

ON TEACHING LITERARY RESEARCH TO UNDERGRADUATE AND GRADUATE STUDENTS
The books, chapters, and articles noted below are worth reading in conjunction with *Teaching Literary Research*, both from the standpoint of presenting ideas and approaches that complement the essays in *Teaching Literary*

Research and also, in some cases, of affirming or reinforcing concepts in this collection, while providing a different perspective.

With the sixth edition of *A Research Guide for Undergraduate Students: English and American Literature*, authors Nancy L. Baker and Nancy Huling update their *Guide* into the middle of the first decade of the 21st century. Their primary goal is to assist the undergraduate in "the search for secondary sources," although they also include "some guidance on the use of [primary sources]." While they pay major attention to "the thirty or so literary research tools that are most likely to be useful," they also include some "basic research strategy," with an emphasis on doing research in "a systematic way."[16] Their audience is the undergraduate student doing research in English and American literature, rather than the instructor or librarian teaching the undergraduates, but, as they work with literature students, both instructors and librarians can borrow from and build on the foundation laid by Baker and Huling.

Janelle Zauha, a librarian at Montana State University, describes her approaches to providing effective information literacy instruction for students of English in her chapter "English Literature" from the book *Information Literacy Instruction That Works: A Guide to Teaching by Discipline and Student Population*.[17] Topics include "Working with Your English Department" and "What to Teach" and feature practical and specific recommendations on meeting the needs of beginning, intermediate, and graduate students, as well as strategies for working with these various groups. She closes with a section on "Anticipated Trends and Developments," addressing the growth of electronic resources and "one-stop-shopping," full-text databases, and the Web. She cautions that "one of the biggest challenges in this new one-stop-shopping environment, however, will be helping students understand the kinds of materials they find. To unsophisticated researchers, it is often not clear what types of information are being jumbled together in one search result set."[18] Results may contain everything from scholarly, peer-reviewed articles to websites garnered through the search. Zauha urges that the librarian "aggressively market her skills" in helping students become critical thinkers who use these resources ethically and judiciously.[19] Packed with ideas and information, this chapter is a useful resource, especially in its inclusion of types of electronic library resources available in the first decade of the 21st century. A CD-ROM with examples of instructional materials is included with the book. Zauha's chapter is one of the best recent examples of how to work with and in the changing environment.

With chapters written by professors of English, professors of library science, and rare book room curators, *Teaching Bibliography, Textual Criticism, and Book History* (2006) addresses a range of topics, many of which are of interest to those engaged in teaching literary research. Ann R. Hawkins states that "when we talk about pedagogy, then, what matters is what works, or appears to work in specific moments and situations. And, answers to pedagogical questions are almost always determined by local context...."[20] Hawkins eloquently describes the importance of "lore" in teaching, as a source of ideas and practices for both the new and experienced teacher. Furthermore, teachers can learn through "reflective interaction" with the essays and their own experiences.[21]

The book is divided into three major sections: 1. Rationales, 2. Creating and Using Resources, and 3. Methodologies (3.1 Teaching 'History of the Book,' 3.2 Teaching Bibliography and Research Methods, 3.3 Teaching Textual Criticism). An accompanying website provides additional resources and examples of assignments and class plans.

The three chapters discussed below are all from the "Methodologies" section of Hawkins' book. In addition to those included in this review, other chapters also describe approaches to teaching literary research skills to undergraduates, graduate students, and library school students.

Ann R. Hawkins' brief chapter on "Teaching Textual Criticism: Students as Book Detectives and Scholarly Editors"[22] provides an overview of her approach to teaching sophomore (often non-English majors), junior, senior, and graduate level classes.

> I teach the skills involved in textual criticism because—at every level—they translate immediately into both practical research skills (the ability to use reference works to find answers) and theoretical understanding (the ability to answer such questions as who is my audience, what kinds of annotations will they need, what is the nature of my text, why is it so unstable over time, etc.).[23]

Students enjoy the research component of this class, in part because it enables them to become an 'authority'.[24]

Shawcross's "The Bibliography and Research Course" outlines subjects that should be included in such a class and describes the time allotted to each topic throughout a semester. While not explicitly focused on graduate students, the course appears to be primarily directed toward the beginning graduate student rather than the upper level undergraduate. The course includes "Finding Information, Considering Past Information, Updating Information," which requires students to complete a series of exercises designed to familiarize them with standard reference resources such as the big national print catalogs, dictionaries, and biographical resources. The topic "Bibliographic Research and Documentation" is followed by "Textual Matters: Setting Up a Text and Approaches to Discussion." The two final units are "Writing and Presentation Skills" and "Presentations."[25] The reader might weigh the time and emphases that Shawcross allocates to various goals and activities against what the reader does.

Maura Ives' "Integrating 'Bibliography' with 'Literary Research': A Comprehensive Approach" describes a course designed for graduate students in English that covers "MLA documentation format; Print and electronic reference sources in English and the humanities; The special characteristics of humanities research; The history of books and printing; Enumerative, analytical, and descriptive bibliography; and Editorial theory and practice."[26] Ives addresses the challenge of trying to teach both bibliography and literary research in the current climate, but adds that in conjunction with Jerome McGann's concerns about texts in the digital age, "a class such as this one is desperately needed to equip our students for the 'digital future.'"[27] Her pedagogical approach can be summarized by her statement that "Only actual research develops research skills." She highlights the "recursive" nature of the process as students work toward completion of their dual assignments to develop "a research guide and an edition proposal."[28]

Most of the chapter details the assignments and types of learning that take place throughout the course.[29] Given the changing research environment, Ives' discussion of the skills needed to thrive in the "digital future" is especially worthwhile.

Some volumes of the Modern Language Association series Approaches to Teaching World Literature include chapters on how to teach literary research. In her chapter on "*The House of Trials* and the Trials of Master's-Level Research,"[30] from the book *Approaches to Teaching the Works of Sor Juana Inés de la Cruz*, Kathryn McKnight, an associate professor of Spanish at University of New Mexico, focuses on "how to train students to articulate a viable and original research question within a clear theoretical framework and to develop a bibliography that will help them answer that research question."[31] She describes the problem that her master's-level students faced: "few students had a clear concept of what it meant to design an original inquiry into a textual problem."[32] She follows by summarizing her approach to teaching the research methods course, based on guiding the students through a set of activities to enhance their research techniques; the rest of the chapter details the activities and approaches she uses to develop her students' skills. The chapter ends with commentary from the students about what they gained from the class. McKnight's chapter directly addresses many of the concerns that readers of *Teaching Literary Research* find as they work with their students, both in the classroom and in the library and should be valuable especially to those working with beginning graduate students.

As of 2008, the first two volumes in the series Literary Research: Strategies and Sources had appeared. Although best suited for the advanced graduate student or the practicing scholar, these volumes have much value for the serious upper level undergraduate and beginning graduate students as well.

Peggy Keeran and Jennifer Bowers, the authors of *Literary Research and the British Romantic Era* (and editors of the series Literary Research: Strategies and Sources) state that their "goal in this volume is to explain the best practices for conducting literary research in the British Romantic era and to address the challenges scholars working in this era face."[33] As this book is designed to help with "[l]earning sound research practices and knowing standard resources,"[34] the authors "emphasize the process, thereby enabling scholars to become effective researchers."[35] Within the volume, the authors provide examples of search strategies and present and discuss a wide variety of print, digital, microform, and archival resources. Chapter 11, "Researching a Thorny Problem," is a neatly written case study that draws on resources and skills covered in the first ten chapters.[36]

The second volume in this series is Angela Courtney's *Literary Research and the Era of American Nationalism and Romanticism: Strategies and Sources*.[37] Courtney's opening chapter on "Basics of Online Searching" presents an excellent, comprehensive explanation of using the MARC record as a path not only into catalogs but also to any electronic records. Sections on both field and Boolean searching, as well as operators such as "near" are included, as are discussions of differences between subject and keyword searches, on how relevancy rankings work, on revising searches, and on the nature of databases and search engines. She concludes the chapter by noting that although many resources for literary research are now electronic, mastery of both the print and electronic resources is necessary.[38] In the rest of the chapters, Courtney uses an approach similar to that of the first book in the series, with the aim of increasing the research fluency of the scholar or student through identifying resources and highlighting best practices.

Both books in the series Literary Research: Strategies and Sources would be valuable used as texts in graduate classes, addressing as they do the mixed print, microform, and electronic resources that all researchers need to utilize skillfully.

G. David Garson's chapter "Quantitative Research Writing in the Humanities" addresses the topic of quantitative research writing in the humanities, a subject not covered by other works included in this literature review.[39] As the author states in his Preface, he tries "to make this [book] one of particular relevance to those engaged in empirical research, in which the writing process is inextricably bound to research design and statistical methodology."[40] Embedded in this book written mainly for students of the social sciences and sciences is the single chapter for the humanities, which most usefully addresses "conceptualizing in the humanities" and then provides a rather brief section on "reviewing the literature of the humanities." A helpful "checklist" contains pertinent questions for the researcher to ask him or herself. The short bibliography is irrelevant to teaching literary research. With its unique focus, this chapter may prove helpful to those engaged in quantitative research on literary matters. It does not, however, address this in depth, nor, given its publication date, does it touch on some of the most recent developments in quantitative literary research, such as the MONK (Metadata Offer New Knowledge) Project.[41]

Along with Coffey's literature review, this update presents the context in which *Teaching Literary Research: Challenges in a Changing Environment* has developed. The chapters and articles reviewed here and the chapters, written by English professors and by librarians, in this collection are voices in the ongoing conversation about the concepts, perspectives, values, best practices, guidelines, and practical experiences surrounding the teaching of literary research. Long may the discussion flourish!

NOTES

1. Reed Wilson, "Researching 'Undergraduate Research' in the Humanities," *Modern Language Studies* 33, no. 1/2 (Spring-Autumn, 2003), 74-79.
2. Ibid., 77.
3. T. H. Howard-Hill, "Introduction to Graduate Research in English at the University

of South Carolina," Literary Research Newsletter 3, no. 4 (1978): 161.

4.   Rosemary Ross Johnston, "Relevant or Not? Literature, Literary Research and Literary Researchers in Troubled Times," Diogenes 50 (2), 2003: 25-32.

5.   Ibid., 26.

6.   Association of College and Research Libraries, Information Literacy Competency Standards for Higher Education (Chicago: American Library Association, 2000) http://www.ala.org/ala/mgrps/divs/acrl/standards/informationliteracycompetency.cfm

7.   Association of College and Research. Libraries Literatures in English Section, Research Competency Guidelines for Literatures in English (2007) http://www.ala.org/ala/mgrps/divs/acrl/standards/researchcompetenciesles.cfm

8.   Richard D. Altick and John J. Fenstermaker, The Art of Literary Research, 4th ed. (New York, London: W. W. Norton & Company, 1993), 20.

9.   Stuart Boon and Bill Johnston, "A Phenomenographic Study of English Faculty's Conceptions of Information Literacy," Journal of Documentation 63 no. 2 (2007): 204-228.

10.   Judy Reynolds, "The MLA International Bibliography and Library Instruction in Literature and the Humanities," in Literature in English: A Guide for Librarians in the Digital Age, ed. Betty H. Day and William A. Wortman, 213-47 (Chicago: American Library Association. Association of College and Research Libraries, 2000), 223.

11.   Ann Grafstein, "A Discipline-Based Approach to Information Literacy," The Journal of Academic Librarianship. 28, no. 4 (July 2002): 197-204.

12.   Ibid., 200.

13.   Ibid., 201.

14.   Ibid., 202.

15.   Ibid., 201.

16.   Nancy L. Baker and Nancy Huling, A Research Guide for Undergraduate Students: English and American Literature, 6th ed. (New York: The Modern Language Association of America, 2006), 1-2.

17.   Janelle M. Zauha, "English Literature," in Information Literacy Instruction That Works: A Guide to Teaching by Discipline and Student Population, ed. Patrick Ragains, 111-127 (New York, London: Neal-Schuman Publishers, Inc., 2006).

18.   Ibid., 125.

19.   Ibid., 125.

20.   Ann R. Hawkins, "Introduction: Towards a Pedagogy of Bibliography" in Teaching Bibliography, Textual Criticism, and Book History, ed. Ann R. Hawkins, 6 (London: Pickering & Chatto, 2006).

21.   Ibid., 12.

22.   Ann R. Hawkins, "Teaching Textual Criticism: Students as Book Detectives and Scholarly Editors," in Teaching Bibliography, Textual Criticism, and Book History, 174-177.

23.   Ibid., 174

24.   Ibid., 177.

25.   John Shawcross, "The Bibliography and Research Course," in Teaching Bibliography, Textual Criticism, and Book History, 109-116.

26.   Maura Ives' "Integrating 'Bibliography' with 'Literary Research': A Comprehensive Approach," in Teaching Bibliography, Textual Criticism, and Book History, 117-123.

27.   Ibid., 117-118.

28.   Ibid., 118.

29.   Ibid., 117, 118.

30.   Kathryn Joy McKnight, "The House of Trials and the Trials of Master's-Level Research," in Approaches to Teaching the Works of Sor Juana Inés de la Cruz, ed. Emilie L. Bergmann and

Stacey Schlau, 161-169 Approaches to Teaching World Literature (New York: The Modern Language Association, 2007).

31.   Ibid., 161.

32.   Ibid., 161.

33.   Peggy Keeran and Jennifer Bowers, "Introduction," in *Literary Research and the British Romantic Era: Strategies and Resources*, ix, Literary Research: Strategies and Sources, No. 1 (Lanham, Md.: Scarecrow Press, 2005).

34.   Ibid., ix.

35   Ibid., xi.

36.   Keeran and Bowers, "Researching a Thorny Problem," in *Literary Research and the British Romantic Era: Strategies and Resources*, 207-215.

37.   Angela Courtney, *Literary Research and the Era of American Nationalism and Romanticism: Strategies and Sources*, Literary Research: Strategies and Sources, No. 2 (Lanham, Md.: Scarecrow Press, 2008).

38.   Courtney, "Basics of Online Searching," in *Literary Research and the Era of American Nationalism and Romanticism: Strategies and Sources*, 1-17.

39.   G. David Garson, "Quantitative Research Writing in the Humanities," in *Guide to Writing Empirical Papers, Theses, and Dissertations*. New York: Marcel Dekker, 2002. Available on *NetLibrary*, http://www.netlibrary.com (accessed May 29, 2008).

40.   Garson, "Preface," in *Guide to Writing Empirical Papers, Theses, and Dissertations*, iii.

41.   MONK (Metadata Offer New Knowledge) Project, http://www.monkproject.org/

Appendix: Research Competency Guidelines for Literatures in English

June 2007
From the Foreword to the Research Competency Guidelines:

> Although based on framework of the ACRL Information Literacy Competency Standards for Higher Education (2000), these guidelines address the need for a more specific and source-oriented approach within the discipline of English literatures, including a concrete list of research skills. [The complete Foreword may be found on web site of the Literatures in English Section of the Association of College and Research Libraries, American Library Association. http://www.ala.org/ala/mgrps/divs/acrl/about/sections/les/lescompetency.cfm]

PURPOSE OF THE RESEARCH COMPETENCY GUIDELINES FOR LITERATURES IN ENGLISH

+ To aid students of literatures in English in the development of thorough and productive research skills
+ To encourage the development of a common language for librarians, faculty, and students involved with research related to literatures in English
+ To encourage librarian and faculty collaboration in the teaching of research methods to students of literatures in English
+ To aid librarians and faculty in the development of instructional sessions and programs
+ To assist in the development of a shared understanding of student competencies and needs
+ To aid librarians and faculty in the development of research methods courses at the undergraduate and graduate levels

Because teaching methods, course content, and undergraduate requirements vary by institution, librarians and faculty may apply these guidelines in different ways to meet the needs of their students. For guidelines on helping students develop general research skills, librarians and faculty may refer to the ACRL Information Literacy Competency Standards for Higher Education at http://www.acrl.org/ala/mgrps/divs/acrl/standards/informationliteracycompetency.cfm.

RESEARCH COMPETENCY GUIDELINES FOR LITERATURES IN ENGLISH: INTRODUCTION

Most research in literary studies begins with the text, whether it is a paperback novel, the electronic text of a poem on an author's Web site, or an illuminated manuscript in a library's collection. Educators encourage students to gain a deeper understanding of a text by exploring the context of the writing and the interpretations of others, and by developing and supporting their own interpretations. Limited only by their imaginations, students face almost endless opportunities for interpretation of a text.

Research plays an indispensable role in the textual discovery process for students. Good research skills help the literary explorer learn more about the author and the author's world, examine scholarly interpretations of the text, and create new studies and interpretations to add to a body of knowledge. Sometimes the goals of textual discovery and interpretation can get lost in the minutiae of database searching and conforming to specific citation styles. However, it is important for librarians and other educators to remember these goals when helping students develop the research skills necessary for literary exploration.

OUTCOMES FOR UNDERGRADUATE ENGLISH OR AMERICAN LITERATURE MAJORS

I. Understand the structure of information within the field of literary research:

I.1 Differentiate between primary and secondary sources

    I.1.i. Learn to discover and use primary source materials in print and in digital repositories, e.g. ECCO and EEBO

I.2 Understand that literary scholarship is produced and disseminated in a variety of formats, including monographs, journal articles, conference proceedings, dissertations, reference sources and websites

I.3 Learn the significant features (e.g., series title, volume number, imprint) of different kinds of documents (e.g., journal articles, monographs, essays from edited collections)

I.4 Differentiate between reviews of literary works and literary criticism

I.5 Understand the concept and significance of peer-reviewed sources of information

I.6 Understand that literary texts exist in a variety of editions, some of which are more authoritative or useful than others

I.7 Understand the authorship, production, dissemination or availability of literary production. This includes understanding the meanings and distinctions of the concepts of editions, facsimiles, and authoritative editions.

II. Identify and use key literary research tools to locate relevant information:

II.1 Effectively use library catalogs to identify relevant holdings at local institutions and print and online catalogs and bibliographic tools to identify holdings at other libraries

II.2 Distinguish among the different types of reference works (e.g. catalogs, bibliographies, indexes, concordances, etc.) and understand the kind of information offered by each

II.3 Identify, locate, evaluate, and use reference sources and other appropriate information sources about authors, critics, and theorists

II.4 Use subjective and objective sources such as book reviews, citation indexes, and surveys of research to determine the relative importance of an author and/or the relevance of the specific work

II.5 Use reference and other appropriate information resources to provide background information and contextual information about social, intellectual, and literary culture

II.6 Understand the range of physical and virtual locations and repositories and how to navigate them successfully

II.7 Understand the uses of all available catalogs and services

III. Plan effective search strategies and modify search strategies as needed:

III.1 Identify the best indexes and databases

III.2 Use appropriate commands (such as Boolean operators) for database searches

III.3 Identify broader, narrower, and related terms or concepts when initial searches retrieve few or no results

III.4 Identify and use subject terms from the MLA International Bibliography and other specialized indexes and bibliographies

III.5 Identify and use Library of Congress subject headings for literature and authors

IV. Recognize and make appropriate use of library services in the research process:

IV.1 Identify and utilize librarians and reference services in the research process

IV.2 Use interlibrary loan and document delivery to acquire materials not available at one's own library

IV.3 Use digital resource service centers to read and create literary and critical documents in a variety of digital forms

V. Understand that some information sources are more authoritative than others and demonstrate critical thinking in the research process:

V.1 Know about Internet resources (e.g., electronic discussion lists, websites) and how to evaluate them for relevancy and credibility

V.2 Differentiate between resources provided free on the Internet and subscription electronic resources

V.3 Develop and use appropriate criteria for evaluating print resources

V.4 Learn to use critical bibliographies as a tool in evaluating materials

VI. Understand the technical and ethical issues involved in writing research essays:

VI.1 Document sources ethically

VI.2 Employ the MLA or other appropriate documentation style

VI.3 Understand the relationship between received knowledge and the production of new knowledge in the discipline of literary studies

VI.4 Analyze and ethically incorporate the work of others to create new knowledge

VII. Locate information about the literary profession itself:

VII.1 Access information about graduate programs, about specialized programs in film study, creative writing, and other related fields, and about workshops and summer study opportunities

VII.2 Access information about financial assistance and scholarships available for literary study and related fields

VII.3 Access information on careers in literary studies and use of these skills in other professions

VII.4 Access information on professional associations

REFERENCES

Altick, Richard D., and John J. Fenstermaker. *The Art of Literary Research*. 4th ed. New York: Norton, 1993.

Association of College and Research Libraries, American Library Association. "Information Literacy Competency Standards for Higher Education." Chicago, IL: ACRL, 2000. 22 March 2007 http://www.acrl. org/ala/mgrps/divs/acrl/standards/informationliteracycompetency.cfm

Gibaldi, Joseph. *MLA Handbook for Writers of Research Papers*. 6th ed. New York: Modern Language Association, 2003.

Grafstein, Ann. "A Discipline-Based Approach to Information Literacy." *Journal of Academic Librarianship* 28 (2002): 197-204.

Jones, Cheryl, Carla Reichard, and Kouider Mokhtari. "Are Students' Learning Styles Discipline Specific?" *Community College Journal of Research & Practice* 27 (2003): 363-375.

Leckie, Gloria J. "Desperately Seeking Citations: Uncovering Faculty Assumptions about the Undergraduate Research Process." *Journal of Academic Librarianship* 22 (1996): 201-208.

Literary Research: LR. College Park, MD : Literary Research Association, 1986-1990.

Literary Research Newsletter. Brockport, N.Y.: Literary Research Newsletter Association, 1976-1985.

Pastine, Maureen. "Teaching the Art of Literary Research." *Conceptual Frameworks for Bibliographic Education: Theory into Practice*. Ed. Mary Reichel and Mary Ann Ramey. Littleton, Colo.: Libraries Unlimited, 1987. 134-44.

Reynolds, Judy. "The MLA International Bibliography and Library Instruction in Literature and the Humanities." *Literature in English: A Guide for Librarians in the Digital Age*. Ed. Betty H. Day and William A. Wortman. Chicago: Association of College and Research Libraries, 2000. 213-247.

Contributors

John C. Bean is Professor of English at Seattle University, where he holds the title of "Consulting Professor of Writing and Assessment." Active in the writing-across-the-curriculum movement since 1976, he is the author of *Engaging Ideas: The Professor's Guide to Writing, Critical Thinking, and Active Learning in the Classroom* (Jossey-Bass, 1996) and is the co-author of *Writing Arguments*, 7th ed. (Longman, 2006), *The Allyn & Bacon Guide to Writing*, 4th ed. (Longman, 2004), and *Reading Rhetorically*, 2nd ed. (Longman 2005). He has published numerous articles on writing and writing-across-the-curriculum as well as on his first love Shakespeare and Spenser.

Austin Booth is Director of Collections for the University Libraries at the State University of New York at Buffalo. Her publications include: *Reload: Rethinking Women + Cyberculture* (Cambridge, MA: MIT Press, 2002), *Re: Skin* (Cambridge, MA: MIT Press, 2007); biographical and critical essays in reference tools such as the *Dictionary of Literary Biography*, *Contemporary American Women Poets: An A-to-Z Guide*, *The Reader's Guide to Lesbian and Gay Studies* and *The Encyclopedia of Popular Culture*; articles about curricular design in the *Journal of Library Administration* and the *Journal of Academic Librarianship*, and reviews in *Choice*, *Serials Review*, and *Victorian Studies*.

Daniel Coffey is Languages and Literatures Bibliographer at Iowa State University. He has published articles in library science and literary studies journals such as *College and Research Libraries* and *Jacket*. His most recent publication is "A Discipline's Composition: A Citation Analysis of Composition Studies," in *The Journal of Academic Librarianship* (March 2006).

José A. Díaz is Associate Professor, Head of Reference Services with responsibility for library instruction, collection management and liaison for Africana Studies, Latin American & Caribbean Studies, and Modern Languages at Hostos Community College (CUNY), whose library is a recipient of ACRL's 2007 Excellence in Academic Libraries Award. He has more than twenty-five years' experience as a reference librarian working with bilingual and ESL students in a bilingual academic setting. His most recent accomplishments include co-translating into Spanish the new CUNY Information Competency Tutorial.

Steven R. Harris is Director of Collections and Acquisitions Services at the University of New Mexico. Previously he was Collection Development and Management Librarian at Utah State University in Logan, Utah. He has also been literature or humanities librarian at the University of Tennessee, Louisiana State University and Texas A&M. He co-authored *Censorship of Expression in the 1980s: A Statistical Survey* (Westport, CT: Greenwood Press, 1994) and helped compile the online bibliography *Tennessee Authors Past & Present*.

Van E. Hillard, Davidson College, has collaborated extensively with library education professionals to develop research methods instruction allied with first-year writing courses. He has published essays in rhetorical studies, literacy studies, and cultural theory.

Sheril Hook is the Coordinator of Instruction Services for the library at the University of Toronto Mississauga. During the project described in this collection, she was the English and American Literature librarian, along with Verónica Reyes-Escudero, at the University of Arizona. She collaborated with James K. Elmborg on *Centers for Learning : Writing Centers and Libraries in Collaboration* (Chicago: ACRL, 2005).

Nalini Iyer is Associate Professor of English at Seattle University. Her fields of specialization include postcolonial studies, feminist theory, 19th and 20th century British literatures, and South Asian and African literatures and cultures. She has published articles in such journals as *ARIEL*, *Alam-e-Niswan: Pakistan Journal of Women Studies*, and *Samar*. Her current research projects include an edited book, *Other Tongues: Rethinking the Language Debates in Indian Literature* (co-editor Bonnie Zare) and a book length study of South Asian American writing.

Kathleen A. Johnson, Professor of Libraries, University of Nebraska-Lincoln, is the subject specialist librarian for English and other humanities at UNL, with special interests in library instruction and collection development in the humanities.

Kate Koppelman is an Assistant Professor at Seattle University where she teaches introductory courses in literature and rhetoric, as well as upper-division courses in medieval literature and culture. Her work has been published in *Essays in Medieval Studies*, and *Comitatus*. An essay is forthcoming in *Exemplaria*, and a chapter on contemporary British Detective Fiction appears in a recent collection.

Miriam Laskin is an Associate Professor at Hostos Community College (CUNY), whose library is a recipient of ACRL's 2007 Excellence in Academic Libraries Award. Dr. Laskin is Coordinator of Instructional Services and a reference librarian, and is the liaison/bibliographer for English and Language & Cognition. Her publications include "Bilingual Information Literacy and Academic Readiness: Reading, Writing and Retention, in *Academic Exchange Quarterly* (2002) and "Making the Teaching Library an Institutional Priority," co-written with Dr. Lucinda Zoe and presented at the 31st national LOEX Conference in 2003. Her other publications and conference presentations range from Internet Resources for Nurses and Nursing Students, to Plagiarism and Academic Integrity issues for faculty and students, and Internet Resources for Indigenous Caribbean Musics.

Vickery Lebbin is a Social Sciences Librarian at the University of Hawaii at Manoa. Her academic interests are information literacy competencies, instructional design, and assessment. She has published articles in *American Libraries*, *Journal of Academic Librarianship*, *Reference Services Review*, and *Research Strategies*.

Kate Manuel is currently a student in the Technology Law Program at George Mason University School of Law. Previously, she worked as the Library Instruction Coordinator at New Mexico State University.

Kristin McAndrews teaches at the University of Hawai`i at Manoa in the English Department. She published *Wrangling Women: Humor and Gender in the American West* in 2006. In addition, she has a chapter in *Culinary Tourism: Explorations in Eating and Otherness*. She has contributed articles to *Folklore*, *Literary Studies East and West: Re-Placing America*, *Conversations and Contestations* and *Etudos de Literatura: Gender* and has also written reviews for *Marvels and Tales*.

Meg Meiman Meg Meiman is Coordinator of the Undergraduate Research Program at the University of Delaware Library, where she works with students to develop short- and long-term research projects and plays matchmaker for faculty and students seeking research partners. Prior to this position, she was a librarian for six years. Engaged in the usual scholarly pursuits – she has given conference presentations about the history of reading, and has taught a class on the social history of the book – she is currently researching scholarly communication issues in higher education.

Verónica Reyes-Escudero is Special Collections Librarian and liaison to the Department of French and Italian at the University of Arizona. During the project described in this collection, she was the English and American Literature librarian, along with Sheril Hook. She has published articles and reviews in *portal: Libraries & the Academy, Criticas*, and *Library Journal*.

Laura Taddeo is the Subject Specialist for the English and Comparative Literature Departments for the Arts and Sciences Libraries at the University at Buffalo. She has published articles on information access and digital reference, including "Information Access Post September 11: What Librarians Need to Know," *Library Philosophy and Practice*, Volume 9, no. 1 (Fall 2006) and "The Nuts, Bolts, and Teaching Opportunities of Real-Time Reference" (co-written with Jill Hackenberg), *College & Undergraduate Libraries*, Volume 13, Issue 3 (2006):63-85.

Elizabeth Williams is an Information Literacy Librarian and an Assistant Professor at Appalachian State University in the mountains of western North Carolina. She has an MLS and a Master's degree in Appalachian Studies, with concentrations in folklore and Appalachian history and literature. She has published articles and book reviews in the disciplines of English and History. Including an article, "Ray Hicks, From Local Storyteller to Cultural Icon: A Bibliography" in *Appalachian Journal* in 2003: 302-30), and she reviewed *Teaching Information Literacy Skills to Social Sciences Students & Practitioners: A Casebook of Applications*, edited by Douglas Cook and Natasha Cooper for *College & Research Libraries* in 2007 (68.4: 369-370).

Helene Williams has served in collection development and instruction capacities at Harvard University, University of Washington, Northeastern University, and Michigan State University. While at the University of Washington, Helene taught the graduate research methods course in the English Department, and she continues to teach the collection development and humanities reference courses for the UW Information School. She participated in the nationally-recognized teaching and technology program known as UWired from 1996-2000, working to improve collaboration between students, faculty, and librarians by effectively incorporating technology into the curriculum. She has published widely in the areas of instruction and usability, including "Teaching Across the Divides in the Library Classroom," with Cheryl LaGuardia, Christine Oka, and Anne Zald. *IFLA Proceedings*, 2002. She also edited the "Literature" chapter in the 12th and 14th editions of *Magazines for Libraries*. She co-edited with Trudi E. Jacobson the book *Teaching the New Library to Today's Users: Reaching International, Minority, Senior Citizens, Gay/Lesbian, First-Generation, At-Risk, Graduate and Returning Students, and Distance Learners.* Neal-Schuman Press, 2000.

William A. Wortman William A. Wortman retired in 2007 after thirty years as humanities librarian (principal librarian rank) at Miami University in Ohio with responsibility for collection management, reference, library instruction, and liaison in the areas of English, theater, and foreign languages. He was also coordinator of the Collection Development Cluster and curator of the Native American Women Playwrights Archive (http://staff.lib.muohio.edu/nawpa). The MLA published his *Guide to Serial Bibliographies for Modern Literatures* (2nd ed.) in 1995; ALA published his *Collection Management: Background and Principles* in 1989; he co-edited *Literature in English: A Guide for Librarians*, 2000, and contributed a chapter on the nature of library collections. He hopes soon to complete a book on the publishing and reception history of Henry James's "Daisy Miller."

Index